# The Family

W. W. Norton & Company has been independent since its founding in 1923, when William Warder Norton and Mary D. Herter Norton first published lectures delivered at the People's Institute, the adult education division of New York City's Cooper Union. The firm soon expanded its program beyond the Institute, publishing books by celebrated academics from America and abroad. By midcentury, the two major pillars of Norton's publishing program—trade books and college texts—were firmly established. In the 1950s, the Norton family transferred control of the company to its employees, and today— with a staff of four hundred and a comparable number of trade, college, and professional titles published each year—W. W. Norton & Company stands as the largest and oldest publishing house owned wholly by its employees.

Editor: Karl Bakeman
Associate Editor: Nicole Sawa
Project Editor: Linda Feldman
Editorial Assistant: Lindsey Thomas
Copy Editor: Janet Greenblatt
Managing Editor, College: Marian Johnson
Managing Editor, College Digital Media: Kim Yi
Production Manager: Benjamin Reynolds
Media Editor: Eileen Connell
Associate Media Editor: Laura Musich
Media Editorial Assistant: Cara Folkman
Marketing Manager, Sociology: Julia Hall
Design Director: Hope Miller Goodell
Photo Researcher: Rona Tuccillo
Photo Editor: Evan Luberger
Permissions Manager: Megan Jackson
Composition: Brad Walrod/Kenoza Type, Inc.
Illustrations: Kiss Me I'm Polish LLC, New York; Jouve
Manufacturing: Transcontinental

Library of Congress Cataloging-in-Publication Data

Cohen, Philip N.
   The family : diversity, inequality, and social change / Philip N. Cohen, University of Maryland. — First edition.
      pages cm
   Includes bibliographical references and index.
   **ISBN 978-0-393-93395-6 (pbk.)**
   1. Families—United States.   I. Title.
   HQ536.C68 2015
   306.850973—dc23                                              2014020492

W. W. Norton & Company, Inc., 500 Fifth Avenue, New York, NY 10110-0017
wwnorton.com
W. W. Norton & Company Ltd., Castle House, 75/76 Wells Street, London W1T 3QT

1 2 3 4 5 6 7 8 9 0

# The Family

## Diversity, Inequality, and Social Change

**Philip N. Cohen**

Author of FamilyInequality.com

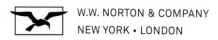

W.W. NORTON & COMPANY

NEW YORK · LONDON

# Contents

# 7   Love and Romantic Relationships

# 8 Marriage and Cohabitation

# 1

# A Sociology of
# the Family

# How the U.S. Census Counts Families

The history of the U.S. Census offers important lessons about the definition of families. It also serves as an example of the emergence of individuality in modern society and the "institutionalized individuality" referred to by the modernity theorists studied later in this chapter (Beck and Beck-Gernsheim 2004).

The U.S. Constitution in 1789 ordered an "actual enumeration" of the population every 10 years, for purposes of apportioning political representatives among the population. A nationwide **census** has been carried out every 10 years since 1790. But the idea of counting everyone in the population is at least as old as the story of the Jews wandering in the desert after fleeing Egypt, in which God commanded Moses to "take the sum of all the congregation of the children of Israel, by families following their fathers' houses; a head count of every male according to the number of their names."

**census**

A periodic count of people in a population and their characteristics, usually performed as an official government function.

In all modern societies, the census plays a crucial role in the development of public infrastructure and the administration of services. These data collection efforts are large government projects, conducted at great expense: the 2010 U.S. Census cost more than $13 billion and employed more than a million people. The census also is one of the government's direct interventions into personal life, requiring the formal definition of all individuals' relationships and family boundaries. So the definitions that government officials use are important for how commonly accepted roles and identities are developed (Coontz 2010).

Until 1840, the U.S. Census recorded only the name of the "head" of each household, with an anonymous count of other people present (slaves were counted as members of their owners' families, though they only counted as three-fifths of a person for purposes of congressional representation). Starting in 1840, individuals were recorded separately, though still listed by household, under the "family head." At that time, census forms were filled out by enumerators, who knocked on doors and recorded information by hand. In 1870, confronted for the first time with large urban buildings that did not separate families into distinct households, the census defined a **household** as a group of people who share a common dining table. That idea stuck, and some variation of the concept of "live and eat separately from others" has been used to define households ever since (Ruggles and Brower 2003).

**household**

A group of people that lives and eats separately from other groups.

## What Is a Census Family?

Today, the Census Bureau uses the legal definition of the family presented in this chapter, but with one qualification: a family lives together in one household. By the personal or legal definitions I presented earlier, members of the same family could live in different households. In fact, one person could be a member of any number of families. When it comes to collecting statistical data, however, that is not practical. So the Census Bureau limits each family to one household, and each person can only be counted in one place. That is why students living in college dorms are not counted as part of their parents' families, but instead are regarded as living in "group quarters" (which is also the case for military personnel abroad or on ships, prisoners, or people in nursing homes). With this definition—putting each person in only one household—the 2010 census showed that among the 301 million people living in 117 million households, there are 78 million families, or groups of people related by birth, marriage, or adoption who live together in one household (U.S. Census 2012a).

But how does the Census Bureau apply the legal definition of family? The task seemed simple at first. The 1880 census was the first to record information about each individual's relationship within the family. After listing the "head" of each family (always the husband in the case of married couples), the enumerator made a list of all other individuals in the household and made a note of the "relationship of each person to the head of this family—whether wife, son, daughter, servant, boarder, or other" (Ruggles et al. 2013). Those six categories now serve as a quaint reminder of a simpler time in family life.

Starting in the 1960s, as families became more complicated, the categories on the census form proliferated, and now people usually fill out the forms without assistance, choosing the category for each person in the household themselves. The idea of a "household head" came under attack from feminists in the 1960s, because they didn't like the presumption of male authority that it implied (Presser 1998). That pressure was successful, and by 1980, the census form dropped the category "household head" and now simply refers to a "householder," defined as anyone who legally owns or rents the home (in married couples it is still almost always the man). That was one of many changes that followed. Figure 1.1 shows the relationship categories for the 2010 census, now including no fewer than 15 ways people can be associated with "Person 1," the householder.

The historical concept of a "man and his family" has clearly been supplanted with a long list

---

Figure 1.1 **"Relationship" question for the 2010 Census**

**2 How is this person related to Person 1?** *Mark (X) ONE box.*

☐ Husband or wife
☐ Biological son or daughter
☐ Adopted son or daughter
☐ Stepson or stepdaughter
☐ Brother or sister
☐ Father or mother
☐ Grandchild
☐ Parent-in-law

☐ Son-in-law or daughter-in-law
☐ Other relative
☐ Roomer or boarder
☐ Housemate or roommate
☐ Unmarried partner
☐ Foster child
☐ Other nonrelative

SOURCE: U.S. Census Bureau (2010b).

of individual relationships and identities. Biological children are differentiated from adopted children, stepchildren, and foster children. In-laws and grandchildren are identified separately, and even "unmarried partners" (cohabiting couples) are counted. In fact, starting with the 2010 census, the Census Bureau started publishing statistics on same-sex married couples, counting 131,729 in that year (I was privileged to serve as a consultant on that report) (O'Connell and Feliz 2011). You might notice another subtle distinction from the list in Figure 1.1. The category "other relative" is at the end of a list of "related" people. The five categories that follow, including unmarried partners and foster children, are not considered "related" and are not used to define families.

the use of some terms and ideas that may seem abstract. But I hope that once we get over the hurdle of these abstractions, you will find that they help make your understanding of families more concrete.

Rather than identify certain groups of people as families or not, this socio- logical definition conceives of the family as the place where family matters take place. I will refer to that as an **institutional arena**, a social space in which relations between people in common positions are governed by accepted rules of interaction. In the family arena, for example, there are positions that people occupy (for example, father, mother, child, brother, sister). And there are rules of interaction, most of them informal, that govern how people in these posi- tions interact. When a social position is accompanied by accepted patterns of behavior, it becomes a role. Family rules include obligations as well as privileges. For example, parents must feed, clothe, socialize, and otherwise care for their children in the most intimate ways. And children are usually expected to obey their parents. The **family arena**, then, is the institutional arena where people practice intimacy, childbearing and socialization, and caring work. Not everyone fits perfectly into these positions or follows these rules, but when they do not conform—for example, when parents abuse or neglect their children—it only serves to reinforce the importance of the rules (Martin 2004).

An institutional arena is not a physical space with a clear boundary, like a sports arena, but a social place where a set of interactions play out. If you think of a game like soccer, there may be an ideal place to play it—a soccer field—but you can sort of play it anywhere. The rules are a little bit different here and there, and many of them are informal. You don't need lines on the ground or fixed goals. A great example of this is the common practice of widening or narrowing the space between the goal posts according to how many players are on the field. In the same way, the family is not a specific social arrangement or something that happens in one home or one type of home. Its rules and positions evolve over time and take place in the area of social interaction where intimacy, childbearing and socialization, and caring work are enacted.

These aspects of family life consume much of our personal, social, and eco- nomic energy and passions. But they do not encompass the domains of two other

**institutional arena**

A social space in which relations between people in common positions are governed by accepted rules of interaction.

**family arena**

The institutional arena where people practice intimacy, childbearing and socialization, and caring work.

important institutional arenas that have direct interactions with the family: the state and the market. To understand the family's place in the society overall, we need to define these overlapping arenas.

The **state** includes many different organizations filled with people in many roles. But at its core, the state is the institutional arena where, through political means, behavior is legally regulated, violence is controlled, and resources are redistributed. The regulation of behavior is set out in laws and policies, and these are enforced with the threat or use of violence (from family court to the prison system to the armed forces). The state affects families directly through regulation, such as granting marriage licenses and facilitating divorces, and by redistributing resources according to family relationships. Redistribution takes place by taxing families and individuals and then spending tax money on education, health care, Social Security, welfare, and other programs.

The state also regulates the behavior of economic organizations and collects taxes and fees from them. In that way, the state has direct interactions with our third institutional arena, the **market**, which is the institutional arena where labor for pay, economic exchange, and wealth accumulation take place. All these activities are closely related to family life. For example, when parents decide whether to work for pay or stay home with their kids, they have to consider the jobs they can get and the costs of day care and other services. These decisions then affect family relationships and future decisions, such as how to divide labor within the family, how many children to have, whether to pursue advanced education—and maybe even whether to get divorced.

The key features of these three institutional arenas are shown in Table 1.1. Each arena signifies a certain type of social interaction, each is composed of organizational units, and each specifies certain roles for its members. Clearly, most people have roles in all of these arenas and take part in different organizational units. For example, a parent might care for his or her own children at home, but also work as a nurse or day care provider in the market arena and act as a citizen on political questions, such as whether welfare programs should use tax money to pay for poor people's day care services. One way to look at such overlapping roles is to see them as interactions between the institutional arenas.

**state**

The institutional arena where, through political means, behavior is legally regulated, violence is controlled, and resources are redistributed.

**market**

The institutional arena where labor for pay, economic exchange, and wealth accumulation take place.

Table 1.1 **Modern institutional arenas**

|  | STATE | MARKET | FAMILY |
|---|---|---|---|
| TYPE OF INTERACTION | Law, violence, and welfare | Labor, exchange, and wealth accumulation | Intimacy, childbearing and socialization, and caring work |
| ORGANIZATIONAL UNITS | Legislatures and agencies | Companies | Families |
| INDIVIDUAL ROLES | Citizens | Workers, owners, and consumers | Family members |

The interaction of institutional arenas is illustrated in the Story Behind the Numbers, which shows examples of overlapping roles. We can see the interaction of family and state arenas in the state licensing of marriages; and the interaction of family and market arenas in the role that commercial services such as day care providers make available to families. An additional interaction (not shown) is between state and market arenas, as when the state regulates the market by restricting companies' behavior. For example, under the Family and Medical Leave Act, the federal government requires large companies to give most of their workers (unpaid) time off from work when a child or another family member is sick. Finally, the figure illustrates one area where all three arenas clearly overlap: welfare policy. As we will see, state support of the poor is based on certain conceptions of family relationships (thus regulating family life), and market forces affect the ability of families to support themselves with or without welfare—even as family decisions affect the market arena (such as poor single mothers entering the labor force).

As we will see in Chapter 2, thinking about institutional arenas can help tell the history of the family. For example, Andrew Cherlin has argued that the growth of individual choice in family relationships signifies a weakening of marriage as an institution as its rules become more flexible (Cherlin 2004). Family history is also a story of changes in how different arenas interact. Returning to the example of parents punishing their children, the state intervenes when its authorities enforce laws against child abuse or acts of violence. The history of change in these two arenas is partly the story of how the line between parental and state authority has been drawn. The state's role also has evolved in the growth of public services in health care and education and in the changing state definitions of marriage, all of which alter the borders of the family arena and the roles of its members.

Throughout this book, we will use the idea of institutional arenas as a way to understand how larger forces interact with individuals and families to shape family life and how the family in turn contributes to larger social trends. Considering the relationship between individual experience and larger social forces is one of the main promises of sociology. And the family has been the subject of sociological scrutiny throughout the history of the discipline. Therefore, before going further into the main subject of this book—the family as a diverse, changing feature of our unequal society—we will need to establish some additional theoretical background.

# The Family in Sociological Theory

In this section, I present some prominent sociological theories and explain how they are useful in thinking about families and changes in family relationships. I want to emphasize that we are not necessarily marrying (to choose a metaphor) any one theory. Rather, we will consider a range of theories and perspectives that offer different kinds of explanations for the patterns we see. If we use theory to

spouse only by observing how they are acted out in the daily lives of the people who occupy them.

**Modernity** People often use the word *modern* to mean "contemporary," but in this book we will use it to refer to a specific period in history, from the eighteenth-century Enlightenment to the present. **Modernity theory** is very broad, but with regard to the family, it concerns the emergence of the individual as an actor in society and how individuality changed personal and institutional relations. Consider the scheme in Table 1.1 as a modern phenomenon. In the state arena, the individual emerged as a citizen, with the right to vote defining that role. In the market arena, the individual emerged as a worker, earning a cash wage to be spent on anything he or she chooses. What about the family arena? Here the individual emerged as an independent actor making choices about family relations freely, based on personal tastes and interests. Individual choice in the family had existed before modernity (more for some than for others), but only in this era did it become institutionalized, or expected of everyone (Beck and Lau 2005).

> **modernity theory**
>
> A theory of the historical emergence of the individual as an actor in society and how individuality changed personal and institutional relations.

Modernity theorists break the modern era into two periods. In *first modernity*, up until the 1960s or so, there was gradual change in family behavior—for example, more divorce, a gradually increasing age at first marriage, fewer children in families, fewer people living in extended families (see Chapter 2), and more choice in spouse selection. These were only incremental changes, however. Even though people exercised free choice, the concept of a "normal" family remained intact as a social standard. Different family types or pathways—such as marriage much later in life, having children outside of marriage, remarrying after divorce, or marrying outside your race—existed, but they were on the margins of acceptability. In *second modernity*, since the 1970s, the chickens have come home to roost. Diversity and individuality are the new norm, and it's up to each person to pick a family type and identify with it. Thus, freedom from traditional restraints "brings historically new free spaces and options: he can and should, she may and must, now decide how to shape their own life" (Beck and Beck-Gernsheim 2004:502). The growth of family diversity is a major theme of this book.

Acting individually is supported (or even required) by other institutions, especially the state and the market, which increasingly have treated people as individuals rather than as family members. This is only natural once family ties such as marriage are considered voluntary, subject to divorce by either individual. For example, some welfare and health care benefits and taxation involve transactions between individuals and the government (although some programs are still geared toward families). And most employers don't consider it necessary to pay a **family wage** to male workers with stay-at-home wives, as they did in the past (see Chapter 2). Compared with the premodern past, this "institutionalized individualization" leads to a tremendous fragmentation of family identities and puts a big psychological burden on people. As a result, a sense of insecurity spreads through the population, driving people into the arms of expert identity fixers, especially therapists and self-help gurus.

> **family wage**
>
> The amount necessary for a male earner to provide subsistence for his wife and children without them having to work for pay.

If all of this freedom implies individual isolation and lack of direction, it also stands to revolutionize the nature of intimacy and family relationships, at least according to modernity theorist Anthony Giddens. In his view, relationships now may be truly based on personal choice and individual fulfillment. Free from the constraints of traditional rules, free from the need to reproduce biologically, and free to negotiate economic survival as individuals, people may now enter into the ideal "pure relationship"—and leave when it suits them—for the first time in history (Giddens 1992).

## Demography and the Life Course

Two additional perspectives warrant attention here, which supplement rather than compete with the theoretical views already presented. Many family researchers study the family in relation to larger population processes. If a population is the number of people in a certain area or place, it may be seen as (a) the number of children who have been born, (b) minus the number of people who have died, plus (c) the number of people who have arrived in the past (minus those who moved away). Demography—the study of populations—therefore focuses on birth, death, and migration. Family researchers who take a **demographic perspective** study family behavior and household structures that contribute to larger population processes. They are especially interested in childbirth, but to understand that, they must study the timing and frequency of cohabitation, marriage, and divorce, as well as living arrangements in general (who lives with whom at different stages in their lives).

The demographic emphasis on timing contributes to an interest in the sequencing of events for individuals and groups in the population. The "normal" family structure of the past included a progression from childhood to adulthood that included marriage and then parenthood. As family life has become more diverse, the common sequences of family events, or family trajectories, have become much more complicated. Researchers using the **life course perspective**

**demographic perspective**

The study of how family behavior and household structures contribute to larger population processes.

**life course perspective**

The study of the family trajectories of individuals and groups as they progress through their lives, in social and historical context.

The decennial census in the United States is a massive project that requires more than a million people to complete. Many are census takers, or enumerators, who visit households that have not submitted a completed Census questionnaire.

study the family trajectories of individuals and groups as they progress through their lives. One important goal of this research is to place family events in their historical context (Elder 1975). For example, if you want to understand attitudes toward family life among Americans who were in their 50s in 2010, you might consider their history as a **cohort**—a group of people who experience an event together at the same point in time (such as being born in the same period). These people were born in the 1950s, when birth rates were very high, so they grew up in a youth-dominated culture. They were in their teens in the late 1960s, when much of the popular culture first embraced ideas of free love and uncommitted romantic relationships. Divorce rates shot up when they were young adults in the 1970s, which had immediate and long-lasting effects on their attitudes toward cohabitation and divorce. Rather than examining individuals at fixed points in time, life course researchers seek to gain a deeper understanding by considering life stories in their social and historical context.

# Studying Families

We have seen how sociologists use theories to make sense of the facts they discover. But where do these facts come from? More important, how can we build a knowledge base to help us understand the reasons behind the facts? In principle, sociologists may gain information from any source at all. However, there are common methods of gathering information that have proved successful. Before examining these sources of data, I need to briefly describe a few of the challenges encountered in studying families.

To develop deeper knowledge often requires using more information than we started out looking for. For example, we know that African Americans on average are less likely to marry than Whites. However, to understand the reasons for that gap, we must look at a variety of factors, including not just individual preferences but also poverty and college attendance rates, income differences between men and women, and even incarceration and mortality rates. In other words, to understand the core facts requires knowledge of the context in which those facts occur.

Another issue we must contend with in research on families is the problem of telling the difference between correlation and cause. Many things are observed occurring together (correlation) without one causing the other. For example, a study of young children's vision found that those who had slept with the light on in their nurseries were more likely to be nearsighted. That is, light at night and nearsightedness appeared to be correlated. The researchers suspected that light penetrating the eyelids during sleep harmed children's vision—that is, that light caused nearsightedness. However, a follow-up study determined that parents who are themselves nearsighted

How did researchers confuse causation and correlation in their study of night lights in bedrooms of nearsighted children?

are more likely to leave a light on in their children's nurseries; it makes it easier for the parents to see. And since nearsightedness is partly genetic, it is possible that the nearsightedness of children who sleep with the light on results not from the light, but from the parents' own nearsightedness being passed on to their children genetically (Zadnik 2000). In this case, despite the correlation of two facts, one does not appear to have caused the other. Researchers could only determine this by gathering contextual information about children's families.

Finally, although there are many sources of information, there are almost as many sources of **bias**—the tendency to impose previously held views on the collection and interpretation of facts. Consider an example: During the summer of 2008, Americans were bombarded by a spate of bad economic news. In response, CNN conducted a "quick vote" on the Internet, asking this question: "Do you believe $139-a-barrel oil and a 400-point loss in the Dow Jones Industrials and the biggest increase in the unemployment rate we've seen in two decades suggest perhaps that we need new economic leadership?" Given the way the question was phrased—and the fact that it was asked during a TV show devoted to governmental failures—it is not surprising that 97 percent of respondents answered "yes" (CNN 2008b). The network asked a biased question and got a predictable result.

We can't always eliminate bias, but we can increase accountability and transparency. That is why most sociologists prefer publicly funded studies, which make their data freely available and which in principle are repeatable by other researchers. That is, nothing is hidden about the way the information is collected and analyzed. And before results are published, a system of peer review is employed in which other scholars review the work anonymously, checking for any sources of error, including bias, logical flaws, or simple mistakes in the analysis.

**bias**

The tendency to impose previously held views on the collection and interpretation of facts.

## Sample Surveys

The most common method of gathering data for sociological studies is the **sample survey**, in which identical questions are asked of many different people and their answers gathered into one large data file. By examining patterns among the responses to the questions we ask, we can find associations that help us understand family life. For example, if we ask people to tell us their gender and how often they do the dishes, we might find out if women do dishes more often than men.

Asking people for information about their lives and opinions is time-consuming and expensive, so we cannot study everyone. We need to find a method of choosing our study subjects. Consider another CNN "quick vote," which asked the simple question, "Who does most of the chores in your household?" More than 30,000 people responded, and 60 percent of them chose "Mom keeps it all tidy," while 27 percent chose "Mom and dad split the work." (The rest were sprinkled across other categories.) (CNN 2008a). That is a big group of people, but how were they selected? Anyone who came to the CNN website was allowed to respond. We don't know who they were, but we might imagine some ways in which they were not representative of the general population—Internet

**sample survey**

A research method in which identical questions are asked of many different people and their answers gathered into one large data file.

users, people interested in reading websites about housework, people who like to click on website polls, and so on. We simply don't know from that survey if those responses represent the population as a whole.

Ideally, we would choose people by random selection, ensuring that each person in the group we want to study has the same likelihood of being interviewed in the survey. That is the best way to ensure that our results are not skewed by who is included or excluded. Students are sometimes skeptical about the principle of random selection. Is it really possible, for example, that the opinions of 500 people can accurately reflect those of 235 million American adults? If it's done right, the short answer is yes; the long answer has to do with probability theory. (If you don't believe me, consider this: when I have my cholesterol checked, why don't I have all of my blood removed instead of just a few ounces?)

We find the clearest evidence of the effectiveness of sample surveys when we can successfully use them to predict people's behavior, as has been done with many political elections. In the 2012 presidential election, for example, a careful analysis of the preelection polls allowed statistician Nate Silver to accurately predict for every single state whether Barack Obama or Mitt Romney would win in the actual election-day voting (M. Cooper 2012). Although there are many ways that surveys can produce errors or lead to ambiguous results, the principle of random selection helps to ensure that we are not misled by research results from relatively small numbers of people.

In addition to random selection, we also make an important distinction between different kinds of surveys. As we have seen, the questions that concern us may involve interrelated sequences of events, such as the connection between nursery room lighting in infancy and nearsightedness years later. Still, although we are interested in events that occur years apart, most surveys are administered only once to each person. Others, known as **longitudinal surveys**, interview the same people repeatedly over a period of time. Tracking people over time is essential for answering questions about sequences of events. For example, researchers have long wondered whether the increase in divorce is the result of women gaining economic independence, so they don't "need" to be married. Or maybe it is the other way around, and women get jobs because they are afraid that a divorce will leave them out on a limb with little work experience (see Chapter 10). Only by carefully following families over time could researchers find that couples do divorce more often when women earn their own income, but marriage quality and satisfaction are even more important (Sayer and Bianchi 2000). Such surveys are time-consuming and expensive, since interviewees have to be tracked down again and again over a period of years, which is why the major longitudinal surveys are at least partly funded by the government, with many researchers sharing access to the data.

Even surveys in which each person is interviewed only once may be repeated at regular intervals, which allows us to track trends in people's answers over time. For example, the federal government has for decades conducted the Current Population Survey (CPS) every month, interviewing representatives from thousands of households to generate such important facts as the national unemployment rate. And because the CPS also includes questions on family structure, we can confidently estimate, for example, that the employment rate of unmarried

**longitudinal surveys**

A research method in which the same people are interviewed repeatedly over a period of time.

Jackie, Sue, and Lynn are three of the subjects in "49 Up," a 2005 documentary in the *Up* series that began in 1964 when they were seven years old. The series has revisited most of them every seven years since.

mothers fell from 73 percent to 65 percent over the decade of the 2000s (see Chapter 11) (Current Population Survey 2014). Similarly, the General Social Survey (GSS) has been asking questions about American attitudes since 1972. From this survey we know, for example, that 36 percent of American adults considered sex before marriage "always wrong" in 1972, but that dropped to 22 percent by 2012 (Smith et al. 2014). These repeated surveys are essential for studying social change, another central focus of this book.

## In-Depth Interviews and Observation

Sample surveys provide much of the basic knowledge we need to understand trends and patterns in family life. However, researchers often must make assumptions or speculate about the meaning underlying the behavior and attitudes measured by sample surveys. Even when we ask people directly about their attitudes, such as whether mothers or fathers should spend more time taking care of their children, the answers may be superficial, and respondents answer only those questions we think of asking in advance. Some researchers prefer not to be limited by brief answers to questions they bring to an interview.

One way to avoid this problem is to arrange much longer, in-depth interviews with a small number of people, usually those who share traits researchers want to study. For example, Pamela Stone, for her book *Opting Out? Why Women Really Quit Careers and Head Home* (2007), interviewed a few dozen successful professional women who had given up their careers to take care of their children. During long interviews, using follow-up questions delving into their decision making, Stone was able to piece together the complicated reasons they had for their choices. Contrary to popular wisdom, most of the women she interviewed did not start out to embrace a homemaker role, but would instead have preferred to maintain their careers. Unfortunately, they were unable to negotiate or maintain the kind of workplace flexibility that such a balance would have required (see Chapter 11).

Even in-depth interviews, however, rely on the answers provided to the researcher. Sometimes, interpersonal dynamics and the subtleties of daily life are best studied through direct observation. This was the method employed by Annette Lareau for her influential study *Unequal Childhoods: Class, Race, and Family Life* (2003). Lareau and her assistants inserted themselves into the lives of 12 families for about a month each, following them from place to place and taking copious notes on how the parents arranged their children's daily lives and interactions with the social world. The results revealed sharp contrasts in parenting style—and the meanings parents attributed to childhood—according to the social class of the family (see Chapter 4).

## Time Use Studies

Most of what happens within families is informal. Unlike the work setting, there is no formal record of who does what, for which rewards, and who answers to whom. And there is no way of measuring how successful families are comparable to sales figures or profits reports in the private sector or services delivered in the government sector. Therefore, researchers studying families often rely on asking people in interviews to describe what they do or observing them firsthand.

To develop a more detailed accounting of what goes on within families, some researchers have produced **time use studies** that collect detailed data on how family members spend their time. Some of these studies are simply surveys in which the questions focus on how people spend their time. Others use time diaries. Rather than asking people, for example, how many hours last week they spent watching TV or reading to their children, time diary studies ask people to record what they were doing, where they were, and who they were with for small increments of time over an entire day.

Time diary studies have been especially valuable in the study of work and families, as we will see in Chapter 11. For example, a large national survey in the 1990s asked men and women to estimate how many hours per week they did various household chores and other work. However, when researchers tallied up the hours spent on all the different activities, it often came to more than the number of hours there are in a week (Bianchi, Robinson, and Milkie 2006)! In contrast, when people are asked to fill out time diaries, recording their activities over the course of the day, the time estimates are more accurate. Recent time diaries show men spending just 10 hours per week on housework and women spending 16 hours per week (Bianchi et al. 2012). This method provides a window into the minute interactions that make up family life, but permits studying larger groups of people than is possible with in-depth interviews or observation.

**time use studies**

Surveys that collect data on how people spend their time during a sample period, such as a single day or week.

# Moving On

In this chapter, we have seen that there are several ways of defining families, from a personal or legal perspective and through the lens of social institutions. Equipped with a clearer idea of what we are studying, we then added to our conceptual framework a set of sociological theories and perspectives, including the opposing views of the consensus and conflict perspectives and the contemporary theories of feminism, exchange theory, symbolic interactionism, modernity theory, and the demographic and life course perspectives. Finally, theories would ring hollow were it not for the factual foundations on which they stand. Therefore, this chapter also introduced a variety of methods that sociologists use

# Theory and Evidence

Different theoretical perspectives and methods of gathering information can help us translate descriptions of particular family events or situations into more general knowledge about families and society.

- Brainstorm several examples of a family conflict, dramatic event, or daily occurrence. Try to think of situations that might be representative of a broader social phenomenon. For example, you might describe a family-related crime story from a TV drama, the changing family structure you or someone you know grew up in, or the real-life saga of a politician or celebrity in the news.

- Choose two theories or perspectives from the chapter that interest you. Describe how a theorist from each perspective might explain the examples you came up with. These do not have to be contradictory; they might simply provide alternative ways of looking at the situations in question or generate ideas about their underlying social causes.

- Select two methods of gathering data described in the chapter. Try to imagine how a researcher might use each method to gather information about the kind of situations or events you are trying to explain—for example, by collecting survey data or directly observing the behavior in question.

- Choosing one of your examples, combine one method and one theory that you think would most fruitfully develop your understanding of the social dynamics in question. Explain why you suggest this approach to turn your description of this case into more general sociological knowledge. What would you hope to discover from your study? How might your study change the way others think about this question?

in less than half of all American households. In its place, we have seen the rise of single-parent families, unmarried couples, and people living alone or in nonfamily group situations.

Each of these trends has changed the character of family life and the place of families in the larger society. We will keep these changes in mind as we trace family history through time, beginning with a brief foray into ancient history.

# Early History

To establish some common background understanding, we will briefly discuss the early history of families, beginning with ancient times and then reviewing some early European history.

## Prehistory: Cooperation and Survival

The Stone Age isn't a big part of this chapter. But there is at least one story worth telling. It took place somewhere in central Europe about 4,600 years ago, when disaster befell a small village. The young adults and older boys had apparently gone hunting. Someone attacked the village—we can't know who—and massacred the defenseless elders and younger children. Their skeletal remains still contain arrowheads and evidence that their bones were broken by the weapons used to overpower them. When the other villagers returned, they buried the victims. According to their custom, they placed food, tools, and weapons in the graves to nourish and protect the dead along their eternal journey. In one grave, they buried an older man and woman, along with two young children. DNA testing of the bones shows that the children were their biological offspring, making this the oldest DNA-confirmed **nuclear family** (see Changing Culture, "Family Types and Terms"). The villagers buried the family members facing each other, with their hands interlinked. Another woman was buried nearby with several other children (not her offspring), this time facing away from each other (Haak et al. 2008).

Why the sad tale? Besides its dramatic appeal, the story shows that the ancient villagers recognized and honored different family arrangements, not just the nuclear family. They also buried stepmothers or aunts—older family members who were not blood relatives, according to the DNA analysis—in family graves with the children they cared for, but the graves were different. This is especially poignant because chemical analysis of their teeth showed that the women had lived in another region when they were children. So these women had married into the village from another group. But their family memberships were nevertheless considered eternal.

> **nuclear family**
>
> A married couple living with their own (usually biological) children and no extended family members.

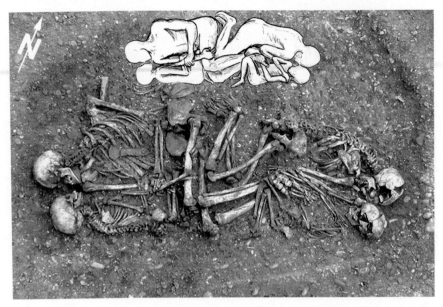

This Stone Age burial site contains the oldest DNA-confirmed nuclear family: a man and a woman (top left and right) and their two children (bottom left and right).

The archaeological record tells us that such flexible family arrangements have always been a crucial element of human social life. Although some people have lived in small, biologically related groups, others mixed and matched in ways that allowed them to survive. In fact, we now understand that the human species could not have survived without a system of family support, providing care for children who couldn't care for themselves. This isn't true of every species. Chimpanzees, one of our closest evolutionary relatives, do not have an extended period of childhood. Their mothers wean them (stop breastfeeding) when they are more or less ready to take care of themselves, at around 5 years of age. Among early humans, however, children were weaned at 2 or 3, an age when they were not able to fend for themselves (G. Kennedy 2005). As a result, the early survival of the species depended on adults caring for children through an extended period. Moreover, human mothers bore their children relatively close together in age, which meant that they couldn't carry them all around at once. The children could only survive with the help of additional adults beyond the mother (Gibbons 2008). These relationships, emerging at the dawn of our species, were the first human families.

The formation of relatively smaller, stable families—including some nuclear families of the kind described earlier—probably occurred only in the last 10,000 years or so, with the beginning of organized food production. The invention of agriculture allowed people to settle down in what are now known as the Americas, the Middle East, and China (Shelach 2006). The domestication of plants made it possible for hunter-gatherers to become farmers. During this time, larger social groups, which had been necessary for low-tech hunting, were augmented by more independent family units. Tiny one-person huts grouped around communal storage spaces were replaced by larger houses with room for four or five people and space for individual property (Flannery 2002). It appears that parents

# Family Types and Terms

The prevailing family system is an important part of any society. And the many different kinds of societies have evolved around a wide variety of family systems. Those traditions help us understand how we came to be where we are today.

Today, most societies have a family system based on monogamy, the marriage of one person to one other person. Monogamous mating occurs in a few species of mammals (maybe 3 percent), but is more common among primates (10 to 15 percent [Fuentes 1998]). Because people are primates, and monogamy has been around for a long time, this has led some people to believe that monogamous marriage is the natural state of humans. But the history of human diversity suggests that it's not that simple. For one thing, different forms of marriage have often been practiced in one society at the same time. For example, polygamy, in which one person has several spouses, has usually occurred in societies where most people practiced monogamy— as is the case in some African countries, where polygamy was pretty common into the 1970s (Welch and Glick 1981). Although less common now, polygamy was the most prevalent form of marriage throughout human history. In prehistoric times, this practice may have given groups a biological advantage, since the more successful men could produce more children if they had multiple partners, while the weaker men had fewer children or none at all. Polygamy has almost always been practiced as men having more than one wife, reflecting the power of wealthy or influential men (Coontz 2005). Not surprisingly, polygamy is found in societies marked by great power inequality between men and women. In imperial China, for example, rich men often had multiple wives, and as a result, many poor men never married (Lee and Feng 1999).

When a monogamous couple live with their own biological children and no extended family members, it is known as a nuclear family. When a nuclear family is also functionally independent of extended family members, some social scientists call it a *conjugal family*. This is the modern ideal many people associate with the 1950s and 1960s, when new suburban homes, with trim lawns and picket fences, reinforced the image of the family as an independent (or even isolated) unit.

As we will see in Chapter 4, families are instrumental in accumulating and maintaining the wealth and status of those at the top of the social hierarchy. When wealth and power are transmitted from fathers to their sons, the family system is known as *patrilineal* (as opposed to *matrilineal*, from mothers to daughters). As we will see, many American Indians had matrilineal traditions, while European Americans were more patrilineal. That's why American wives and children usually take their surnames from the man of the family.

Suburbanization encouraged young couples to move away from their parents, but Americans had been a relatively mobile population since the westward expansion of the nineteenth century. In other societies, young couples often live with or near the husband's family home, in a living arrangement we call *patrilocal*, or near the wife's family (*matrilocal*). Contemporary societies are not usually rigidly gendered in this way, but in some cases strong traditions remain. In rural China, for example, it is still common for young women to move into their husband's household, where they play an important role in the family care system, especially in caring for the older family members. For this reason, having a son is more economically advantageous than having a daughter, because the son is likely to bring a wife/worker into the family, whereas a daughter may marry and leave her parents with no one to support them when they are old (Hvistendahl 2011).

Finally, we may speak of family systems as being either *patriarchal,* which means that power is wielded by men within the family, or *matriarchal,* in which women hold power. Although there certainly have been matriarchal families, truly matriarchal societies have been very rare in history; even in matrilineal American Indian tribes, for example, men usually had more power on questions of war (Eggan 1967). As we follow the history of families up to the present, we will see how men's power within society at large and their power within the family are mutually reinforcing.

Each of these terms represents whole systems or patterns of family life, different ways of acting and thinking from the moment we wake up till our heads hit the pillow (if we have one). Looking at all the different forms of marriage and family structure throughout history, and recognizing how successful those systems have been at maintaining their respective societies, it seems unreasonable to believe that there is one normal, or natural, family form ordained by God or evolution. There is simply too much diversity in the human historical record for that to be true.

As an aside, note that all of these terms have been used for families based on marriages between men and women. Now that an increasing number of states and countries permit marriage between couples of the same sex (see Chapter 8), we should have an appropriate adjustment of terms. I have suggested that we call marriage of man to woman **heterogamy** and refer to same-sex marriage as **homogamy**—from the Greek *hetero* for "different," *homo* for "same," and *gamos* for "marriage" (P. Cohen 2011). But it's too early to know if this idea will catch on.

**heterogamy**

Marriage between a man and a woman.

**homogamy**

Marriage between two people of the same sex.

and young children lived together in these homes, along with grandparents if they were still alive (Steadman 2004). Still, even if prehistoric human societies formed nuclear families, they would not have survived if small families were responsible for all of their own needs. Cooperation beyond the immediate family was always essential.

# From Europe to the United States

For most of this chapter, we will focus on the European origins of American family history. That's not because Europeans are more important than other groups, but because their traditions and practices dominated the legal, political, and cultural landscape in the early years of the country. Europeans were the most

Edouard Victor Durand's *Whitsunday* (1888): What role (if any) does religion play in your family's life?

**patriarchy**

The system of men's control over property and fathers' authority over all family members.

powerful group in early American society; they not only set cultural standards but enforced them by virtue of their political and economic power. Their model of the family was not adopted by everyone, however. In this chapter we will see how the historical experience of other groups diverged from the European-American story. We will return to this theme in Chapter 3, which examines racial and ethnic diversity in contemporary American family life through the intertwined stories of American Indian, African-American, Asian-American, and Latino families.

To help set the stage for American history, we will start with some themes pertaining to families in Europe (I have drawn from several sources, including principally historian Stephanie Coontz [2005]). The first is the important role played by the Christian (Catholic and Protestant) churches. Religious regulation of family life has varied considerably over the centuries, but from the time the Catholic Church consolidated its power throughout the Roman Empire in the late fourth century CE, Christianity set guideposts along the road of family life. With regard to marriage, state-established churches played the role held by government authorities today, determining the validity of marriages, presiding over marriage ceremonies, and allocating power and property among family members.

The second theme we see in European families is the extreme inequality and the separate family worlds of rich and poor. While rich families had elaborate marriage schemes—complex deals that involved land, armies, unwilling princesses, and domineering kings—the poor had no such luxury. They married and reproduced as matters of economic survival, often picking spouses based on whose family had a nearby plot of land or farming tools they needed for their crops. The children of the poor were workers in a family-based economy, not innocent cherubs sheltered from the harsh realities of life. To us, their lives would have seemed hard, bitter, and short.

Both rich and poor, however, shared a common third trait. Regardless of how marriage and family life were structured, family relations were not matters of personal preference or choice. Marriage was a political and economic institution that served important functions in society. For the rich it was necessary for maintaining their lineages and creating ties between powerful families. For the poor it was about arranging cooperation in labor, especially in working the land. In the countryside, survival depended on the division of labor between husband and wife. In those circumstances, marrying for love was far too risky a proposition to be practiced widely. In fact, being too passionate about one's spouse was highly suspect, raising concerns about social stability or even idolatry. Among Christians before the 1600s, the word *love* was usually reserved to describe feelings toward God or one's neighbors, not family members (Coontz 2005).

Finally, a pervasive theme through European family history and family structure is **patriarchy**, a system of male control over the family property and fathers' authority over the behavior of the family's women and children. That authority was not always absolute, but it was almost always present and acknowledged, both formally and informally. Each of these aspects of the European family system left a legacy that formed the backdrop for family life in the American colonies.

# Origins of the American Family

To establish the background for modern American families, we set the stage with two periods: the Colonial period before 1820, and the early modern period of the nineteenth century.

## Colonial America (before 1820)

From the settlement of Europeans through the early nineteenth century, American family history was primarily the story of three interrelated groups: American Indians, White Europeans, and African Americans. In the passages that follow we will examine their stories separately, and consider how they intersected to create the complex set of family practices, dynamics, and traditions that emerged in the modern era.

### American Indians: The Family as Social Structure
The Europeans who founded the colonies that would become the United States encountered a vast and diverse population of what we now call American Indians (or Native Americans). Through a long, painful process (which continues to this day), the descendants of those indigenous tribal groups were incorporated into the fabric of the dominant European-American society. We will investigate American Indians' contemporary family patterns in the next chapter; here we will consider their precolonial traditions.

Despite the diversity among American Indian groups, some historians have attempted to make generalizations about their family traditions. These include a strong respect for elders and a reliance on extended family networks for sharing resources and meeting essential needs. In most cases, family connections were the basic building blocks of social structure. Family relations were the model for nonbiological relationships, including those between members of the larger community and people's connections with the environment and animals (Weaver and White 1997). We know some of this from analyzing their languages. For example, Sioux Indians used family relationship terms for all members of the community, based on the nature of their cooperation. If a grown man moved into a community, he might be considered a stranger until an older woman with

A quilt created by a Sioux woman around 1900 depicts scenes of traditional daily life, including hunting and cooking.

whom he had a relationship started referring to him as her son, at which point he would become brother to her children, uncle to her grandsons, and so on (DeMallie 1994).

One common (although not universal) characteristic that set American Indians apart from Europeans was matrilineal descent, in which people were primarily considered descendants of their mothers rather than their fathers (see Changing Culture, "Family Types and Terms"). Among the Hopi Indians in the high deserts of the Southwest, families lived in clans following mothers' descent, with the oldest daughter inheriting the family home and living there with her husband and children. Because women were the property owners in the household, and men were relative outsiders surrounded by their wives' kin, women had greater authority within the clan (Queen 1985).

On the other hand, American Indians had some family traits in common with Europeans. Most practiced monogamous marriage—although their marriage bonds were not as strong as other relationships, and divorce was more common than among Europeans (Queen 1985). Like Europeans, American Indians also practiced a gender division of labor. For example, in groups that mixed hunting with agriculture, men did most of the hunting, while women grew and prepared food and reared young children (Gearing 1958). Even where matrilineal traditions increased women's power in the household, men usually had more political authority in the larger group (Eggan 1967). However, the relations between American Indian men and women in general remained more equal than they were among Europeans (Coontz 2005:42–43).

## Colonial Americans: "So Chosen, He Is Her Lord" Coming from Europe, colonial Americans brought traditions for marriage and family life to the New World. Marriage for them was a practical arrangement that was considered necessary for civilization, not a source of love and affection. When in 1620 the English colonists in Jamestown, Virginia, showed signs of becoming undisciplined and unruly, a shipment of 90 intended brides was dispatched from the home country. The hope was to provide a stabilizing influence and encourage the male settlers to take a more mature view of the colonial enterprise. (The wives were also a valuable asset to the colonists, who were expected to trade 150 pounds of tobacco for each woman [Ransome 1991].)

Even if these early "mail-order brides" felt more like indentured servants than beloved wives, the male colonists endorsed the idea of choice in principle and rejected the Old World practice of arranged marriages. Still, colonial husbands' authority within marriage was virtually unchecked, and given the dependence of women on their husbands for survival, their choices were in fact very limited. As with the relationship between God and man under Protestant doctrine, the idea of free choice in marriage only served to reinforce the wife's duty to serve her husband. "The woman's own choice makes such a man her husband," wrote Massachusetts governor John Winthrop in the Founders' Constitution in 1645. "Yet being so chosen, he is her lord, and she is to be subject to him" (Winthrop 1853). In the Massachusetts Bay colony, local authorities were more likely to discipline husbands for failing to control their wives than for abusing them (Coontz 2005:141).

For the common people of colonial America—woman or man, free or slave, native or European—government was mostly a distant symbol when it came to family matters (Cott 1976). The system of marriage that prevailed in colonial times was supported by the Christian Church and by the power vested in local community leaders, who imposed their interpretation of Christian doctrine on marriage and divorce. Women could not vote, hold political office, or even serve on juries, so they had little choice but to comply with the marriage system. Their status as members of the local community—and often their very survival—depended on conformity to the standards of the time. Once married, any property that a woman brought to the marriage, as well as the products of her labor, became her husband's. In fact, a wife's legal existence disappeared when she got married: under the legal doctrine of **coverture**, which lasted until the late nineteenth century, wives were incorporated into their husbands' citizenship.

## Children and Families: More Work and Less Play
Colonial American families were large. The average woman bore about seven children in the course of her life, but one or more of them were likely to die at a young age. Children, like everyone else, played an economic role in the family, contributing to its survival and prosperity. Although this seems a shame or even a tragedy to us now—children growing up without a true childhood—the idea of childhood as a uniquely innocent stage of life was not common at that time. Most colonists held to the Calvinist view that children were guilty of original sin, and their evil impulses needed to be controlled through harsh discipline and hard work (Griswold 1993). Many families sent their children to live and work in the homes of others. Even rich parents did not spend much time interacting with their children (by today's standards). Because the bonds between family members in general were much less sentimental than they are now, these decisions did not provoke the kind of guilt or parental anxiety they would today (Coontz 2005).

Although couples had many children, most people did not live in large **extended families** under one roof. Households were mostly made up of nuclear families, plus any boarders or servants they had. Even though they didn't all live together, extended families played an important support role. Most people lived close to their siblings' families, and they shared labor and other resources. Among extended families, a **stem family** was the household formed by one grown child remaining in the family home with his or her parents. The favored child—typically the oldest son—would inherit the family home or farm, while the other siblings started their own households after marriage. This arrangement was common among farm families and those wealthy enough to leave an estate to their children (Ruggles 1994).

**coverture**

A legal doctrine that lasted until the late nineteenth century, under which wives were incorporated into their husbands' citizenship.

**extended families**

Family households in which relatives beyond parents and their children live together.

**stem family**

The household formed by one grown child remaining in the family home with his or her parents.

The colonial way of family life represented the first phase of a transition from the rural family, dominated by European Christian ideology, to the modern, urban, and industrial family system that was to come. As with all such transitions, the old ways were not completely left behind, but the pace of change in the nineteenth century would be so dramatic that many Americans felt powerless to understand, much less control, it.

### African Americans: Families Enslaved

African families had gone through their own transitions, of course, of a particularly devastating nature. From the arrival of the first slaves in Jamestown in 1619 until the mid-1800s, Africans were forcibly removed from their homelands in western and central Africa and subjected to the unspeakable horrors of the Middle Passage aboard slave ships, slave auctions, and ultimately the hardships of plantation labor in the American South (as well as in the Caribbean and South America). Because they were thrown together from diverse backgrounds, and because their own languages and customs were suppressed by slavery, we do not know how much of slave family life was a reflection of African traditions and how much was an adaptation to their conditions and treatment in America (Taylor 2000).

But there is no doubt that family life was one of the victims of the slave system. The histories that have come down to us feature heart-wrenching stories of family separation, including diaries that tell of children literally ripped from their mothers' arms by slave traders, mothers taking poison to prevent themselves from being sold, and parents enduring barbaric whippings as punishment for trying to keep their families together (Lerner 1973). In fact, most slaves only had a given name with no family name, which made the formation and recognition of family lineages difficult or impossible (Frazier 1930). Slave marriage and parenthood were not legally recognized by the states, and separation was a constant threat. Any joy in having children was tempered by the recognition that those children were the property of the slave owner and could be sold or transferred away forever.

A slave family in a Georgia cotton field, c. 1860.

Nevertheless, most slaves lived in families for some or all of their lives. Most married (if not legally) and had children in young adulthood, and most children lived with both parents. This was especially the case on larger plantations rather than small farms, because slaves could carve out some protection for community life if they were in larger groups, and husbands and wives were more likely to remain together (Coles 2006). Even if they had families, however, African Americans for the most part were excluded from the emerging modern family practices described in the next section until after slavery ended.

# The Emerging Modern Family (1820–1900)

During the Roman Empire (roughly 27 BCE–476 CE), the Latin word *familia* meant not just a man's wives and children, but also his slaves and servants, who would bear his name after they were freed (Dixon 1992). In some ways, patriarchal power has been declining ever since. But with the spread of democracy and industrial capitalism, from the time of the American Revolution into the nineteenth century, new ideas, new laws, and the growth of the market economy hastened the erosion of fathers' absolute authority, bringing "profound changes in record time" (Coontz 2005:145).

**Marriage: New Ideals, New Traditions** Ironically, the period of rapid change brought about by democracy and industrialism also created a family characteristic that we often think of as "traditional": the sharply divided roles of fathers as breadwinners and mothers as homemakers. Even though most families still depended on the economic contributions of wives, the ideal of man as the economic provider became a powerful symbol in American culture. That ideal made men even more powerful and dominant within the family, even as women started embracing for themselves the growing ideology of individualism and personal freedom. The principle of autonomy for the country, as enshrined in the Declaration of Independence, also applied to individual citizens. As a result, individual free choice in marriage, as in democracy, was an ideal that was widely shared in the early years of the United States.

However, not everyone was happy with the idea that individuals, like colonies, had a right to independence and self-determination. A conservative backlash grew in the nineteenth century, led by those in positions of power who had used the language of independence during the American Revolution, but who grew increasingly uneasy with the spread of that idea throughout the population (even though slaves obviously were not included). These conservatives believed that women's freedom threatened the traditional family. And they had some success. In the decades after the American Revolution, most states went out of their way to pass laws denying women's right to vote, instead of merely assuming they were forbidden from doing so.

But it was too late. Independence, once promised, proved hard to revoke. The result was what Coontz calls "a peculiar compromise between egalitarian and patriarchal views" (2005:153). Women were still considered free, and the concept of male authority began to be replaced by the idea of men as "protectors" of women, while women cared for, loved, and nurtured their husbands. These gender roles came to be known as the separate spheres.

Meanwhile, with the recognition of individual rights and the spread of industrialization in the 1800s, the essential political and economic functions of marriage began to erode. That left young adults freer to consider the emotional aspects of their future marriages and to challenge parents or other authorities who tried to impose marriages on them for their own reasons. Companionship, affinity, love, and affection in marriage all began to grow more important in the minds of young adults—especially women—seeking a spouse.

John George Brown's *The Music Lesson* (1870) and *Courtship* (c. 1870) illustrate middle-class and working-class couples, respectively. Note the difference in their surroundings.

Not surprisingly, youthful ambition for happy marriages sometimes came into conflict with parental concern for economic or social status. The practice of **courtship** emerged as a compromise to reconcile these competing interests. Young couples themselves initiated courtship, which normally began with supervised contact in some public or semipublic place. Among the wealthy or middle class, that might mean a formal party or private social event. Despite having a choice at the outset, young people remained under their parents' watchful eyes. If the couple's interest persisted, additional meetings would take place in the woman's home, possibly leading to marriage if the parents approved. The system made it difficult for young women to act entirely against their parents' wishes, but offered some elements of free choice.

Among the poor and working class, parental control in spouse selection was less complete, but it was usually acknowledged that parents should approve their children's choices. Life at the low end of the income scale did not permit the luxury of shaping families around individual emotional desires. But the seed of the idea was planted, and whenever the standard of living permitted it, the poor would embrace the principles of choice and independence in family life. This would emerge as an important theme in the late twentieth century.

**Children and Families: Fewer and More Tender** One of the most monumental changes in family life in the nineteenth century was the drop in the number of children in each family. For White families, the average number was cut almost exactly in half over the century (see Figure 2.1). This was partly the result of couples learning how to prevent pregnancy. Mass production of condoms began in the mid-1800s (Gamson 1990), although most couples practiced withdrawal or limited the frequency of intercourse, as birth control information was not widely available in many places. But the declining birth rate was also the result of couples *wanting* fewer children. For one thing, many fewer children

Figure 2.1 **Children per woman, White women, 1800–1900 (average number ever born)**

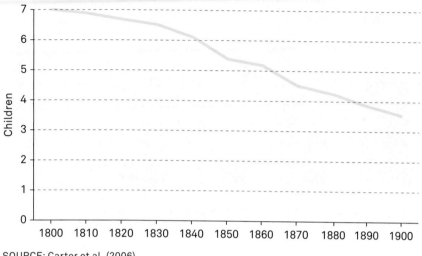

SOURCE: Carter et al. (2006).

died after the mid-nineteenth century; the rate of infant deaths (those in the first year of life) was cut almost in half in just 50 years and has declined even more dramatically since 1900 (see Figure 2.2).

The emerging modern childhood also changed the logic of child rearing. During the nineteenth century, children's individuality emerged as a valued ideal, reinforced by the drop in the number of children and their greater likelihood of surviving. For example, children more often had their own rooms in the family home, with toys and books made especially for them. And they were less often named after their parents, helping to instill an independent identity. The prevailing view of children's morality also changed, as a new generation of experts declared that children were a blank slate of innocence, displacing the Calvinist notion that they harbored evil spirits that needed to be crushed. That change in thinking occurred as men started to work outside the home more often. So it was mothers who embraced the new, tenderer form of parenting, replacing the harsh discipline of fathers (Griswold 1993). Gradually, the parent-child relationship became more emotionally close.

Even between fathers and children—especially their sons—there were new emotional bonds. Instead of being tyrants with unchecked power, fathers took on the role of moral authorities who (ideally) led more by persuasion than by force. And children (again, especially sons) began to question fathers' domination in the family (Mintz 1998). As the historian Robert Griswold put it, "Hierarchy and order, the watchwords of older forms of paternal dominance, gave way to a growing emphasis on mutuality, companionship, and personal happiness" (1993:11).

Smaller families also meant that there were fewer adult children with whom elderly parents could live. As in colonial America, elderly parents mostly lived in their own homes with one of their grown children. However, most adults still

Figure 2.2 **Infant mortality, 1850–2000 (deaths per 1,000 births)**

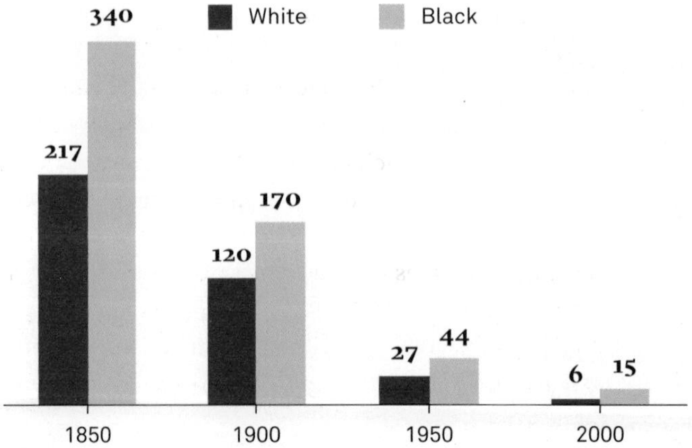

SOURCE: Carter et al. (2006).

did not live with elderly relatives, chiefly because there weren't many old people in the population. Only 4 percent of Americans were age 60 or older in 1850, compared with 19 percent today (Ruggles et al. 2014).

**Institutional Arenas** In Chapter 1, we introduced the idea of three inter-related institutional arenas: the family, the market, and the state. These concepts help us understand the change in family form and function that has taken place over the last 200 years. Beginning in the nineteenth century, the market and state emerged as dominant features of modern society, and as a result, the family arena was transformed. I will briefly explain how the family lost its status as the center of the economy and began to be more directly regulated by the state. At the same time, the state started providing services that lightened the load on family care providers.

## Family and Market: Men and Women, Separate and Together

In the nineteenth century, for the first time in history, "most people worked for someone else during their entire adult lives" (Katz 1986). Although that might not sound liberating, these workers were called "free labor" (as opposed to slaves) because their self-image was one of independently acting members of the new industrial economy (Foner 1995). That wage-labor relationship helped foster a sense of individual identity, reflecting American democratic ideals. Men's new identities—and the new workers were mostly men—were reinforced outside the walls of the family home in the factories and workshops of the industrial economy, where income-generating work took place.

Although there was no plan to make it happen this way, the industrial revolution also helped to reinforce the division of gender roles for men and women. Under the new doctrine of **separate spheres**, women were to make the home a haven, a sanctuary from the harsh realities of the industrial economy in which men worked for pay. This separation—women at home, men at work—was said

**separate spheres**

The cultural doctrine under which women were to work at home, to make it a sanctuary from the industrial world in which their husbands worked for pay.

to provide the balance necessary for social harmony (Strasser 1982). There were important exceptions, such as the hiring of young women to work in the early industrial mills of New England, but this only highlighted the rule that real workers were supposed to be men, because young women were expected to leave the workforce once they married.

Not surprisingly, the ideal of separate spheres was most strongly embraced among the expanding white-collar middle class in urban areas and promoted in new magazines targeted at that audience, such as *Harper's* and *Ladies' Magazine* (Mintz 1998). Men from these middle-class families, working at the growing number of desk jobs—wearing shirts with white collars—could be seen commuting on streetcars from suburban homes to their jobs in the central cities as early as the middle of the nineteenth century (Griswold 1993). Although separate spheres were not attainable by the great majority of working-class families, the ideal nevertheless was shared by men and women of most racial and ethnic groups and among the poor as well.

An important exception to these trends was farm families, many of whom continued to work in the older "family mode" of production. However, by the end of the nineteenth century, only 38 percent of the labor force worked in agriculture, while the proportion of the population living in urban areas (places with more than 2,500 people) climbed steadily to 40 percent (Figure 2.3). Further, the change in economic organization brought by industrialization was so pervasive that even farmwork increasingly operated along market principles, with workers leaving home to work for wages on a farm run as a business.

In the end, industrialism and separate spheres increased economic inequality between husbands and wives, with men's advantage growing. Because these new waged workers were men, the shift of economic power from the home to the workplace left men positioned to wield that power. And although women's

Figure 2.3 **From farms to cities, 1800–1900**

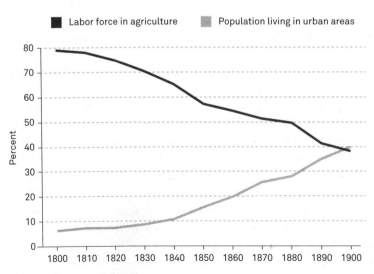

SOURCE: Carter et al. (2006).

labor in the home remained crucial for economic survival, the fact that it did not generate as much income as men's wage work created the impression that wives were dependent on their husbands.

But if these changes strengthened husbands' authority, they also strengthened that of wives. Although men wielded more economic power, women's influence over the children and household was enhanced. Emboldened by their newfound status as "managers" of the home, middle-class women especially sought recognition for the work they did. When that recognition was not forthcoming, many grew frustrated, steeped as they were in the cause of individual liberty and freedom. In 1869, for example, Harriet Beecher Stowe—who had published the sensational abolitionist novel *Uncle Tom's Cabin* almost two decades earlier—and her sister Catharine lamented men's high status, complaining that the "honor and duties of the family state are not duly appreciated" (Beecher and Stowe 1869:221). The two women listed the vast array of responsibilities burdening the typical (wealthy) wife:

> She has a husband, to whose particular tastes and habits she must accommodate herself; she has children whose health she must guard, . . . whose temper and habits she must regulate. . . . She has constantly changing domestics, with all varieties of temper and habits, whom she must govern. . . . She is required to regulate the finances of the domestic state, and constantly to adapt expenditures to the means and to the relative claims of each department. She has the direction of the kitchen. . . . She has the claims of society to meet, visits to receive and return, and the duties of hospitality to sustain. She has the poor to relieve; benevolent societies to aid; the schools of her children to inquire and decide about; the care of the sick and the aged; the nursing of infancy; and the endless miscellany of odd items, constantly recurring in a large family.

In the nineteenth century, the explosion of market relationships took families out of the center of economic life. However, it also reinforced the family as a separate social space, a place where a new kind of relationship developed. Less economic and more emotional, the modern family was emerging as a distinct institutional arena.

### Family and State: "Monogamous Morality"

The family household under the principle of separate spheres was increasingly seen as a private place, caring for its members and raising its children instead of producing goods and services for public trade and consumption. In most cases, the state did not interfere with husbands' authority. Under coverture, a wife was incorporated into her husband's citizenship, under his name, and the husband was the family's representative when it came to interacting with the authorities or the law. Politicians generally believed that social stability required peace within the family. In fact, President Abraham Lincoln, warning against the conflict between slave-owning states and free states that was leading to the Civil War, knew that the public would understand him when he used the family as a metaphor, saying, "a house divided against itself cannot stand" (Cott 2000:77). Peace within the family required strong male leadership, just as peace within the nation required a strong federal government.

But if the government didn't interfere with male authority within the household, it nevertheless became much more assertive about regulating who was married and under what conditions. In colonial times, most marriages had been blessed by local authorities alone, if at all, and there was very little civil regulation of family life. In the industrial era, however, the state's practical authority increased. For most people, the most powerful evidence of this authority may have been the spread of public education, which used local taxation to fund schools for most of the free population by the middle of the nineteenth century (Goldin and Katz 2003). In addition, such apparently simple functions as law enforcement agencies and the national postal service began reaching further and further into daily life.

The federal regulation of family life revolved around marriage and citizenship. Because a married man was the real citizen in the household, representing the rest of the family in the political arena, it made sense to insist that his marriage credentials were legitimate. In the name of safeguarding the character of the nation, then, the government began enforcing a sort of national "monogamous morality" when it came to family definition (Cott 2000:136).

Monogamous morality was not a new standard. It drew heavily from the Christian tradition, writing into law what had previously been religious or local custom. Rules for marriage included **monogamy** and a moral standard that required women to be faithful to their husbands (though not necessarily the other way around), while husbands supported their wives and children economically. For example, when the government supported Civil War soldiers' widows, officials made sure they had not remarried, in which case the burden of support would pass to their new husbands (Cott 2000).

**monogamy**

A family system in which each person has only one spouse.

The reach of moral enforcement can also be seen in the Comstock Act of 1873, which banned shipment of "obscene" material in the U.S. mail. That meant not just pornography, but also literature promoting birth control and even nonmonogamous relationships such as those advocated by some "free love" communes at the time. But monogamy itself was a key target of federal policy. Under the Dawes Act of 1887, a federal statute that granted individual landholding rights only to those male American Indians who were legally and monogamously married, Christian standards were effectively imposed over Indian family traditions (see Chapter 3). The enforcement of monogamy led to a long-running legal and political feud with the new Mormon Church, a feud that ended only after the Mormons officially renounced **polygamy** and Utah was permitted to become a state in 1896 (Cherlin and Furstenberg 1986). This burst of federal family regulation in the second half of the nineteenth century was mirrored by state laws and decisions at lower levels of government—for example, prosecuting and even jailing men who remarried after deserting their wives. In many ways, then, at the end of the nineteenth century, the government at all levels laid a much heavier hand on the family lives of its citizens than it had a century before.

**polygamy**

A family system in which one person has more than one spouse, usually one man and multiple women.

## No Families: Widows and Orphans Families had become less central as sites of economic activity, but they remained an essential source of economic support for most Americans: despite their inequality in the marketplace, husbands and wives were in fact dependent on each other, just as children were

The Sisters of Charity created the New York Foundling in 1869. It still exists today as a foster home and child welfare agency.

dependent on their parents. Yet in the new male-centered wage economy, many widows and orphans had no one to provide monetary support and joined the ranks of the chronically impoverished or the mentally or physically disabled. In this period, being short on family members often went along with being short on necessities.

In the past, people in these predicaments had been cared for by their extended families (if they got any care at all). But starting in the mid-nineteenth century, a new set of specialized institutions arose to provide for, or at least supervise, those who could not earn their keep in the industrial economy. This was a weak, disorganized patchwork of poorhouses, orphanages, penitentiaries, and almshouses, which often started out as charitable institutions before being taken over by local or state governments. There were two common features of this emerging welfare system. First, it isolated those in need of assistance from the rest of the population in residential institutions, sometimes for their entire lives. Second, the care provided was usually inadequate, since a lack of resources and ineffective or nonexistent government regulation made it impossible for institutions to provide a decent life for their wards (Katz 1986).

The plight of widows in particular was widely known. In fact, the federal government's ability to recruit soldiers for its army in the Civil War relied on the promise of widows' pensions, without which many soldiers would not have volunteered, for fear of leaving their wives and children destitute. The resulting bureaucracy was the precursor to our modern welfare system, providing federal support for hundreds of thousands of veterans and their widows (Skocpol 1992). This breakthrough made it possible for Americans without the means to support themselves—and without the support of employed family members—to survive under the care of the state. That made living without a family possible, a rare feat in the history of our species, although in the century to follow it would become increasingly common (Klinenberg 2012). Not everyone in need was able to benefit from early pension and welfare programs, which were selective in whom they assisted, but the modern state increasingly stepped in when people could not draw sustenance from the market or the family (Gordon 1994).

## African, Asian, and Mexican Americans: Families Apart

Being without a family was one of many problems that confronted members of America's minority groups in the nineteenth century, whether African Americans emerging from slavery, Asian-American immigrant communities, or Mexicans who found their lands annexed within growing U.S. boundaries. Each group developed its own family arrangements and practices in ways that were related to, but distinct from, those of Whites.

For African-American families, the Civil War marked a decisive turning point. The abolition of slavery in 1865 did not mean their liberation from racial oppression; many African Americans entered into a new agricultural system of sharecropping in which they worked on land owned by Whites in conditions of desperate poverty, albeit not formal slavery. And in the South their very citizenship was far from guaranteed. But slavery's demise did make possible a family revival, allowing some former slaves to reunite with long-lost spouses and children and allowing many others to marry, have children, and live together in the manner of their choosing for the first time in America (Gutman 1976). For the first time, also, African-American families could be legally recognized. In fact, the federal government, under monogamous morality principles, required legal marriages among those who qualified for federal relief provided to former slaves (Cott 2000).

The African-American families that emerged in the late nineteenth century exhibited more gender equality, based on the greater economic role of women, than Whites families did. But their marriages also were more fragile, partly as a result of the persistent poverty and hardship they suffered, and ended more often in divorce or widowhood. On the other hand, African Americans developed stronger extended family networks of caring and cooperation. This was especially necessary for children, who were frequently cared for by extended family members and foster or adoptive parents (Furstenberg 2007).

The first large Asian group in the United States was the Chinese. These immigrants began arriving in significant numbers during the gold rush years in the West, starting in 1852. Over the next few decades, several hundred thousand

An 1857 wood engraving that depicts Chinese miners living and working in California during the Gold Rush.

Chinese came to work in the mines and build the railroads of the growing western states, making up a substantial part of the manual labor force (Fong 2008). Almost all of them were men, most of whom had wives and children in China, where they eventually returned (Chew and Liu 2004). This arrangement—married workers spending years separated from their spouses—has been called the split-household family (Glenn and Yap 2002). In response to anti-Chinese racism in the West, Congress passed the Chinese Exclusion Act of 1882, which cut off most new immigration. As a result, few Chinese women could join the single men who remained. And because Chinese men were forbidden from marrying Whites (at least in California, where most of them lived), these men remained unmarried and childless. In the next chapter, we will see how the Chinese community—along with other groups from Asia—eventually flourished in the twentieth century.

Unlike the Chinese, who migrated to the United States in search of jobs, the first major group of Latinos in the United States were not immigrants. They were the descendants of Spanish colonists and Aztecs, and they became Americans when the United States won the Mexican-American War in 1848, laying claim to more than half of Mexico in what is now the American Southwest (Nostrand 1975). The new Mexican Americans were mostly poor farmers, but as large commercial farms began taking over their land, and as new railroads reached the territory, many traveled around the country for work. Like the Chinese and African Americans, then, family life for Latinos in early America often included long periods of separation, which required strong family bonds and extended family care relationships (Baca Zinn and Pok 2002). This experience contributed to Mexican Americans' *familism* (see Chapter 3), a strong orientation toward family needs and obligations that persists today (Landale and Oropesa 2007).

# The Modern Family (1900–1960s)

During the nineteenth century, a number of forces had pulled men and women toward a nuclear family arrangement in which one employed man was stably married to, and economically supporting, one homemaking woman and their children. These included the cultural ideal of separate spheres, economic forces pushing men toward paid labor outside the home, and government attempts to enforce "moral" marriage. But most Americans couldn't live that way even if they wanted to. Most men didn't make enough money to "keep" a woman at home, and most families couldn't afford a home that provided the kind of privacy the ideal demanded.

By the middle of the twentieth century, however, the goal of the male breadwinner–female homemaker household was for the first time within the reach of most American families. Those who achieved that goal attempted to create a new kind of marriage, in which men and women were friends and companions as well as romantic partners. On the surface, by the 1950s the dream of the **companionship family** appeared to have become a reality. Beneath the surface, however, the foundation was decidedly shaky.

**companionship family**

An ideal type of family characterized by the mutual affection, equality, and comradeship of its members.

## Marriage: Unequal Companions

Around the turn of the twentieth century, many young men lived independently, and many others lived with their parents or as boarders until they married in their late 20s. Women usually stayed in the family home until they married. In 1900, the typical man married at about age 26, the typical woman at 22 (see Figure 2.4).

Marriage was becoming more attractive to young people for cultural, economic, and political reasons. First, the nature of marriage—and the ideal of marriage—was undergoing a cultural shift that has been described as "institution to companionship." That was the subtitle of a textbook you might have read if you took this course in the 1940s. The author, Ernest Burgess, saw a new,

Figure 2.4 **Median age at first marriage, 1890–2011**

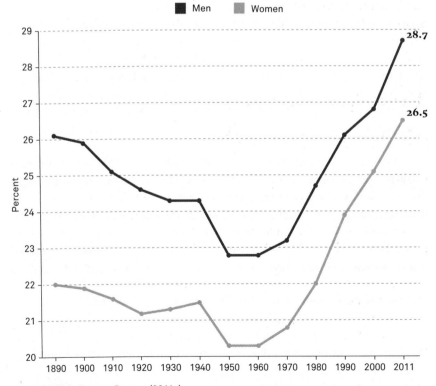

SOURCE: U.S. Census Bureau (2011c).

Table 2.1  **The companionship family ideal**

|  | PATRIARCHAL FAMILY | COMPANIONSHIP FAMILY |
|---|---|---|
| BASIS FOR CHOOSING A SPOUSE | Parental influence, social status, and economic needs | Self-directed motivation based on affection and personality |
| HUSBAND-WIFE RELATIONSHIP | Subordination of wife to husband | Equality based on consensus |
| BONDS HOLDING FAMILIES TOGETHER | Father's authority | Mutual affection and common interests |
| FAMILY SIZE | Extended | Nuclear |
| FAMILY GOALS | Duty and tradition | Happiness and personal growth |

modern family type, which he described as "the companionship family, characterized by the mutual affection, sympathetic understanding, and comradeship of its members" (Burgess 1963:vii). I summarize the ideal of the companionship family and how it differed from the patriarchal family of the past in Table 2.1.

The companionship family ideal was just that—an ideal, not a reality. But the description Burgess offered shows the direction in which many people thought families were headed: smaller families, freely chosen, that make decisions based on mutual interests, in the service of the individual happiness and personal growth of husband and wife. It was an ideal shared by many Americans, especially (but not exclusively) the White, middle-class families that dominated popular culture, politics, and the business world in the mid-twentieth century (May 1988).

The core relationship of the new model family was the **companionate marriage**, which was a companionship, a friendship, and a romance, rather than being a practical platform for cooperation and survival, as marriage seemed to have been in the past (Cherlin 2009). The companionate ideal was especially attractive to men working in the growing sector of white-collar corporate jobs, many of whom, even if well paid, felt alienated and frustrated by their impersonal bureaucratic work (Mintz 1998).

The promise of companionate marriage also contributed to the breakdown of the courtship system—the old compromise between free choice and parental supervision in choosing a spouse. The independence of young people was no longer so easily controlled. In the growing urban areas, there was plentiful opportunity for unsupervised interaction, fueled by cash in the pockets of employed young men, and driven—at least in part—by cars.

In this way, courtship was replaced by the freewheeling system of **dating**, in which young adults spent time with a variety of partners, before making

**companionate marriage**

A view of marriage as a companionship, a friendship, and a romance, rather than as a practical platform for cooperation and survival.

**dating**

The mate selection process in which young adults spend time with a variety of partners before making a long-term commitment.

long-term commitments (see Chapter 7). The authority of parents was severely compromised in the process, replaced by the authority of young men, who now initiated and paid for dates. The companionate marriages that resulted from dating—despite their ideology of sharing—thus started off with a man in the driver's seat.

Beyond the symbolic importance of independence, however, the economic opportunity necessary for achieving the ideal—an employed man supporting a homemaking wife in their own home—became more accessible. For many years, American workers (and their unions) had demanded from their employers a **family wage,** the amount necessary for a male earner to provide subsistence for his wife and children without their having to work for pay. As American industry grew and the threat of labor unrest became more unsettling to employers, more companies started paying their workers enough to support a whole family. Ford Motor Company crossed a symbolic threshold when it dramatically increased pay, introducing the "Five Dollar Day" in 1914. That wage was intended to promote workforce stability, home ownership (and car buying), as well as worker loyalty (May 1982). And it succeeded.

The federal government also gave marriage a political boost in the early twentieth century, replacing the stick with a carrot. The strict moral tone of marital regulation of the nineteenth century gave way to a pattern of economic incentives for marriage (Cott 2000), including Social Security and Aid to Dependent Children (discussed shortly). These programs indirectly promoted marriage because women who never married or who got divorced were not eligible at first to receive their support. After World War II, the government provided extensive benefits to male veterans, especially low-interest loans to buy homes, which also had the effect of encouraging marriage (Cherlin 2009).

Taken together, all of these factors—the cultural shift toward the companionate marriage and away from parental authority, the economic opportunities for independence provided to men through industrial development, and the political incentives to marry offered by the government—increased the motivation and ability of young people to marry in the first half of the twentieth century. Because most married couples conformed to the separate spheres ideal, or tried to, some observers assumed that the family as an institution was stable and secure. Talcott Parsons, the sociologist most identified with the theory of structural functionalism (see Chapter 1), was one such naive observer, writing in 1955: "It seems quite safe in general to say that the adult feminine role has not ceased to be anchored primarily in the internal affairs of the family, as wife, mother and manager of the household, while the role of the adult male is primarily anchored in the occupational world" (Parsons and Bales 1955:12–14). That image might have applied to the 1950s, but it would not last much longer.

**family wage**

The amount necessary for a male earner to provide subsistence for his wife and children without their having to work for pay.

The companionate marriage made the combination of companionship, friendship, and romance between equals the new marital ideal; however, the companionate marriage still left the man in the driver's seat.

# Children and Families: From Bust to Boom

On average, Americans married younger and younger over the first half of the twentieth century, but the birth rate continued to decline—an unusual combination. White women had an average of 3.6 children each in 1900, and that fell to 2.3 children by 1940, continuing the steady decline we saw in the nineteenth century (Carter et al. 2006). But all that changed—at least temporarily—from the end of World War II to the mid-1960s. The **baby boom**, which refers to the period of high birth rates between 1946 and 1964, reversed the long-standing pattern of declining fertility (see the Story Behind the Numbers), producing a huge population bubble of "baby boomers" who are now in their 50s and 60s.

To understand this seismic event in family history, we need to look at the experience of the cohort of adults who married in the 1940s and 1950s. There was a sudden drop in age at marriage between 1940 and 1950 as the young couples who would produce the baby boomers got married (look again at Figure 2.4). If you work back from marriages that took place in, say, 1945, you'll see that those couples were born in the early to mid-1920s and thus experienced childhoods marked by the deprivation of the Great Depression of the 1930s. The economy revived and eventually soared as a result of American participation in World War II (1941–1945), when increasing numbers of women entered the workforce to replace men who were serving in the military. Even though millions of men returned to their jobs after the war (and women resumed their roles as homemakers), the nation faced a cumulative shortage of workers brought on by the decline in birth rates in the first half of the century. That shortage of workers, combined with the growing economy, produced a dramatic spike in wages beginning in the late 1940s.

Baby boom parents experienced a rare sequence of events, with severe economic depression and all-consuming war followed by sudden prosperity (Cherlin 2009). After difficult childhoods and a long period of uncertainty about the future, they embraced the prospect of stability. They married, and an unprecedented number of them bought homes, encouraged by a boom in housing construction in the suburbs (connected to cities by the new interstate highway system, begun in 1956) and made affordable (to Whites) through new federal mortgage guarantees (Freund 2007). The historian Elaine Tyler May writes that American families after World War II perceived an "intense need to feel liberated from the past and secure in the future" (1988:10). To achieve that feeling, they turned inward toward family life—and they had a lot of children.

In light of these long-term trends and the unique circumstances of the postwar years, it is clear that the 1950s

**baby boom**

The period of high birth rates in the United States between 1946 and 1964.

Television shows from the mid-twentieth century, such as *The Adventures of Ozzie and Harriet*, showcased the ideal of the breadwinner-homemaker family.

were a highly unusual decade. Since that time, the 1950s have come to be seen as the pinnacle of the "traditional" American family, epitomized by the stably married and loving couple, headed by one male wage earner and made possible by a homemaking wife. And in fact, that model was never more prevalent than in the 1950s, but it was a tradition that was invented in the nineteenth century and it had very shallow roots. The traditional family had always been more an ideal than a reality. In fact, it seems most realistic to describe it as a myth (Coontz 1992).

# New Family Diversity (1960s–Present)

There are many dimensions to the family changes that occurred after the 1950s, but I think they can best be captured by the concept of increasing family diversity. More individuals and families were arranging their lives and relationships in more different ways than ever before. The 1950s-style "traditional" family persisted as an ideal for many people. But as a reality it shrank further and further from its dominant position. In its place emerged a wide range of families and living arrangements, most prominently including individuals living alone (both younger and older adults), single parents (some of them divorced), blended stepfamilies, and unmarried couples. Each of these changes will be featured in later chapters; but here I want to focus on the growth of family diversity itself.

Why did family patterns depart so dramatically from the 1950s ideal? Two institutional factors were important in the postwar period. First, market forces more than ever challenged some of the core functional tasks of modern families. With the growth of modern services, such as laundries and restaurants, and new technology, such as washing machines (see Changing Technology, "Laborsaving Devices"), much of the work that housewives did was taken over by paid service workers or machines. One government analyst went so far as to predict that "the final result might be virtually to eliminate the home as a place of work and housewives as a functional group" (Durand 1946).

But the biggest challenge to the 1950s ideal was women's increased tendency to leave home for paid work. Women's employment had increased gradually from the beginning of the century into the 1950s. During that time, most employers only hired single women. But starting in the 1950s, as women married at younger ages and the growing economy needed more workers, there simply weren't enough single women to go around. Employers opened their doors to married women, and women responded eagerly (Goldin 1990). After 1960, employment rates for both married and unmarried women rocketed upward in a 30-year burst that would radically change the foundation of marriage and family life in the United States (Cotter et al. 2004). Women's work finally moved primarily from the home to the market, following men's movement of the previous century. This didn't eliminate housework and care work done at home, but for the first time, a majority of women's work was done as part of the paid labor force (Thistle 2006).

# Decline in birthrates, increase in women workers

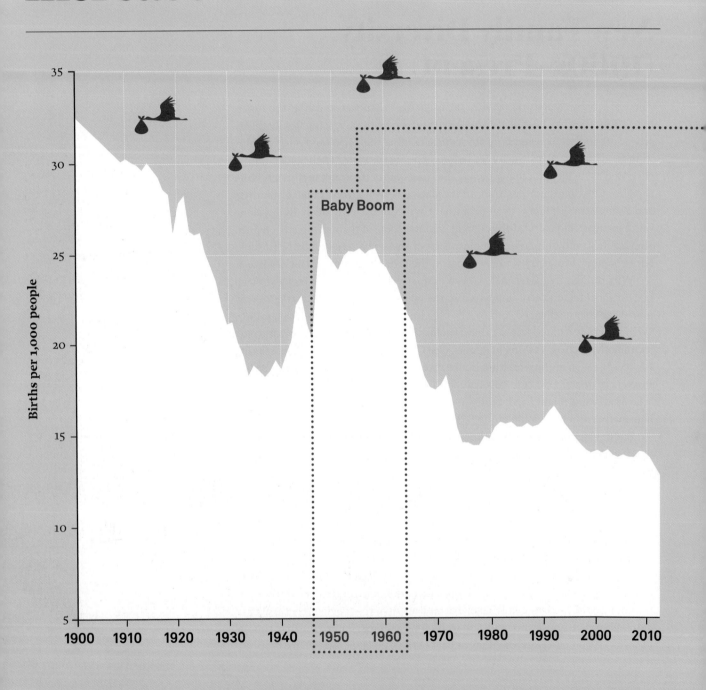

From 1900 to 2010 the birth rate dropped roughly 60 percent, from more than 32 births per 1,000 people in the population to 13. During that time, women entered the paid labor force in growing numbers, working everywhere from factories and restaurants to schools and hospitals. But the story isn't that simple. Starting at the end of World War II, in 1945, there was a huge increase in birth rates—the baby boom. Why? The children of the Great Depression (from the 1930s) found economic prosperity after World War II (in the 1950s). Men had good jobs, and the suburbs beckoned. They bought homes and married young at record rates, and went on to have a lot of children. But in the end, despite the baby boom, the big stories of the century were still falling birth rates and rising employment for women.

*Sources: Vital Statistics of the United States, Statistical Abstracts of the United States, Current Population Surveys.*

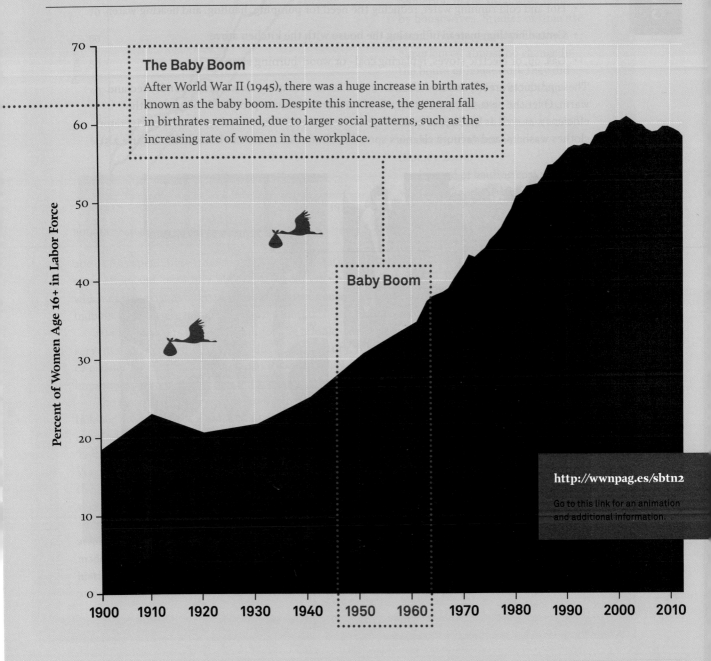

### The Baby Boom

After World War II (1945), there was a huge increase in birth rates, known as the baby boom. Despite this increase, the general fall in birthrates remained, due to larger social patterns, such as the increasing rate of women in the workplace.

Baby Boom

**Percent of Women Age 16+ in Labor Force**

http://wwnpag.es/sbtn2

Go to this link for an animation and additional information.

That shift to market work reinforced women's independence *within* their families as well as *from* their families. Women freed from family dependence could live singly, even with children; they could afford to risk divorce; and they could live with a man without the commitment of marriage.

State forces were the second institutional factor promoting family diversity. A combination of pension and welfare programs offered the opportunity for more people to structure their lives independently. The greatest program, in terms of social impact and economic cost, was the pension plan known as Social Security. Created in 1935, Social Security provided pensions to wives after their husbands retired or died. It also freed millions of Americans from the need to live with their children in old age (Engelhardt and Gruber 2004). At the beginning of the twentieth century, the census counted only 1 in 10 people age 55 or older living with no relatives; but by the end of the century, the proportion was more than 1 in 4. Most of that change occurred between 1940 and 1980.

For younger adults, growing welfare support made marriage less of a necessity, at least for poor women with children. The federal program known as Aid to Families with Dependent Children had been created as part of the Social Security Act to support widows and women who had been abandoned by their husbands. In the 1960s and 1970s, the program grew explosively, eventually supporting millions of never-married mothers and their children. Although it always carried a shameful stigma and provided a minimal level of monetary support, welfare nevertheless underwrote the independence of many poor single women, thereby increasing the options available to them (Mink 1998).

The growth of women's employment was more striking among those with higher earning power, especially college graduates (Cohen and Bianchi 1999). Poor women, especially African-American women, had long been more likely to work for pay, but their lower earnings did not offer the same personal independence that those with better jobs enjoyed. On the other hand, welfare support was a bigger factor in the growing independence of poor women. Thus, market forces increased the independence of middle-class and more highly educated women, while state forces increased the independence of poor women.

As a result of these trends, after the 1950s more people had more choices for how to live and arrange their family lives, and the diversity of family arrangements increased dramatically. One way of representing that change is shown in Figure 2.6. Here I have categorized each household into one of five types and calculated what percentage of households were in each arrangement, from 1880 to 2010. The largest category is households composed of married couples living with no one except their own children. If there was any other relative living in a household, I counted it as an extended household. The third category is individuals who live alone. Fourth are single parents (most of them mothers) living with no one besides their own children. In the final category are households made up of people who are not related (including unmarried couples).

Figure 2.6 shows that the married-couple family peaked between 1950 and 1960, when two-thirds of households represented this arrangement. After that decade, the proportion of married-couple households dropped rapidly to less than half (45 percent) in 2010. The greatest increase during this period was in the categories of individuals and single parents, which together accounted for

Figure 2.6 **Distribution of household types, 1880–2010**

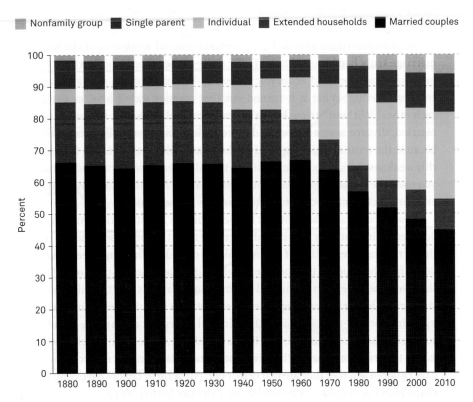

Note: Data for 1890 are not available; these are interpolated.

SOURCE: Author's calculations from U.S. Census data as compiled by IPUMS
(Ruggles et al. 2014).

39 percent of all households in 2010. Extended households are less common than they were a century ago, mostly as a result of the greater independence of older people (although their numbers have increased again in the last several decades). In sum, the chart shows that the dominant married-couple household of the first half of the twentieth century was replaced not by a new standard, but rather by a general increase in family diversity.

## Marriage: Out with the Old

The increase in women's paid work was an important factor in the decline of married-couple family dominance. It highlighted a crucial weakness in the companionate marriage model. Although in principle based on equality and consensus, the relationship between husbands and wives in the companionate marriage was far from equal: husbands had more power because they earned all or most of the family's income. This became more apparent when women started pouring made possible the transformation of marriage from a necessity to a voluntary arrangement. And that, in turn, changed the nature of the marriage relationship.

In each of the three institutional arenas that we are focusing on in this book—the state, the market, and the family—a form of independence is possible and becomes desirable for most people. That is, each arena includes an independent role to which people may aspire, even if it is not attainable by everyone all the time.

In the state arena, independence is marked by the role of citizen and the rights it prescribes. The state certifies that independent role as an individual right, available to all citizens in a modern democratic society. For women, independence was formally achieved only with the passage of the Nineteenth Amendment to the Constitution, giving them the right to vote, in 1919. For African-American women and men in much of the country, it wasn't achieved until the passage of the Civil Rights Act of 1964 and the Voting Rights Act of 1965.

Independence in the market arena is chiefly expressed by the role of worker, as we saw with male workers in the nineteenth century. Women increasingly moved into that role in the second half of the twentieth century. In the market arena, everyone is a consumer, but only workers who have their own incomes can act independently in their consumption behavior, rather than acting on behalf of someone else (such as a husband).

In the family arena, with the development of the love-based marriage and the expectations of mutuality and affection within the family that it entails, the role of family member now implies independence as well. That independence is represented by the marriage choice. Just as you can vote and work for whomever you want, so you are free to marry whomever you want—and to walk away from a spouse whenever you want.

Independence in each of these arenas is, naturally, a double-edged sword. In the state arena, citizenship rights come with responsibilities that restrict our choices, from taxation to regulation to (at the extreme) compulsory military service. In the market, the freedom to contract our own labor also gives employers the freedom to hire and fire without regard for loyalty. In the family arena, the independence achieved in the twentieth century introduced a sense of instability that once was unfamiliar but now has become a way of life. As insecurity in the market and family arenas has increased—epitomized by job loss, falling wages, divorce, and single parenthood—some people argue that the state should provide additional protections to individuals (Saraceno and Keck 2011). This question is at the center of much of the policy debate we will explore in Chapter 13.

## Children and Families: Emotional Bonds

As marriage has changed—becoming more emotional and less essential, more an expression of independence than of dependence—how have the relationships between parents and children changed? Falling birth rates, especially after the baby boom, mean that children have fewer siblings today than they did in previous eras, so the interactions between parents and their few children may have

women to keep their family
husband's name. Although t
forbid women to keep their
that the question had becom

In recent years, only 3 pe
name that differs from their
age 30 (Gooding and Kreider
different surnames, this clea

Naming children present
and potential anxieties. Mo
as a project in the twentiet
project with respect to thei
name their children after th
name simply because they li
it signals a certain style (suc
the kind of person they hope
celebrity), or because it show
has become important enoug
articles, and websites to help
book called *Baby Names for D*

The result of all these cho
of names. Using a technique
this trend by showing the pe
popular names in each decad
can see, in the 1940s, the to

Figure 2.8 **Top 100 girls' nai**

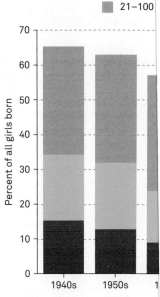

SOURCE: Author's calculations fr

# If I Could Change One Thing...

It might be hard to imagine yourself living in a different historical time period. If everything were different, you wouldn't be the same person anyway. But what if you could change just one thing? Imagine how just one aspect of your life would be different if it had taken place in a different time.

For example, Judy and I married after college and were together more than 10 years after that before we decided to have children. During that time, we lived in five different cities, we each earned two advanced degrees, and we experienced many aspects of independent adult life without the responsibilities (and joys!) of parenting. But such a decision would have been unusual 50 years ago and almost unheard of 100 years ago. The acceptability of "starting a family" so long after starting our family—just that difference—changed the whole structure of our lives. If we had felt more pressure to have children earlier, I could imagine a whole sequence of events—paths not taken—that would have changed everything.

- Looking at your own family history, identify a key decision point or event that shaped your family life in the years that followed. For example, it could be a marriage or divorce, the birth of a child, or a change in family structure.

- Make a list of family events and decisions that followed from that turning point—things that depended on that historical event: for example, how divorce set different family members heading in their own directions or how births changed a family dynamic.

- Using your imagination, relocate that turning point to a different historical moment. For example, consider the family living in colonial America, the Industrial Revolution of the nineteenth century, or the 1950s.

- In a short essay or even a brief outline, describe how the decision or event you selected might have been different in the alternative time period. How would cultural or economic pressures have led family members to make different decisions?

- In your essay or in a class discussion, try to spin out the implications of this imaginary scenario. What would be different for the family if that turning point had been reached at a different time in history? Your answers might help explain how historical context shapes the paths of our lives in ways we don't notice at the time.

grown more individually intensive. The period of parenting also seems longer, as the typical young adulthood has been extended by more years of education, delays in starting careers, and later marriage (Furstenberg 2000). We will return to parenting attitudes and practices in Chapter 9.

Although multigenerational living has in general become less common (as shown by the declining number of extended households in Figure 2.6), some grandparents have grown emotionally closer to their grandchildren than they

What are some reasons grandparents [play a] role in their grandchildren's lives?

of all names. Now the top 100 account for only about one-third. The five most popular names alone dropped from 15 percent to less than 5 percent of the total during that time.

Another way to view this trend is to focus on the most common girl's name, which was Mary from 1880 (the first year records were kept) all the way up to 1961, except for six years in the 1950s, when Linda topped the chart. Since then, no name has been in the number 1 spot for more than 15 years (Jennifer, 1970–1984). Emily had a chance, from 1996 to 2007, but her reign ended in time to fit the pattern of declining name dominance over time. In fact, in 2009, Mary herself dropped out of the top 100 for the first time and has now fallen to 123rd as of 2012.

We can't assume that these naming trends mean that people are just more individualistic or less conformist than they used to be—although they may be. Rather, the fact that people have to choose—to make an active choice, rather than follow a tradition—naturally leads to a greater diversity of outcomes. Family life in the last half-century reflects the same tendency. As people become *free* to make choices, they are also *compelled* to make choices. And when people choose, the outcomes are much more varied than when there are no choices to make.

This insight about the increasing diversity of personal names opens a window onto a different source of family diversity, as well as inequality and change: the racial and ethnic variations in the United States, both in the past and in the present. Building on the history of families told here, the next chapter will help us understand the story of family diversity.

## KEY TERMS:

nuclear family    heterogamy

homogamy    patriarchy    coverture

extended families    stem family

courtship    separate spheres

monogamy    polygamy

companionship family

companionate marriage

dating    family wage    baby boom

# Questions for Review

1. What are the prehistoric origins of family life?

2. Compare the relationship between men, women, and children in American Indian families, Colonial American families, and enslaved African families prior to 1820.

3. How did married life change during the nineteenth century? Why?

4. How was family life disrupted for many African Americans, the Chinese, and Latinos in the nineteenth century?

5. How is the companionship family different from the patriarchal family? What led to the emergence of the companionship family in the twentieth century?

6. Why was there a baby boom in the middle of the twentieth century?

7. Beginning in the 1960s, why did family patterns depart so dramatically from the 1950s ideal?

8. What factors led to the decline in the number of married couples in the late twentieth century?

9. How have the relationships between parents and children changed since the 1960s?

# 3

# Race, Ethnicity, and Immigration

Before we can learn how race and ethnicity connect to questions of family diversity, inequality, and social change, we need to know what race and ethnicity are. Not surprisingly, this is a complicated issue, as the following example illustrates.

In 2005, Kylie Hodgson and Remi Horder, a British couple who each had a White mother and Black father, had twins. The twins were fraternal, meaning they share many but not all of the same genes. Although both parents would likely be seen as Black (or African American) in the United States, the twins differ from each other by skin color. The genetic difference between them is very small. And yet if they had been separated at birth, they would likely have different outcomes in life—not because of the inherent differences between them, but because of how others would see them and how they would come to see themselves. (A couple with a similar experience is pictured on the next page.) Do they belong to different races?

Sometimes, as in this case, race appears to be a simple accident of birth. But the community we are born into—and the category we inhabit as we grow up and interact with our family and the wider world—are the result of much larger social forces. These forces have profound effects on everyone, directly and indirectly, through our families.

# What Are Race and Ethnicity?

We begin with some terms and definitions that will help us make sense of the facts and stories that follow.

Sophia Greenwood's drawing of her family. Sophia's mother had Black and White parents and Sophia's father is White. Through interracial marriage and adoption, Sophia also has close relatives from Costa Rica and South Korea.

Twins who look like they are of different races challenge social ideas of race and ethnicity. Dean Durrant, who is of West Indian origin, and Alison Spooner, who is White, have two sets of twins. In each set, the twins would probably be labeled as different races by strangers. How might they be treated differently?

## Biology and Race

The surface differences between groups of people around the world led scientists in the eighteenth century to attempt to categorize people into "races," which roughly corresponded to populations of the different continents (Banton 1998). After Charles Darwin's theory of evolution gained currency, nineteenth-century scientists ranked the races in hierarchical order, believing that the more advanced (that is, richer and more powerful) populations were more evolved (Gould 1996). Now, however, biologists understand that the groups commonly called "races" do not fit the scientific criteria for racial classifications we see in other animals, where subspecies, or "breeding populations," are genetically more distinct from each other (Keita et al. 2004). That is because modern humans emerged from Africa quite recently in evolutionary time—less than 100,000 years ago—to populate the other continents. And even then they did not remain truly separate populations, but rather continued to migrate around and produce mixed children, preventing the formation of very different races.

Ironically, the difference on the surface—skin color—is perhaps the most important biologically. Among people who lived near the equator, dark skin was an important adaptation that improved survival dramatically. Because they were more likely to live long enough to become parents, dark-skinned people quickly grew to dominate the populations near the earth's equator. Other differences between groups, such as facial shape or hair type, do not appear to affect survival, so scientists now believe that they evolved randomly from groups living apart (Berg et al. 2005). After being separated for just a few tens of thousands of years, the worldwide remixing of human groups in modern society is further undermining genetic differences between groups of people.

# Definitions

So *biology* doesn't support the classification of people into races. But deeply felt divisions between groups of people remain important *socially*. In the United States, the federal government collects information about race and ethnicity mostly to enforce civil rights laws against discrimination. According to the U.S. Census Bureau, the government's main statistical agency, the racial categories they measure are "not an attempt to define race biologically, anthropologically or genetically," but rather "reflect a social definition of race recognized in this country" (U.S. Census Bureau, 2012e). So how do we arrive at that social definition?

One important modern principle used in almost all data collection about race and ethnicity involves self-identification: the race and ethnicity you choose are up to you (or your parents, if you're too young to fill out the form). And you don't have to offer any proof to justify your choice. In practice, however, the definitions that people apply to themselves usually conform to how others see them as well. That means that self-identity is partly a social product. This quality—self-definition as a social product instead of a fixed, objective category—is one reason we say that race and ethnicity are *socially constructed*. The categories we use, and the assignment of individuals to categories, are the outcome of social interaction and beliefs; they change over time, and they differ from place to place.

The original American definition of *Black* is a good example of social construction. During the period of slavery, anybody who had any identifiable African ancestry, no matter how remote, was considered Black in the eyes of both the law and White society. That was the so-called "one-drop" rule, referring to one drop of African blood (also known as the rule of hypodescent). It was not based on a scientific understanding of race, but rather on the economic interests of male slave owners, who wanted to make sure that the children they fathered with Black slave women remained their property instead of becoming their heirs (R. Moran 2001). By this one-drop rule, a White woman could give birth to a Black child, but a Black woman couldn't give birth to a White child (Fields 1982:149). Although the U.S. Census included the racial category "mulatto" for mixed-race individuals for several decades after 1850 (see Changing Law, "How the U.S. Government Measures Race"), this peculiar rule has largely stuck (mostly informally) to the present day. That is why Barack Obama grew up with a Black self-identity and was labeled the first Black president, because his father was Black, even though his mother was White.

Race and ethnicity are both socially constructed, but the two concepts reflect different ideas. Racial identities reflect perceptions about biological traits. A **race** is a group of people believed to share common descent, based on perceived innate physical similarities (Morning 2005). Note that common descent and physical similarity remain a matter of perception, not biological certainty. Racial identity is usually passed from parents to children within families, and family interaction is the first site of racial self-awareness.

**race**

A group of people believed to share common descent, based on perceived innate physical similarities.

# How the U.S. Government Measures Race

The U.S. government currently counts five distinct races—White, Black, American Indian or Alaska Native, Asian, and Native Hawaiian or Pacific Islander—and allows people to identify with as many of these races as they like. It also counts, in a separate category, Hispanic or Latino ethnicity. These categories are established by the federal government and implemented by agencies across the country, the most prominent of which is the U.S. Census Bureau, which is mandated by the U.S. Constitution to conduct a count of the population every 10 years (Snipp 2003).

The latest racial identification question, from the 2010 census form, is shown in Figure 3.1. You will notice several confusing things about the question. For example, although Asian

Figure 3.1 **2010 Census race question**

**What is Person 1's race?** *Mark* ☒ *one or more boxes.*
- ☐ White
- ☐ Black, African Am., or Negro
- ☐ American Indian or Alaska Native — *Print name of enrolled or principal tribe.* ↗

| | | | | | | | | | | | | | | | | | | |
|--|--|--|--|--|--|--|--|--|--|--|--|--|--|--|--|--|--|--|

- ☐ Asian Indian        ☐ Japanese        ☐ Native Hawaiian
- ☐ Chinese             ☐ Korean          ☐ Guamanian or Chamorro
- ☐ Filipino            ☐ Vietnamese      ☐ Samoan
- ☐ Other Asian — *Print race, for example, Hmong, Laotian, Thai, Pakistani, Cambodian, and so on.* ↗        ☐ Other Pacific Islander — *Print race, for example, Fijian, Tongan, and so on.* ↗

| | | | | | | | | | | | | | | | | | | |
|--|--|--|--|--|--|--|--|--|--|--|--|--|--|--|--|--|--|--|

- ☐ Some other race — *Print race.* ↗

| | | | | | | | | | | | | | | | | | | |
|--|--|--|--|--|--|--|--|--|--|--|--|--|--|--|--|--|--|--|

SOURCE: 2010 Census race question (U.S. Census Bureau 2010b).

is considered one of the "race" groups, the form actually lists a series of national origins (e.g., Chinese, Filipino), and there is no check box labeled "Asian." That is because many people from these groups don't express a racial identity beyond their country of ancestral origin. To make matters still more complicated, the Latino group, which is considered ethnic, not racial, is identified in a separate question altogether (not shown here). As a result of the multiple-race option ("one or more boxes") and the separate Latino identification, any one person may be a member of many racial and ethnic combinations.

Figure 3.2 **U.S. population, by race and ethnicity, 2010**

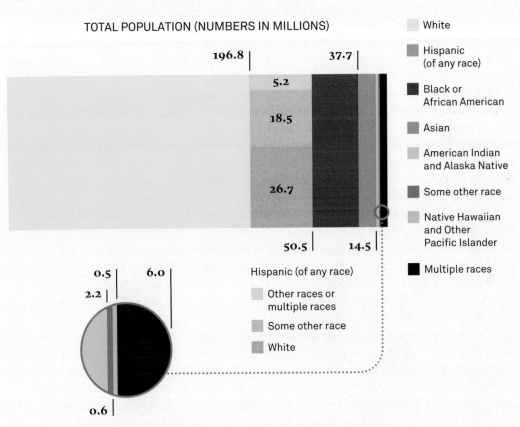

Racial and ethnic identification are complex. Of the 309 million people counted by the 2010 U.S. Census, the largest group, non-Hispanic Whites, was 196.8 million. About 50 million were Hispanic, more than half of whom (26.7 million) considered themselves White as well. Most of the Black, Asian, American Indian, or Pacific Islander people only used one racial category. Finally, six million non-Hispanic people identified as more than one race.

SOURCE: Adapted from Humes, Jones, and Ramirez (2011).

The 15 possible check boxes on the 2010 census form represent only the latest attempt by the government to keep up with America's changing demography and culture. In fact, since 1880, the race and ethnicity categories on the census form have changed every single decade. For example, the only Asian category in 1870 was "Chinese." The category for Americans of African descent was "Black" in 1850, along with "Mulatto"—used for those of mixed African and European descent. In 1930, both were dropped for "Negro," which became "Negro or Black" in 1970 and "Black, African American or Negro" in 2000 (Farley and Haaga 2005). Finally, in 2013, the Census Bureau announced it would drop the category "Negro" on future forms, leaving simply "Black or African American" (Yen 2013).

The most important recent change to this system of categories was the option to check more than one race identification box, implemented in 2000. This policy was a response to the growing presence of interracial couples, who resisted the instruction to impose one racial category on their children (Brunsma 2005). The change also was aimed at the millions of immigrants, most from Latin America and Asia, for whom the American system of racial classification was uncomfortable and often confusing (J. Lee and Bean 2004). For example, many Latinos consider themselves to be White but also another race, such as Indian (referring to the descendants of Central and South America's indigenous populations).

In practice, however, relatively few people identify as more than one race. In 2010, a total of 9 million out of 309 million people in the United States chose more than one race, and one-third of them were Latinos (see Figure 3.2). Nevertheless, this relatively small population of multiracial people is very diverse, representing many different combinations. Allowing them to choose more than one racial category has improved the identification process for them, even though it has complicated the work of demographers and government statisticians.

Figure 3.2 shows one convenient way of handling the complexity of these categories. In the column for total population, I have included each person in only one category, with all Latinos placed together (50.5 million) regardless of which racial category they identified. The main column also shows the 6 million people (not including Latinos) who chose more than one race. In most of the statistics in this book, however, I follow a common convention by including multiracial people in the largest non-White group they identify (for example, people who choose Black and White are included in the Black category).

One consequence of the option to choose more than one race is a weakening of the informal rule of "one-drop" identification of African Americans. Rather than simply identifying children of any Black parent as Black, an increasing number of interracial couples are identifying their children as members of both of their parents' races. Although their numbers remain relatively small, this may be an important historical development within families. In 2011, for example, the Census Bureau recorded about 50,000 children born to married couples in which one parent was White and one was Black, and in 69 percent of those families, the infants were identified as both White and Black (American Community Survey 2011 via Ruggles et al. 2014). This simple response to the multiple-race option shows the symbolic power of a government category to alter such intimate details of individuals' lives as their racial identity.

On the other hand, ethnic identities are focused on cultural traits. An **ethnicity** is a group of people with a common cultural identification, based on a combination of language, religion, ancestral origin, or traditional practices. One important difference between ethnicity and race is the sometimes voluntary nature of ethnic identity. Ethnicity can change over a person's lifetime—for example, when a child grows up and leaves the family. It can even change from one social setting to another, as when we move from a group of friends to a family celebration. Racial identity is more stable.

In the United States, the concepts of race and ethnicity often overlap. Thus, many people use the ethnic term *African American* and the racial term *Black* interchangeably, because that group includes both perceived physical similarities and common cultural identification. On the other hand, Latinos (also known as Hispanics) are usually thought of as an ethnicity because of a shared cultural heritage. But in other ways they are thought of in racial terms, as when a person is said to "look" Latino. As a result, both African Americans and Latinos fit the combined concept of a racialized ethnic group, or a **racial ethnicity**, which is an ethnic group perceived to share physical characteristics. (To make it clear that I am referring to cultural groups instead of skin colors, as the names imply, in this book I capitalize *Black* and *White* along with other racial-ethnic groups.)

In light of such confusing concepts and categories, it is worth asking why sociologists and government bureaucrats go to the trouble of classifying people this way. I believe such classifications make sense for two reasons. First, many aspects of family and social life still reflect persistent separation between people along racial-ethnic group lines. Despite a remarkable loosening of the boundaries in this country, most people still live, marry, reproduce, and raise children primarily within their own racial-ethnic group. This practice of marriage and

**ethnicity**

A group of people with a common cultural identification, based on a combination of language, religion, ancestral origin, or traditional practices.

**racial ethnicity**

An ethnic group perceived to share physical characteristics.

If you didn't know who this man was, would you describe him as "African American"? (He's Usain Bolt.)

# Why are there so many single Black women?

**http://wwnpag.es/sbtn3**

Go to this link for an animation and additional information.

The drop in marriage rates has been felt by all groups, but it has been steepest for African Americans. One reason is the situation of Black men. In 50 large metropolitan areas, unmarried, young Black women outnumber unmarried, employed Black men in their age group by about 2 to 1. Many of the Black men are unemployed, in prison, or no longer living. As a result, Black women experience a shortage of men to marry. The economy, job discrimination, incarceration policies, and health disparities all combine to hurt the life chances of Black men and women, including their chance of marriage. For Whites the "marriage market" numbers are much more even.

**Due to larger social forces—the economy, job discrimination, incarceration policies, and health issues—Black men under age 35 are:**

**6x**
more likely to be incarcerated than White men

**1.8x**
more likely than White men to be poor

**1.5x**
more likely than White males to die before age 35

**2x**
more likely to be unemployed than White males

*Sources: Author calculations from U.S. Census Bureau data provided by IPUMS.org (Ruggles et al. 2014); Glaze (2011); Hoyert and Xu (2012); U.S. Census Bureau (2012d); U.S. Bureau of Labor Statistics (2014b).*

# Average of 50 large metropolitan areas

| 51.1 employed, unmarried Black men | 100 unmarried Black women | 92.8 employed, unmarried White men | 100 unmarried White women |

---

## Four Largest Metropolitan Areas

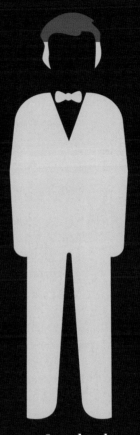

| New York City | Chicago | Los Angeles | Washington, D.C. | New York City | Chicago | Los Angeles | Washington, D.C. |
|---|---|---|---|---|---|---|---|
| 53.4   100 | 39.8   100 | 52.9   100 | 60.1   100 | 90.5   100 | 94.1   100 | 97.3   100 | 94.8   100 |

## Figure 3.8 Family profile of Latinos, by national origin

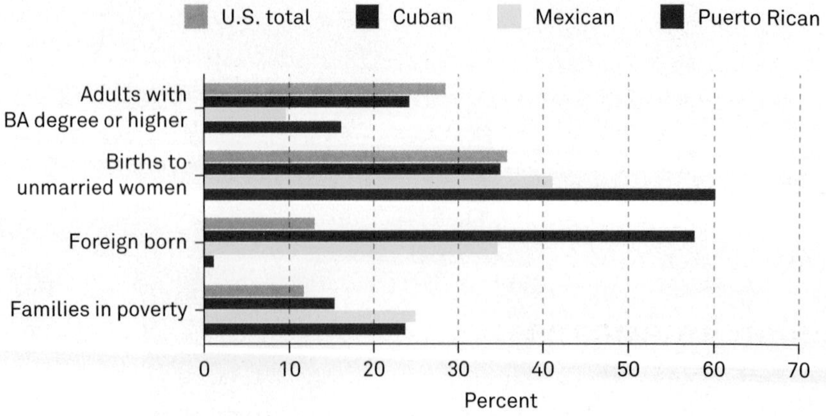

Legend: U.S. total, Cuban, Mexican, Puerto Rican

SOURCE: American Community Survey 2011 via American FactFinder 2014.

young group on average, with a median age of 27.5, which is 10 years younger than the national average (American Community Survey 2011 via American FactFinder 2014).

As a result of their diverse origins and history, we should not generalize too broadly about different Latino groups (Baca Zinn and Wells 2000). For example, with regard to family structure, Mexicans and Cubans are much more likely to live in married-couple households than are Puerto Ricans, who have much higher rates of births to unmarried women (see Figure 3.8). Still, all Latinos trace their history back to Spanish-speaking countries dominated by a Catholic culture. In colonial days, these societies were generally more tolerant of cultural mixing with Europeans, African slaves, and native people than were the Protestants of the U.S. colonies (Coles 2006). Thus, language, religion, and less rigid racial divisions constitute common elements of Latino culture.

**Familism** One cultural trait that many observers associate with Latino culture is **familism**, a personal outlook that puts family obligations first, before individual well-being. Even if the extent of this attitude is sometimes exaggerated, family relationships—including strong intergenerational ties—play a central role in daily life for most Latinos. Latinos are two to three times more likely to live in extended families than most other groups. This is especially apparent among Latino immigrants, most of whom maintain close family ties back home. And many have joined relatives in the United States who migrated earlier, creating family chains of immigration (Carrasquillo 2002).

Although some critics believe that strong familism makes the Latino community inward looking and slows their integration into the American mainstream, there is no doubt that family cooperation has also helped immigrants survive and even thrive in their new American context (Sanchez 1993). In fact, if poverty and hardship drive families together for support, strong intergenerational ties among

**familism**

A personal outlook that puts family obligations first, before individual well-being.

Latinos are probably as much a response to such challenges as they are a reflection of cultural tradition (Baca Zinn and Wells 2000).

Younger average age, more children per family, and extended households all make the average Latino family substantially larger than that of any other major group (Figure 3.9). However, in many respects, Latinos exhibit the same trends followed by the rest of the country. In particular, they, too, have seen a decline in marriage at young ages and a rapid increase in the number of children born to unmarried parents (Landale and Oropesa 2007).

## Asian Americans

In Chapter 2, we saw that the first large group of Asians in the United States was Chinese workingmen in the nineteenth century, most of whom did not intend to stay in the country. And because those who did stay were legally forbidden from marrying Whites, their numbers dwindled. However, in waves of migration over the twentieth century, immigrants from many other Asian countries eventually joined them (Takaki 1998). Thus, like Latinos, most Asians are within a few generations of their families' immigration to the United States. Today the U.S. population is 6 percent Asian American. The largest groups trace their ancestry to China (23 percent), the Philippines (20 percent), and India (18 percent; Hoeffel et al. 2012). Asian immigrants today are mostly professionals, students, or the family members of previous immigrants (Reeves and Bennett 2004). And because so many Asian families include immigrants, 70 percent of Asian Americans speak a language other than English at home (American Community Survey 2011 via American FactFinder 2014).

**Family Traditions, Modern Times** Several features of Asian-American families are common—although not universal—among the different national-origin groups. In some communities, especially among Chinese and other East Asians with a Confucian religious background, there is a tradition of striving for educational excellence. Historically, this derives from the ancient Confucian exam system, through which even poor children could achieve success through diligent study (Chao 1995). Parental support for education—some might say parental pressure, as represented by the figure of the "tiger mother" popularized by author Amy Chua (2011)—is one reason why only 3 percent of Asian Americans 16 to 24 years of age are high school dropouts, compared with 8 percent of the total population (American Community Survey 2011 via American FactFinder 2014).

Most Asian cultures also include strong imperatives to respect and care for elders. Although it is not safe to assume that cultural practices from their homelands are uniformly followed today, Asian Americans remain relatively likely to

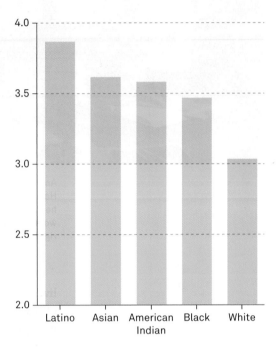

Figure 3.9 **Average number of family members living together**

SOURCE: American Community Survey 2011 via American FactFinder 2014.

## 1924: Immigration Act

After decades of European immigration brought millions to America, Congress virtually shut the door with the Immigration Act of 1924, permitting only a few immigrants per year according to a country-based quota system—and completely shutting off immigration from Asia. As a result, immigrant communities were not "replenished" and their children's integration into mainstream society accelerated.

## 1945: War Brides Act

Tens of thousands of U.S. military servicemen married local women while serving in Europe or Asia during World War II. The War Brides Act permitted the immigration of their wives and children and later was extended to Korean wives of U.S. soldiers from the Korean War (1950–1953). The immediate welcome these women received was not always warm. Ruth Poore, who had married an American air sergeant in England, arrived in New York with almost 1,000 other women and children. "They had to lock the buses we were held in," she remembered. "We were being picketed by women who were mad at us" (Foley 2004:72).

## 1942–1964: Bracero Program

Faced with both the need for agricultural workers and popular resistance to full-scale immigration, the United States extended "temporary" work permits to millions of Mexican workers through the Bracero Program. Instead of preventing whole families from immigrating, however, the program opened a door that many families eventually went through. Repeated trips over the border often led to permanent settlement on the U.S. side, where many braceros (Spanish for "manual laborers") made the connections necessary to bring family members as well.

Catalina Corella and her daughter Margarita Flores in 1948. They joined Catalina's husband, Jesus Corella, when he worked on a ranch in the Bracero Program.

# 1965: Amendments to the Immigration and Nationality Act

Among the most important immigration laws of the twentieth century, these amendments to the original 1952 act (which was highly restrictive) lifted all numerical restrictions on the immigration of spouses, children, and parents of U.S. citizens. They also ended the country-based quota system. As a result, most immigrants now arrive as family members, and most of them are from Latin America and Asia.

# 2002: Homeland Security Act

After a decade of attempts at policing the United States–Mexico border to control illegal immigration, the newly created Department of Homeland Security took over immigration enforcement. Through fence building and patrols along the border, the government has made illegal crossing much more difficult and dangerous. The result, ironically, is that male undocumented immigrants, who used to travel back and forth between work in the United States and their families in Mexico, are more likely to establish permanent residence in the United States and bring their families here to live.

# 2005: International Marriage Broker Regulation Act

American citizens have been allowed to bring their spouses and prospective spouses to the United States since 1952. But in 2005, recognizing the growing abuse of immigrants within marriages arranged by brokers, including those operating over the Internet, Congress passed the International Marriage Broker Regulation Act to require that potential immigrants be notified if their would-be spouses have a criminal history or have filed many immigrant petitions. However, a 2008 report from the Government Accountability Office showed that the law has not been effectively implemented, leaving so-called "mail-order brides" at risk of abuse by their American sponsors.

Families"). This change in policy opened the door to family reunification through immigration, and most legal migration since that time has been family related. Without this principle, immigration would result in an influx of individual workers rather than families; under the law, whole immigrant communities have grown and thrived. Family-based immigration also ensures that immigrant communities are regularly "replenished," which helps the leading immigrant groups—such as those from Mexico, China, and the Philippines—continue to grow as families flourish around the first few members who move here (Waters and Jimenez 2005). On the other hand, a family-based immigration system may increase the social distance between immigrant groups and the rest of society by encouraging them to interact within their own community.

# Generations

When people move from one society to another, they adapt to their new cultural environment through "a complex pattern of continuity and change" (Berry 1997:6). Immigrants and their children learn the ways of their new homeland through **acculturation**, the acquisition of a new culture and language. For families, that acculturation may be *consonant*, when parents and children together gradually transition away from their home culture and language; or it may be *dissonant*, when children develop English ability more quickly and integrate into the new society more easily than their parents (Portes and Rumbaut 2001).

Immigrants do not simply join the new culture, however, and leave the old one behind. New groups blend into American society to varying degrees through a process sociologists call **assimilation**, the gradual reduction of ethnic distinction between immigrants and the mainstream society. Both the immigrant group and the mainstream culture adapt to each other, moving toward the point—perhaps never fully reached—when the ethnic distinction is no longer recognized at all (Alba and Nee 2003). Unlike acculturation, assimilation is successful only when the host society accepts the new group (Gans 2007). In America, new groups have received very different levels of acceptance, depending on the timing of their arrival, the economic and social role they play, and the attitudes of the dominant group toward them (Portes and Rumbaut 2005).

Researchers refer to immigrants according to their relation to the family's migration. So the "first generation" is the immigrants themselves, the "second generation" is their children, and so on. Each generation has its own experience, and in some cases that fosters a strong self-identity. That was the case for Japanese immigrants, known as *issei* (first generation) and *nisei* (second generation). The original immigrants were cultural standard-bearers, and their children played the role of mediators between the old ways and the new society (Glenn 1986). As studies have become more detailed, researchers have discovered that the age at which people immigrate, not just their generation, has a major impact on their role in the family's acculturation (Rumbaut 2004). Table 3.2 shows some of the issues they face, using the terms for these partial "generations."

Generational change is evident among Latino immigrants on such key family indicators as age at marriage (or cohabitation), number of children, and overall family size. For example, Latinas overall average 2.4 children per woman (J. Martin et al. 2012). But married Latinas born abroad average more than 5 children each (Swicegood, Sobczak, and Ishizawa 2006). So those who are removed by a generation from the immigration experience show family patterns more similar to the dominant culture. Conflicts can arise when the children change more rapidly than their parents, a pattern exacerbated by children's access to new

文化変容

**acculturation**

The acquisition of a new culture and language.

同化

**assimilation**

The gradual reduction of ethnic distinction between immigrants and the mainstream society.

Table 3.2 **Immigrant generations**

| GENERATION | AGE AT IMMIGRATION | FAMILY ISSUES |
|---|---|---|
| .5 generation ("point-five generation") | Retirement age | Joining their families in the United States at older ages, without command of English or regular employment, these immigrants may feel isolated and dependent on their children. But they provide a connection to their homeland for the grandchildren. |
| First generation | Working-age adulthood | These are the classic immigrants, whose fateful decision brings the family to the United States, usually for employment or a better future. Despite success at work, they may never feel fully integrated into the new society, especially if they do not learn English well. |
| 1.5 generation | Childhood (especially ages 6–12) | Having learned to speak a different language first, this generation may speak English imperfectly, but they are often the most acculturated members of the immigrant family. |
| Second generation | Children of immigrants | Born and raised in the United States, but members of an immigrant family, they are the transitional generation, whose easier acculturation may lead to conflict with their parents. |
| Third generation | Grandchildren of immigrants | They may retain their identity as part of an immigrant family, but come to see their ethnicity as family history rather than their own experience. |

technology, including online media, in addition to their quicker language acquisition. On the other hand, there are many cases in which children of immigrants choose to affirm their ethnic identity by showing their commitment to caring for family members and demonstrating loyalty to their families' collective needs (Pyke 2004).

One recurring theme in the conflicts that arise among immigrant families is the choice of marriage partners made by the young immigrants and those of the second and later generations. The barriers between groups—and the possibility of overcoming them—are perhaps never more clearly exposed than they are when two families view each other across the chapel aisle.

# Intermarriage

**intermarriage**

Marriage between members of different racial or ethnic groups.

Racial and ethnic groups can only exist if the categories they represent stay distinct in the minds of society's members. And the idea of separate groups can only persist as long as there is some actual separation between groups in daily life. For that reason, **intermarriage**, or marriage between members of different racial or ethnic groups, is the "litmus test" of racial and ethnic difference. We can use the frequency of intermarriage to measure the degree of integration between two groups. At the same time, the experience of intermarriage *creates* the integration of two groups. In the United States, the stiffest barrier to integration has been between Whites and African Americans.

## Black and White

The first U.S. law prohibiting marriage between Blacks and Whites was passed in Maryland in 1661, and most African Americans lived under such laws until the 1960s (Moran 2001). During slavery, White male slave owners fathered many children with Black slave women, and the "one-drop rule" ensured that their children remained slaves, protecting the perceived integrity of the White race. But the possibility of Black men fathering children with White women remained an unacceptable affront to southern White public opinion.

Throughout the period of slavery and well into the middle of the twentieth century, many Whites were willing to resort to violence—legal or illegal—to prevent mixing between the races. Several thousand African Americans were the victims of lynching from the 1880s to the 1930s, and in more than a third of these cases, the mob sought to avenge an alleged interracial sex crime (Tolnay and Beck 1995). In the words of anti-lynching crusader Ida Wells-Barnett (1892), they acted on "the old thread-bare lie that Negro men rape white women." Within the legal system, the process was different, but the outcome was often the same: death. In the twentieth century, 455 Americans were executed for the crime of rape, and 89 percent of them were Black, mostly convicted of raping White women (U.S. Census Bureau 1996:table 357).

Laws against interracial marriage were common in the twentieth century and were on the books in 16 states when they were declared unconstitutional in the 1967 U.S. Supreme Court case *Loving v. Virginia*. (Loving was the name of the White man whose marriage to an African-American woman led to their arrest, in their bedroom, by local police.) But old attitudes die hard. In 1973, President Richard Nixon was privately discussing abortion rights (which he opposed) when

Figure 3.11 **Black–White marriages, 1970–2010**

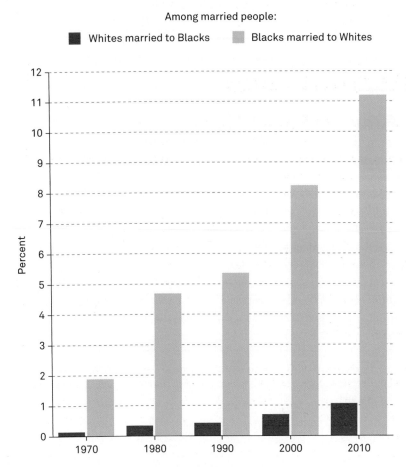

Among married people:

■ Whites married to Blacks    ▨ Blacks married to Whites

SOURCE: U.S. Census Bureau 2008 and 2010a.

a hidden microphone captured him saying, "There are times when an abortion is necessary. I know that. When you have a Black and a White. Or a rape" (Savage 2009). That a Black–White pregnancy was at the same level of shame as one resulting from rape pretty well illustrates the strength of the taboo.

Since the 1970s, we've seen steady but slow growth in the rate of interracial marriage. You might say it's grown from "nearly non-existent to merely atypical" (Pew Research Center 2006). By 2010, some 11 percent of married African Americans were married to Whites. But because Whites are the larger group, that translated into just 1 percent of married Whites (see Figure 3.11).

African Americans remain the minority group that is least likely to marry outside their own race. And it is even less common among Black women than it is among Black men, which is especially notable given the shortage of Black men described earlier (Crowder and Tolnay 2000). On the other hand, some groups have high rates of intermarriage. In 2000, more than half of American Indians and native Hawaiians were intermarried. Asian Americans and Latinos were in between, with about 15 percent of each group married to those outside the group (S. Lee and Edmonston 2005). From an ethnic perspective, it is perhaps not surprising that Asians and Latinos are much more likely to marry outside their specific national-origin group (for example, Chinese, Mexican) than they are to marry outside the larger racial-ethnic group (Waters and Jimenez 2005). (We'll have more to say about intermarriage between racial-ethnic groups in Chapter 8.)

## The Future of Social Distance

**social distance**

The level of acceptance that members of one group have toward members of another group.

The level of acceptance that members of one group have toward those of another has been called **social distance**. Some sociologists believe that intermarriage is itself a good measure of social distance, because it shows the breakdown—or lack thereof—of society's most rigid taboos (J. Lee and Bean 2004). In fact, because marriage rates reflect concrete actions toward integration, studying them may tell us more than we can learn from surveys in which people say what they *think* about other groups. However, because most people end up marrying someone who lives, works, or goes to school near them, and given the persistence of residential segregation, many people do not have a reasonable opportunity to marry people from other races. This is especially true of Whites, because as the

Figure 3.12 **Percent of Whites who say they would be "somewhat opposed" or "very opposed" to a close relative marrying a Black person, by age**

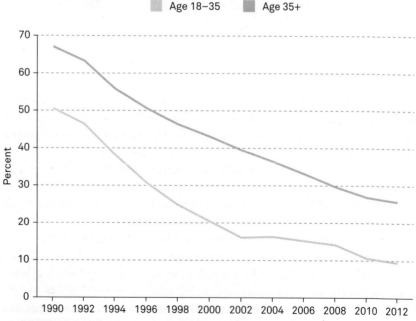

SOURCE: Author's calculations from the General Social Survey, 1990–2012 (Smith et al. 2014).

# Social Distance

Research shows that attitudes toward relationships that cross racial and ethnic lines are often affected by the nature of the relationship and the social perspective of the observer.

| | | Your relationship with a member of _____ group | | | |
|---|---|---|---|---|---|
| | | Close friend | Date | Live together | Marry |
| Would anyone disapprove? | You | | | | |
| | Your parents | | | | |
| | Your grandparents | | | | |

The table presented here shows four relationships, ranging in level of intimacy from close friendship to marriage and expressing different levels of social distance. Consider the attitude that you yourself, your parents, and your grandparents might take (or have taken) toward such a relationship between you and a member of a specific racial-ethnic group (or just write in "a different" group).

Perform this exercise on your own, in small groups, or as a class exercise: Use a photocopy or drawing of the table and insert comments reflecting the attitudes for each situation. You can also just mark an X in each spot where disapproval is likely or has occurred.

Does the level of disapproval you anticipate (or have experienced) depend on which group is considered? Do you think the views of your family members differ across the generations? If so, do you believe that those views simply reflect generational attitudes, or some other factor? Try to explain the pattern you find.

largest group, they are the most likely to marry within their own race even if they have no racial preferences at all. To track the attitudes of the whole population, then, surveys remain very useful. What do they show?

The American public clearly has an increasing tolerance of interracial relationships. This change has occurred partly because older generations are being replaced by cohorts born and raised more recently. When the General Social Survey asked Whites in the early 1990s how they would feel about a close relative marrying a Black person, the majority expressed either some opposition or strong opposition (see Figure 3.12). In the two decades since, there has been a steep drop in such attitudes. There is still a large generational difference, however. One quarter of those age 35 or older expressed some opposition in 2012, compared with just one-tenth of those under age 35.

Clearly, the trend is in the direction of narrowing social distance. And the generation gap in Figure 3.12 suggests that a greater change in public attitudes is on the way. The generational pattern is also apparent among immigrants. Both Asians and Latinos are considerably more likely to be intermarried in the second or third generation after immigration, compared with those who immigrated themselves (Stevens, McKillip, and Ishizawa 2006). That was also the case for Italian and other European immigrant families in the first half of the twentieth century, which suggests that these newer immigrants could be on a similar path of social integration (Pagnini and Morgan 1990). With regard to the Black-White family divide, U.S. society may be moving in the same direction—at least toward a breakdown of the strictest barriers—but the pace of change remains quite slow.

America's increasing racial and ethnic diversity makes very visible the idea of different families enacting different traditions in their own way. Maybe that makes family diversity seem more natural or inevitable. But it doesn't eliminate the social conflicts that arise over the different forms and expressions of family life. In the remainder of the book, we will delve more deeply into the many forms of family diversity. And we will see that inequality is both a cause and a consequence of that diversity.

## KEY TERMS:

race   ethnicity

racial ethnicity

endogamy   exogamy

minority group

familism   acculturation

assimilation   intermarriage

social distance

# Questions for Review

1. How are race and ethnicity different from each other?

2. How has the U.S. government changed how it measures race? Why are these changes important to sociologists?

3. How have the racial and ethnic populations in the United States shifted in the twentieth century?

4. Describe three disruptions in American Indian family life that have occurred in the last century.

5. According to historians and sociologists, what are some of the legacies of slavery and the Southern agricultural economy that have shaped African-American families?

6. How have extended households eased the burdens of racial inequality for Black families?

7. What is familism and how does it play a role in Latino family life?

8. How did the immigration reforms of 1965 affect families?

9. What are some of the factors behind the growing intermarriage rate in the United States?

# 4 Families and Social Class

The documentary *Born Rich* (2003) starts as Jamie Johnson is about to celebrate his 21st birthday—at which point he will suddenly have many millions of dollars of his own. He wonders, "What did I do to earn the kind of money I'll own at midnight tonight? All I did was inherit it." His great-grandfather and two brothers started the Johnson & Johnson company. His grandfather, Seward, bought his first yacht in his 20s (S. Warner 2005), and his last wife was worth $3.6 billion when she died (Forbes 2013). The rich descendants of those Johnson brothers—children, grandchildren, spouses, nieces, and nephews—may have had jobs, but they didn't earn their fortunes through their own efforts. Their wealth came through the family.

We all know that there are rich people and poor people and people in between. But for sociologists concerned with families, social class is more complicated than that. Within families, not everyone is in the same financial position: what about a doctor married to a nurse? We might also ask who controls the money and who inherits it when someone dies. As we saw in Chapter 1, even who belongs to a family is not always clear, since different people have their own definitions of family relationships and obligations.

It might seem intuitively obvious that the Johnson family is not just exceptionally rich; they are in a different category from almost everyone else. That raises a fundamental question: Is social class experienced as a continuous gradation from poor to rich or as a set of discrete conditions? In other words, does social class refer to individuals or to groups?

Many people think of class as a ladder of economic resources, with richer people (and their families) climbing higher than those with fewer resources. But most sociologists—myself included—are interested in classes as *categories*, in which people share a common set of circumstances and perspectives (Tilly 1998). These two different views of social class are depicted in Figure 4.1,

The recession and long-term unemployment have contributed to more families and working-class people going to food banks for help. Unfortunately, the recession also reduced private donations and government funds to food banks.

Jamie Johnson's documentary *Born Rich* featured several other young adults with vast family fortunes, including Ivanka Trump, Michael Bloomberg's daughter Georgina, and a Vanderbilt scion.

with the ladder climbers representing the continuum-of-resources view and the stacked boxes representing the discrete-groups view. Both views show people in richer-versus-poorer stations, but the ladder accentuates their status as individuals and their ability to move up and down. The boxes, on the other hand, highlight the shared positions of people in groups and also the barriers between groups that make it difficult to climb around. Which perspective captures the modern experience of class matters because it may reflect how people see themselves and how they behave in everything from marriage decisions to parenting styles to political action (Lareau 2011).

For our purposes, the difference between the ladder view and the boxes view is vital to understanding families—which are, after all, groups of people with a lot in common. To address this distinction more systematically and to understand its importance for modern families, we will need to revisit some of the sociological theories we introduced in Chapter 1, especially the consensus and conflict perspectives. And we will meet two new theorists: Max Weber and Pierre Bourdieu.

# Theories of Social Class

Both the consensus and conflict perspectives provide important insights into the role of social class in modern society. But their assumptions about how society works lead to very different interpretations of class and inequality. These

## Figure 4.1  **Two perspectives on social class**

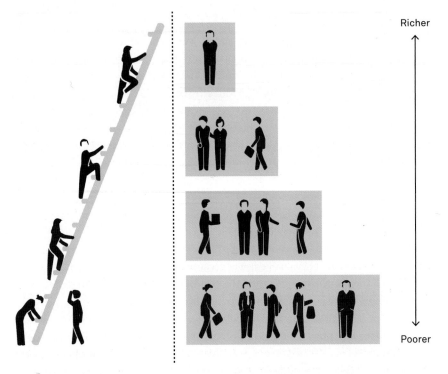

A continuum of resources is shown on the left, with richer people above poorer people on the socioeconomic ladder. A set of discrete groups is shown on the right, with smaller, higher classes stacked on top of larger, lower classes and with the people in each box sharing a common set of circumstances.

differences regarding social class are best understood through the issue of **division of labor**, the social process of determining who does what work and for what rewards, a central concern from the early years of sociology (Durkheim 1893/1997).

Consistent with the precepts of functionalism, consensus theorists have worked backward logically from the prevalence of social inequality in all societies, albeit to widely varying degrees, to the assumption that inequality therefore serves an essential function. In a classic statement of this position, Kingsley Davis and Wilbert Moore (1945) argued that some jobs are more important and more difficult to do than others. Society therefore needs a way to find and train the most talented people for these jobs and motivate them to perform well. (Think of surgeons or airplane pilots.) The system that fulfills this need, they believed, is a pattern of unequal rewards that creates incentives for people to strive for the best jobs they can get. Unequal rewards, therefore, are necessary to entice people to seek the extensive training required for difficult and important work. In this view, social class is a continuum from lower to higher rungs on the economic ladder, with the different levels of reward determined by the kinds of jobs people have. And the inequality between those

**division of labor**

The social process of determining who does what work and for what rewards.

lower and those higher on the ladder is not only beneficial but necessary to the functioning of society.

The conflict perspective, drawing especially from the work of Karl Marx in the nineteenth century, also takes the division of labor as the crucial element in defining the class system (Marx 1867/1990). But rather than seeing classes, and the inequality between them, as necessary and beneficial, conflict theorists see inequality as the result of economic **exploitation**, the process by which the labor of some produces wealth that is controlled by others. Scholars in this tradition believe that the fundamental class division is not one of skills and expertise, but one of ownership. In a capitalist society, capitalists—those who own and control property (capital)—dominate those who have no capital and therefore must subsist by selling their labor on unfavorable terms. Social classes are distinct categories, in this view, defined by their ownership (or lack of ownership) of capital. By extension, the classes are defined by their relationship to each other; capitalists and workers exist only in relation to each other. The class structure of modern societies has grown more complicated since Marx's time, especially with the growth of large middle-class categories (E. Wright 1997). However, the conflict perspective on social class still carries great weight in sociology.

Neither the consensus view nor the conflict view, as described so far, does much to explain the complication of social class for families. For example, consider college students, who may not have jobs or live off their own income and whose future class position may differ from that of their origins. To what social class do they belong? To address this, let's consider the work of another classical sociologist, Max Weber (1864–1920). Weber believed that the opportunity to succeed is crucial to the definition of class. Weber's work (Weber 1946) is the source of the sociological concept of **life chances**, defined as the practical opportunity to achieve desired material conditions and personal experiences. For Weber, it was not abstract freedom but the *practical* ability to achieve that defines a person's life chances. This concept is different from the conventional American view of opportunity, which focuses on the absence of formal obstacles to success. For example, in a capitalist economy, a person with few material resources or skills does not have high life chances, even if that person has the hypothetical possibility of becoming rich, because the practical chance of doing so is very small (E. Wright 1997).

The concept of life chances helps explain how social class works within families. The job or income of a parent, for example, clearly affects the life chances of his or her spouse and children. (For example, children whose parents have high incomes are much more likely to complete college.) Similarly, the spouses of rich people have historically had the chance to live a lifestyle far more lavish than their own income or career would have permitted (although wives in such marriages often remain subordinate to their husbands). Thus, the income and other resources of those we are connected to influence the life chances of each of us and therefore our class position (Szelenyi 2001).

This brings us to the broader idea of **social capital**, the access to resources a person has by virtue of relationships and connections within a social network (Portes 1998). The French sociologist Pierre Bourdieu (1930–2002), who developed this idea (Bourdieu 1986), believed that families are only one such social

**exploitation**

The process by which the labor of some produces wealth that is controlled by others.

**life chances**

The practical opportunity to achieve desired material conditions and personal experiences.

**social capital**

The access to resources one has by virtue of relationships and connections within a social network.

The Missoni family's fashion company is based in Italy and its zigzag pattern is famous worldwide. Founded by Rosita (center) and her husband, Missoni employs several family members in executive positions.

network, but perhaps the most important one. Belonging to a group, such as a family or an exclusive club, makes it possible for people to draw from the resources held by all of its members. For example, think of parents paying for college, an uncle getting someone a job interview, or the chance to meet potential spouses at an exclusive party. Naturally, the resources of the group are not automatically shared equally with everyone. Instead, getting access to those resources depends on being a group member in good standing, which requires effort and upkeep. In family terms, that may mean offering one's own resources to other family members, protecting the family name and reputation, and obeying one's elders—or at least being polite at Thanksgiving dinner.

Social capital is not something that only rich people have. After all, poor people might get jobs from their uncles as well. But the amount of social capital—in addition to the amount of money in their pockets—is one of the things that divide those in lower classes from those in upper classes.

## Families in Their Social Classes

To illustrate this divide more concretely, let's consider two very different extended families. The first is a wealthy family. I pieced together their story from public sources, such as wedding announcements, corporate biographies, alumni newsletters, and obituaries. The second is a snapshot of a working-class family drawn from Katherine S. Newman's book *No Shame in My Game: The Working Poor in the Inner City* (K. Newman 1999). These descriptions are meant to illustrate how a class may hold together through families and across generations.

**Generations of Wealth and Privilege** Audrey Winston has two sisters, Dorothy and Elizabeth (I've altered their names and a few details to protect their privacy). Their parents, William and Barbara, were White and wealthy. William had two engineering degrees from Columbia University; Barbara was a graduate of an Ivy League university as well and worked for an elite private high school. Two of the girls attended that same high school, whose alumni include a former U.S. president as well as many other prominent politicians, writers, scientists, and celebrities. The third sister went to a different New England private school. For college, the sisters went to Brown, Yale, and Skidmore College. This is an elite New England family, wealthy and well educated—the sort of family whose weddings are reported in the *New York Times* (which is how I found them, in the wedding announcements). The family is diagrammed in Figure 4.2, with the Winstons shown in orange.

Two of the three daughters married, and those marriages give a further glimpse of the class to which they belong. Audrey married a banking executive, himself a graduate of an elite private high school and an Ivy League university. His parents were successful professionals. Dorothy married a lawyer, Robert Whittaker, also a product of prep schools and an elite private college, whose father was an Episcopal Church leader.

Figure 4.2 **An elite extended family**

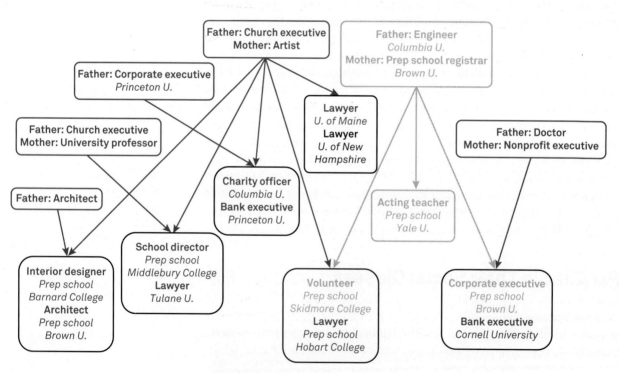

The Winstons (orange) and the Whittakers (pink), along with their in-laws (purple), formed a wealthy family network through marriages among their children. The couples are shown in boxes together. Most are graduates of prestigious private prep schools and universities, working in high-paid professional or corporate careers.

To look one step further, consider Robert's siblings (his family is shown in pink). His brother was a lawyer who married a lawyer; one sister married a lawyer, another married a banking executive, and the third married an architect. Between them and their spouses, they attended Barnard College and Columbia, Princeton, Brown, and Tulane Universities. The spouses' parents (shown in purple), in turn, were all college-educated professionals, including some who attended Ivy League schools and worked as corporate executives.

This is a small slice of the American upper class. Showing their interconnections is important for understanding that this class is not just people with very high salaries and professional jobs, but a *group of connected families full* of people with high salaries and professional jobs. Substantial wealth passes from generation to generation, along with the lifestyle, education, and social connections of their extended networks, enjoyed in their big houses (and summer homes) and private schools for their children. When they marry, they usually marry endogamously, that is, within their group. Although not formally named, like the aristocracies of old Europe, this class still uses family ties to forge a cohesive social group. And unlike the poor or working class, this is a very exclusive group, membership in which is closely guarded. As a class, they share common interests, experiences, and ways of looking at the world, which are reinforced in their selective schools and tightly connected social interactions (Khan 2011). And when they need a job or a spouse or a friend, they have a network of potentially like-minded people to whom they may turn—people who may be in their alumni association, school PTA, or yacht club. Their class membership is not just a result of inherited wealth, high-income jobs, and high education, but a result of a huge stock of social capital to which all members have access—and life chances that reflect these opportunities.

Identifying a friendship network is more difficult than tracing a group related by marriage, as I have done here, because friendships are not usually publicly recorded. However, I found one easy example: a short visit between Audrey and two of her college friends was reported in the gossip section of the alumni newsletter. The couple, who were married, stayed with Audrey and her husband while they were in town. This couple, I discovered, are not only Ivy League graduates but also successful corporate executives themselves, with MBA degrees. She was a commercial banker and marketing manager who left the workforce to be home with the children, while he was a managing director at one of the biggest financial firms in the country. Thus, friendship connections also appear to be highly selective.

**Generations of Working Poverty** Now consider a family from the other side of the tracks—an old phrase that refers to people from different social classes living on different sides of the railroad tracks, which have long been prominent physical and social barriers in American cities (Du Bois 1942). In her book, Katherine Newman details the struggles of the working poor—that is, people who often have jobs but are unable to achieve economic security or stability. She tells the story of Evie, a Black woman in her late 50s who works as a letter carrier (K. Newman 1999:164–165). She has seven daughters between her ex-husband, William, and her current partner, Harry, who is retired from a job parking cars.

Three of the daughters have jobs—as a medical secretary, a corrections officer, and a hairstylist. All seven daughters have husbands or partners, whose jobs include truck driving, bus driving, and construction work. Two of the men are military veterans; several of the families receive public assistance. Three of the daughters have children with former partners. None of the daughters has been to college, but a few of their children have started (and one granddaughter is attending law school after marrying an accountant).

As the family tree expands to include cousins and their families, we find that the adults have jobs as postal workers, fast-food workers, military service members, and clerical workers. College attendance is very rare, while poverty and public assistance are very common. In the three generations represented, there is little evidence of movement out of the working class and its meager material conditions; only one of Evie's descendants has married or cohabited with someone who has a professional degree. What social capital they have doesn't provide the needed resources for much improvement in life chances.

**Family Networks** Drawing from the ideas presented so far and the examples of the two extended families—each of which has grown within its own social class borders—we can now bring in the idea of social networks (see Chapter 6). Like the Winstons and their affluent relatives, Evie's working-poor family is a network of people with similar class backgrounds and economic circumstances. Seeing families this way helps make sense of the relationship between family and social class. In the network diagram in Figure 4.3, each circle represents an individual in an immediate family, represented by the clusters of circles. When someone joins another family (usually through marriage), the clusters are connected with a thick solid line. The clusters of families are separated into two groups by the railroad tracks, representing two different social classes.

In this scenario, most families have connections only to those within the same class, and only a few marry across the tracks (represented by the dotted pink lines). These groups are not just at different levels from each other; rather, they occupy distinct social spaces, and the barriers between them are formidable—like the railroad tracks that separate city neighborhoods. The clearest example is marriage patterns, such as those in the extended families just described. What is the chance that these two families would ever be joined by marriage? Exogamy that cuts across social classes is no less fraught with potential problems than the intermarriages between racial-ethnic groups that we discussed in Chapter 3.

Figure 4.3 is just an abstract representation; the true number and nature of the connections would need to be determined by research. Such research can take the form of case studies (like the ones considered here) or analysis of demographic data. For example, we will see in Chapter 8 that 4 out of 5 American marriages include spouses on the same side of the college/no-college divide—and that pattern has grown stronger in recent decades. In different societies or different periods in history, we might find looser or denser groups of families, with more or less contact across the tracks.

Thinking about families grouped into a social class helps us to understand a crucial aspect of class: **class identity**, which we can define as the awareness of, and sense of belonging to, a specific social class. If people did not have class

**class identity**

The awareness of, and sense of belonging to, a specific social class.

**Figure 4.3 Families in social class networks**

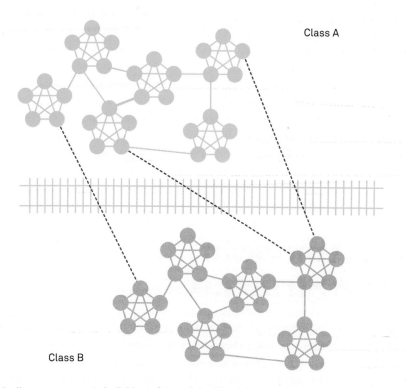

Class A

Class B

This diagram represents individuals (circles), families (clusters of circles), and social classes (orange versus blue), with social classes separated by a symbolic social boundary (railroad tracks). There are many more connections within each social class than there are across the tracks.

identities, we might think of social classes as just statistical groups of people with similar economic profiles. But with class identity, they become familiar social settings with distinctive ways of life and patterns of interaction. Because social class involves intimate, lifelong family relationships, classes develop shared patterns of thinking and acting. These patterns are partly the result of similar economic circumstances and experiences, such as owning wealth and property (or not), working for others versus managing others at work, and so on (Kohn 1977). But they also follow from the everyday interactions their members have with each other, through which they socialize with each other and build a repertoire of expected and acceptable behavior, similar to the process that happens within families.

The concept of class identity, in turn, helps us with another problem in figuring who belongs in which social class—the fact that many people have fluctuating incomes. For example, poorer families may see their incomes bobbing up and down around the bare minimum as they navigate between different jobs and income sources. Middle-class families experience fluctuations as well, even if they don't usually rise to the level of threatening the family's survival. Class identity, on the other hand, is more durable, persisting for years, if not generations (Roksa and Potter 2011). That is because people are raised and socialized according to their family's class perspectives and the behavior and expectations of those around them (Irwin 2009). Further, their social capital helps smooth out the unevenness in their circumstances from year to year: during good years they may help friends and relatives, and during lean years they may draw on help from others.

In general, when the barriers between classes are strong, class identity tends to be stronger as well, because it is reinforced by close contact among people belonging to a given class. On the other hand, when people flow easily between classes, the tendency to identify with their own class origins is weaker. In fact, the number of classes, or even the existence of discrete, identifiable classes, is not always certain. We turn next to that issue.

# The American Class Structure

Combining various approaches to social class and the way Americans see themselves, and analyzing the distribution of income and occupations, sociologists have developed a common description of the contemporary structure of social classes (E. Wright and Rogers 2011). I use the phrase "common description" because it reflects the fact that most sociologists have given up attempting to precisely define social classes in modern society. Instead, we are satisfied if we can use concepts and measures that help explain the nature of social life and the problems we face, both individually and collectively (Lareau and Conley 2008). With that in mind, the following four categories provide a useful framework for learning about social class.

- *The capitalist and corporate managerial class.* This very small group is sometimes called "the 1 percent," although the actual number is not certain; "upper class" may be a more appropriate label. In the General Social Survey (GSS), 3.2 percent of American adults identify themselves as "upper class" (see Figure 4.4). They have an extremely high standard of living, as well as both economic and political influence far beyond their numbers.

- *The middle class.* This much larger group has historically had relatively stable jobs based on their higher education or technical skills and credentials. Although their standard of living is much more modest than that of the upper class, they are able to meet basic needs, including health care and education, and usually own homes. Almost half the U.S. population (43.2 percent) chooses this category to describe themselves.

- *The working class.* Although lacking the higher education or training of the middle class, this large group has a standard of living similar to that of the

Figure 4.4 **Percentage of Americans who identify as . . .**

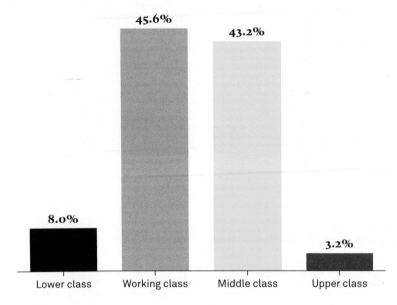

SOURCE: Author's calculations from the General Social Surveys, 1972–2012 (Smith et al. 2014).

middle class, but with much less stability. Their jobs, once based in industries with strong labor unions or government protections, are less secure, and they more often experience economic shocks that threaten their way of life—as was painfully apparent during the recession of the late 2000s. In the GSS, this group is slightly larger, 45.6 percent.

- *The lower class.* Most people in this group do not have higher education or skilled jobs, so their families have low incomes and a high degree of economic insecurity. As their job situation fluctuates, they may experience periods of outright poverty, including lack of adequate medical care and housing. Among this group are the very poor, who are unable to compete for the jobs that might lift them out of poverty. They usually depend on government assistance for much of their food, medical care, or housing. Only 8 percent of the population identifies as "lower class" in the GSS, but based on their economic conditions, most sociologists believe that this group is larger. As we will see, the official poverty rate was 15 percent in 2012.

Clearly, social class categories and identity are important parts of family life, for better or worse. What we have not addressed explicitly to this point, however, is social class inequality. If classes represent higher and lower levels of economic status and security, then the distance between them is social class inequality. And one of the most important trends in U.S. history for the last half-century has been the growth of such inequality.

# Increasing Inequality

To think about income inequality, we need to make two kinds of comparisons. First, we have to consider the relative difference between people with more money and people with less money. Second, we need to understand how the overall level of inequality in society changes over time. What seems like extreme inequality in one context may not be as severe in another context. (An additional, very important dimension beyond the scope of this book is inequality between societies; Korzeniewicz and Moran 2009.) As people view those who are richer or poorer than themselves, their perception is affected both by the social distance between them and others and by how that distance has changed over time. We will discuss each of these issues briefly.

Figure 4.5 offers a simple view of the current distribution of family income in the United States. Family income is the combined income of all related people who live in the same household. If you line up all families according to income, with the poorest on the left and the richest on the right, and add up their incomes

Figure 4.5 **U.S. family income distribution, 2011**

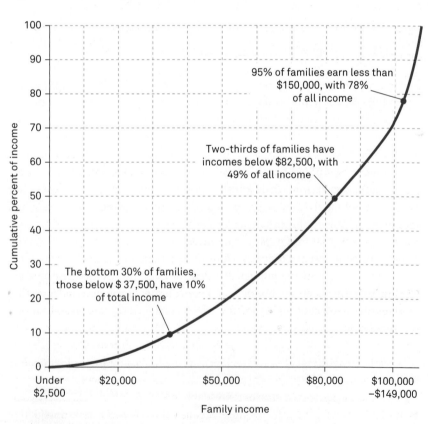

SOURCE: Author's calculations from U.S. Census Bureau sources.

Figure 4.6 **Family income inequality, 1947–2011**

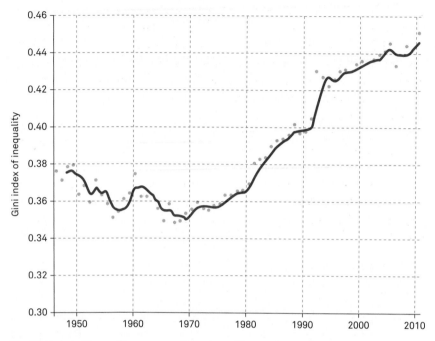

The Gini index of inequality measures the extent of income inequality, with a score of 1 representing complete inequality (one family has all the income) and 0 representing complete equality (all families have equal income).

SOURCE: Author's calculations from U.S. Census Bureau sources.

as you move from left to right, the result will be the pink line shown in the figure. The highlighted points on the line help explain the pattern. The first shows that 30 percent of families had incomes below $37,500 in 2011, and together those families have just 10 percent of the total national income. The bottom two-thirds of families were all below $82,500 each, and together they had 49 percent of all income. Finally, the top 5 percent of families all had incomes of $150,000 or more, and their share of all income was 22 percent.

If the top 5 percent of families received 22 percent of the income in 2011, is that "a lot" of inequality? One way to answer that is with a measure called the **Gini index** (Allison 1978). The Gini index is a score between 0 and 1, with 0 representing complete equality (all families have the same income) and 1 representing complete inequality (one family has all the income). The income distribution shown in Figure 4.5 has a Gini index of 0.45. When we compare that number in 2011 with the level of inequality in previous years, as I've done in Figure 4.6, it becomes clear that income inequality has increased dramatically, and almost continuously, since the end of the 1960s. To understand the reasons behind this trend, we need to consider changes that have affected those on the bottom, in the middle, and at the top of the economic ladder (Levy 1998).

**Gini index**

A measure of inequality in which 0 represents complete equality and 1 represents complete inequality.

- *At the bottom: keeping the poor from improving their lot.* Among the lowest earners, there have been changes in public policy and family structure that have kept their incomes from rising. For example, the legal minimum wage, which is set by the federal government (although some states set theirs higher), has been allowed to fall as inflation eroded its value. From its peak in 1968, the minimum wage had fallen 30 percent by 2012, after inflation is taken into account. At $7.25 per hour, this translates into just $15,000 per year for a full-time job. (In response to the falling value of the minimum wage, some places have implemented "living wage" laws, as we discuss shortly.) Meanwhile, the growing number of single-parent families (see Chapter 9)—most with only a mother's income to live on—has contributed to the number of poor families as well (McLanahan and Percheski 2008).

- *In the middle: divergent fortunes.* In the middle-income ranges, some trends have pulled families down while others have lifted families up, resulting in a greater degree of inequality. On the one hand, the decline of the manufacturing sector in the face of global competition hurt many middle-income workers, who had previously been able to earn a good income without the benefit of a college degree (but with the help of labor unions that used to be stronger). Noncollege jobs now are likely to be low-wage service jobs (think of fast-food jobs). On the other hand, in the new service-oriented economy, those with higher education are doing much better (think of lawyers). Further, many women now receive higher earnings than they did in the past, but these gains have largely benefited women with more education (Karoly and Burtless 1995). On top of these economic forces, the increasing tendency of people to marry at their own education level has exacerbated the split between families with two high earners and those with two low earners (Schwartz 2010).

- *At the top: the new superrich.* Finally, a new pattern of very high incomes has emerged, spurred by government policies that include the deregulation of the finance industry, reduced taxes on certain kinds of income earned by the very rich, and relaxed restrictions on corporate lobbying for those policies (Stiglitz 2013). This includes three groups: chief executives at major corporations, whose incomes include stock in the companies and huge bonuses; investment bankers and financial managers who handle vast sums of money; and celebrities and superstar athletes, whose growing audiences have propelled their incomes upward (R. Gordon and Dew-Becker 2008). As a result, the richest 1 percent of individuals more than doubled their share of the total national income in the last four decades, from less than 10 percent to more than 20 percent (Piketty and Saez 2007).

These factors all contributed to increasing inequality between families (Allegretto 2011). As the gap between rich and poor has grown, the threat of slipping down from the upper class or the middle class has become a constant worry for many families. In fact, insecurity and instability are potential issues for all but the richest of American families. As we will see in Chapter 10, job loss and economic stress in general increase the likelihood of marriages ending in divorce. And sometimes an economic crisis threatens a family's class identity as well as its material well-being. In the United States, where owning a home is often considered a marker of middle-class status, the breaking point may occur when the family is at risk of losing a house. Consider a working-class family described in a 2011 *New York Times* report (Tavernise, Deparle, and Gebeloff 2011):

> Jennifer Bangura works at Georgetown University Hospital as a cashier. Together with her husband, a driver for a catering company, their family income is just under $50,000, enough to pay a mortgage of $800 on a house she purchased in 1992. But after taxes, medical costs and the gas to get to work, they slip into the category of near poor. Their situation has been made worse by a second mortgage, taken out several years ago to raise money for their daughter's college tuition. The monthly payment shot up to $2,200, an amount she says is now untenable. "It's killing me," said Ms. Bangura, who is 50 and originally from Jamaica. She said she has been making payments for years and that "to lose it now would tear me apart."

Although this family's basic needs are not immediately threatened, they may have to choose between college and homeownership. A crisis of this type is more than just financially destabilizing. One of the young adults that Kathleen Gerson (2010:48) interviewed about their childhood experiences explained how her father's business failures shook up her parents' marriage as well:

> Things would look okay and then all of a sudden my mother would find out we were seven months behind on the mortgage. It felt like every time you made a step forward, you ended up getting hit with something else. The most obvious thing was the economic instability, but it created so much instability in the family 'cause we were so busy just trying to survive each day.

One of the most important questions about inequality, both for analysts and for those attempting to make policy, concerns poverty. What is poverty, who is poor, and what can and should we do about the problem? We turn next to that issue.

## Poverty and Policy

The class categories described earlier are not official definitions. Still, social class is important for government policy, especially tax and welfare policy. Although the amount of government intervention is lower in the United States than in many other countries, the government does distribute income downward to assist the poor. To do this, it has to identify richer people to tax and poorer people to receive benefits. Toward this end, various laws establish dividing lines between those with higher and lower incomes.

The federal government uses income categories to set tax rates, so that rich families usually pay higher tax rates than poor families—a practice known as *progressive taxation*. In fact, a majority of the American public agree that the rich should pay higher taxes (Saad 2011). The rules are complicated, and there are a lot of exceptions, but taking all federal taxes and credits into account, the poorest fifth of households pay 4 percent of their income in taxes, compared with 26 percent for the richest fifth of households (Congressional Budget Office 2009).

In addition to setting tax rates, the government also defines poverty and uses that definition to determine who may get government benefits. In 2012, a family of four was considered "poor" if their combined income was less than $23,283. This is the official **poverty line**, the level of income below which the federal government defines a family or individual as poor. This definition was created in the 1960s based on a formula that simply multiplied a family "economy food plan" times three, because at the time food accounted for about one-third of a family's expenses. Since then, the poverty line has been adjusted annually according to the inflation rate (Iceland 2003).

If the intention of the poverty line is to identify those families that are unable to meet their basic needs, there are at least three problems with this measure (Short 2011). First, the price of food has risen more slowly than the price of housing and medical care, so living on a food budget times three is no longer adequate. Second, the calculation doesn't include important government benefits that some low-income families get, especially medical assistance and tax credits. Finally, it doesn't take into account the different cost of living in different places; that $23,283 might be enough to live on in a small midwestern town, but not a

**poverty line**

The level of income below which the federal government defines a family or individual as poor.

The feasibility of the "SNAP Challenge," in which participants try to eat an average of $4–5 worth of food a day, is hotly debated by Democrats and Republicans. Logistics aside, it is a question many fortunate people might not have to ask themselves every day: How much do your meals cost?

big coastal city. Nevertheless, although it is a crude measure, the benefit of the poverty line is that it allows us to assess the problem of poverty in a consistent way over time and for different groups (S. K. Danziger 2010).

Research on poverty encompasses many research methods and data sources. It also involves difficult questions of politics and public policy as well as morality. Some people say that the government has no right to redistribute money from the rich to the poor. Others argue that those of us with money to spare must fulfill society's moral obligations to care for the poorest of the poor—and the government is our agent in that endeavor. One source of that perspective is Christianity. According to the Gospel of Matthew (25:31-46), Jesus promised salvation for those who met this obligation:

> Take your inheritance, the kingdom [heaven] prepared for you since the creation of the world. For I was hungry and you gave me something to eat, I was thirsty and you gave me something to drink, I was a stranger and you invited me in, I needed clothes and you clothed me, I was sick and you looked after me, I was in prison and you came to visit me.

For those who did not rise to the moral challenge of caring for the poor, Jesus instead promised "eternal fire."

Regardless of our moral or political perspectives, however, we need a basic understanding of the problem. To that end, I have organized some key facts about poverty in the United States:

- *Poverty increased dramatically during the 2000s.* In 2012, the official poverty rate in the United States was 15 percent. That is, 46.5 million people were living in families (or alone) with incomes below the federal poverty line. That was the largest number ever recorded and an increase of about 15 million from the year 2000 (see Figure 4.7). On a percentage basis, the poverty rate in 2012 was as high as it had been at any time since the 1960s. The increase in poverty was caused by a combination of the factors that increased inequality (discussed earlier) and by the severe economic crisis that began in 2008.

- *Poverty is concentrated by race/ethnicity.* We saw in Chapter 3 that poverty rates differ widely for various racial-ethnic groups (see Figure 4.8). In fact, American Indians, Latinos, and African Americans are all about three times more likely to be poor than Whites. This long-standing pattern has been exacerbated by recent trends (Edin and Kissane 2010).

- *Poverty is closely related to family structure.* People who live in households headed by a single mother are much more likely to be poor than other groups in the United States. As we will discuss in Chapter 8, African Americans and people with less education are less likely to marry. And we know that women with less education have more children, on average (see Chapter 9). A single woman who lives with her children is especially likely to fall into poverty—or be unable to rise out of it. As a result, although there are many poor people living in married-couple families—14 million, almost as

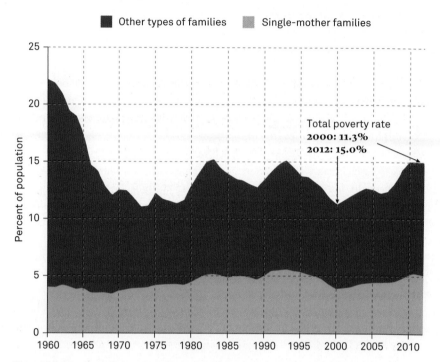

Figure 4.7 **Percentage of U.S. population in poverty, 1960–2011, by family type**

■ Other types of families    ▨ Single-mother families

Total poverty rate
**2000: 11.3%**
**2012: 15.0%**

Percent of population

1960  1965  1970  1975  1980  1985  1990  1995  2000  2005  2010

Note the large share of the poor who are in single-mother families (but the even larger share who are not).

SOURCE: U.S. Census Bureau (2013d).

many as live in single-mother families—the poverty *rate* for single-mother families is more than four times higher (34 percent versus 8 percent). This is illustrated in the Story Behind the Numbers.

- *People in poverty suffer from serious deprivation.* Even in a rich country like the United States, those at the bottom of the economic scale go without many of the things most people consider necessary. Sometimes such deprivation is episodic—it comes and goes—but it still looms large in the lives of the poor. For example, about half of the children in families below the poverty line experience at least one of these hardships in a given year: periods of food shortage, overcrowded housing, being late on the rent or mortgage, and not going to the doctor when necessary (A. Sherman 2011). Not many people freeze or starve to death in the United States, but many do live in families that have to make painful tradeoffs to keep the heat on and put food on the table.

- *Homelessness has declined but remains a serious problem.* About 600,000 people are homeless, that is, living in homeless shelters, on the streets, in cars, in abandoned buildings, or in other places not intended as dwellings. Although this is a lot of people, it is a small percentage of the population

**Figure 4.8  U.S. family poverty rates, by race/ethnicity, 2011**

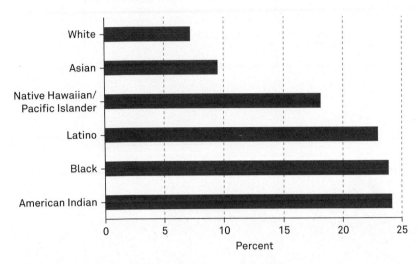

Families are defined by the race/ethnicity of the householder. Races are for those who specified only one race; White group excludes Latinos.

SOURCE: American Community Survey 2011 via American FactFinder (2014).

(about 0.2 percent). About a third of homeless people are living with their families, while the rest are alone (National Alliance to End Homelessness 2013). The problem declined through the 2000s—even with the major economic crisis—because of concerted efforts by the federal government and local partners to identify and house homeless people.

- *Many people move in and out of poverty.* We tend to think of how many people are poor at any one time. But poverty is an experience that many more Americans have at some point in their lives. For example, even though 15 percent of people are in poverty now, about twice that number experienced at least one year of poverty during the last 15-year period (Sandoval, Rank, and Hirschl 2009). That is because the number of people who are near the poverty line—and at risk of falling below it in short order—is much greater than the number of poor at any one time. In fact, one thing that poor people and those at risk of poverty share—and something many more remember from their childhood—is the experience of uncertainty, of not knowing whether more serious hardship is right around the corner (Western et al. 2012).

Federal, state, and local governments operate many programs to assist people in need. The poverty line is often used as a guide for who should receive such assistance, but it's not a strict cutoff. For example, the federal Women, Infants, and Children program makes millions of low-income families eligible for nutritional support based on an income cutoff of 1.85 times the poverty line (Food and Nutrition Service 2013). Other programs that define eligibility in relation to the poverty line are Medicaid (medical assistance for the poor), food stamps, the school lunch program, and dozens of others (S. K. Danziger 2010).

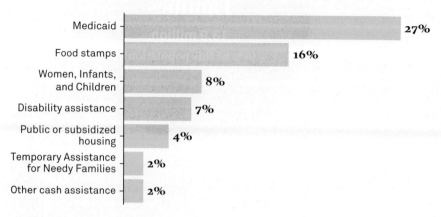

Figure 4.9  **Percentage of people in U.S. households where someone receives each type of federal assistance, last quarter of 2011**

| Type of assistance | Percentage |
| --- | --- |
| Medicaid | 27% |
| Food stamps | 16% |
| Women, Infants, and Children | 8% |
| Disability assistance | 7% |
| Public or subsidized housing | 4% |
| Temporary Assistance for Needy Families | 2% |
| Other cash assistance | 2% |

SOURCE: U.S. Census Bureau (2013j).

The most common poverty assistance programs are shown in Figure 4.9. They range in size from Medicaid, which supports more than one-quarter of the population, to Temporary Assistance for Needy Families (TANF), which supports mostly poor single mothers as they seek employment.

Despite the hardships that poor people experience, this patchwork of government assistance programs helps prevent many of the worst outcomes associated with economic deprivation. Some analysts have concluded that the various benefits reduce the number of people in real poverty by more than half (Ben-Shalom, Moffitt, and Scholz 2011). Still, even after taking into account government support, almost 1 in 6 Americans do not have the income necessary to support their basic needs (Short 2011). In terms of the social class categories outlined earlier, this would include the lower class as well as a significant portion of those in the working class who, even if they have jobs, do not command enough stable income to rise above a minimal standard of living.

# Social Mobility and Class Persistence

We saw in the families described earlier that the children mostly followed in the social class footsteps of their parents, as indicated by the education and jobs they got and the people with whom they married and had children. Clearly, however, this is not always the case. How exactly the system repeats itself from generation to generation—or doesn't—is a major issue in sociological research (Beller and Hout 2006).

In sociological terms, this is the question of **social mobility**, or the movement,

**social mobility**

The movement, up or down, between social classes.

up or down, between social classes. The basic issue is people's class origin versus their class destination—that is, the social class status of their parents compared with their own class position in adulthood. Most Americans believe that we live in a society with a high degree of social mobility—a society in which anyone can rise from meager origins to achieve higher status or wealth (Ferrie 2005), as in the classic "rags-to-riches" stories popularized by Horatio Alger in the nineteenth century. And many people do rise—but many more do not.

In classical sociology studies, social mobility was studied by comparing the occupations of fathers with the occupations of sons (which made more sense when a father's income alone usually determined the status of a family). These studies produced a tool known as the "mobility table," an example of which I show in Table 4.1. This table shows men classified according to five job categories, ranked roughly from highest (upper professional) to lowest (unskilled and service). The numbers on the dark-green diagonal are the highest in the table, showing that sons are most likely to share their fathers' occupational category. Sons whose fathers were upper professionals are 2.2 times as likely to be upper professionals themselves, compared with sons whose fathers were in other occupations. (The pattern is similar for mothers and daughters.)

Is this a lot of mobility? Compared with most other wealthy countries, the United States has less social mobility. That is, American children are more likely to end up in economic situations similar to their parents' (Ermisch, Jäntti, and Smeeding 2012). This is particularly true of people at the opposite ends of the economic spectrum. Studies show that it is especially difficult to escape deep poverty and highly unusual to fall from extreme wealth (Beller and Hout 2006).

We can think of the flip side of mobility as social class persistence—the tendency of children to relive their parents' class status. The most obvious way for

Table 4.1 **Mobility table of sons' occupations in relation to their fathers' occupations**

| | SON OCCUPATION | | | | |
|---|---|---|---|---|---|
| **FATHER OCCUPATION** | UPPER PROFESSIONAL | LOWER PROFESSIONAL/ CLERICAL | SELF-EMPLOYED | TECHNICAL AND SKILLED | UNSKILLED AND SERVICE |
| Upper professional | 2.2 | 1.0 | 0.7 | 0.5 | 0.5 |
| Lower professional/clerical | 1.1 | 3.9 | 0.1 | 0.8 | 0.7 |
| Self-employed | 0.6 | 0.9 | 2.0 | 1.3 | 1.2 |
| Technical and skilled | 0.6 | 0.8 | 1.1 | 1.5 | 1.4 |
| Unskilled and service | 0.6 | 1.0 | 1.0 | 1.1 | 1.6 |

Numbers above 1.0 (shown in green) indicate that sons are more likely to be in the occupational category listed above if their fathers are in the category listed on the left; numbers below 1.0 (shown in yellow) mean that the outcome is less likely for sons.

SOURCE: The author's calculations from the General Social Surveys, 2006–2010 (Smith et al. 2014), using the categories from Beller and Hout (2006).

that to happen is for parents to pass their fortunes—if they have them—on to their children. Through inheritance, children of the rich may inherit wealth while children of the poor do not, resulting in a replication of the previous generation's inequality (E. Wolff and Gittleman 2011). Historically, inheritance taxes as high as 77 percent on the largest estates have mitigated this economic inequality. At its peak in the late 1970s, the federal estate tax was taken on the richest 7 percent of people when they died, but the limit has since been lowered so that now less than 1 percent of estates are taxed (D. Jacobson, Raub, and Johnson 2011). That change is part of what has made the tax structure in the United States less progressive, contributing to increased inequality.

Regardless of our individual efforts to succeed, then, the passing of wealth from one generation to the next adds a strong element of yesteryear's class structure into the present. In fact, by giving—or even just promising—money with strings attached, parents also may attempt to shape the values and behaviors of the next generation. For example, parents may withhold or withdraw financial support if they do not approve of their children's marriage choices. If such parents are successful, their children may inherit not only their assets, but crucial aspects of their behavior and perspectives on society as well (Angel 2008:80).

Besides the money that passes directly from one generation to the next, I will discuss two important dimensions of family life that have consequences for the life chances of children in the next generation. The first is family structure itself, which can have cascading effects in many areas of children's development, and the second is parenting behavior.

## Family Structure

In subsequent chapters, we will see a number of ways that family behavior differs according to social class. For example, people with lower incomes are less likely to marry (see Chapter 8). And people with less schooling have more children than those with higher levels of education (see Chapter 9) and have a higher risk of divorce (see Chapter 10). Combined with the forces that have increased economic inequality in recent decades, these trends mean that we now find children who live with married parents concentrated in higher-income families and those who live with a single parent (most often their mother) skewed toward the lower end of the income scale, often in poverty (McLanahan and Percheski 2008). This discussion is intended to prepare us for those later investigations.

The pattern of income and family type is shown in Figure 4.10. You can see that the most common situation for children of single mothers is a family income below $25,000. There are almost 10 million children of single mothers living in that income bracket. In contrast, the most common situation for children of married parents is a family income of between $50,000 and $100,000. If it is true that children are likely to remain in the same social class as the one in which they grow up, this would suggest that today's children of single mothers are most likely to dominate the lower and working classes of tomorrow.

Because of the stark contrast shown in Figure 4.10 and the growing number

**Figure 4.10 Distribution of children by family type and family income, 2010**

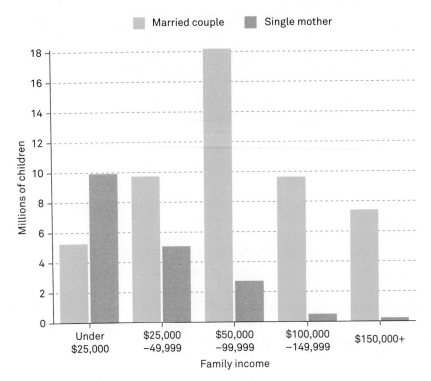

SOURCE: Author's calculations from U.S. Census Bureau sources.

of families in poverty, much of the concern about family structure and social class focuses on single-mother families (Mayer 1997). Those growing up with a single parent face three kinds of scarcity that can make it more difficult to reach the middle and upper classes (McLanahan and Sandefur 1994):

- *Money*. The most important factor separating children of single mothers from those whose parents are married and living together is simply their lower incomes (Musick and Mare 2006). It may be difficult for these families to meet their basic needs, much less such benefits as better housing or private education. And the children in these families live with economic uncertainty and insecurity, which increases their stress and threatens their self-confidence.

- *Time*. Single mothers have less time to spend with their children than do married parents (Vickery 1977). That is partly because there is only one parent, but also because of the time demands on low-income mothers who must work to support their families (Kendig and Bianchi 2008). In fact, some welfare programs exacerbate this problem by requiring mothers' employment, which tightens the time squeeze in single-parent families (Albelda 2011). The lack of parental time cuts down on the supervision and support

# Working and Poor

Consider the budget of a single mother living in Buffalo, New York (see Table 4.2). With two children, ages 6 and 3, her biggest expense is child care—more than $1,000 per month for a licensed, home-based center for her youngest and a small family care provider for her 6-year-old's after-school hours. After that, she needs about $700 for her rent, $500 for food, and $300 for transportation (maintaining, insuring, and fueling a car). Once the rest of her basic expenses are added up, she needs a total of $3,134 per month, or $37,602 per year.

But what does she earn? If she's a hotel housekeeper, she probably earns $20,000 per year (the median wage for a full-time, year-round housekeeper). A preschool teacher or nursing aide would make $24,000 or $25,000. If she had been working for a while and got promoted to manager in the food service industry, she could expect to earn $36,000—still not enough.

But the government helps. The housekeeper's salary—the only one below the official federal poverty line—would allow her to receive $2,000 per year in food stamps and free lunch for her 6-year-old in school. A teacher or nursing aide would qualify for reduced-price lunches. And then there are tax breaks—the Earned Income Tax Credit, a tax credit for each child, and a child-care benefit. But even with government support and tax credits, none of these jobs would bring her total income up to cover her basic necessities. What can she do?

In this exercise, breaking into groups for a discussion or working on your own, consider this woman's scenario and address these questions:

- Does the scenario seem realistic and/or reasonable?

- Looking over her budget, see where you might cut first or what you would do to make ends meet.

- Besides the budget, what else needs to change in this situation?

Then consider her children:

- How does the bare-bones budget affect their daily lives?

- What about their long-term development and future prospects?

- Besides monetary adjustments, what changes or adaptations can their mother make for them?

Finally, what—or who—is missing from this story? How might other family members, neighbors, community members, charities, or the government help (or hurt) the situation?

Table 4.2 **Budget worksheet: Single parent with children ages 3 and 6, living in Buffalo, NY**

| EXPENSES | Annual | Monthly |
|---|---|---|
| Rent and utilities | $8,448 | $704 |
| Food | $5,691 | $474 |
| Child care* | $12,760 | $1,063 |
| Health insurance (employee contribution) | $2,609 | $217 |
| Out-of-pocket medical | $456 | $38 |
| Transportation | $3,821 | $318 |
| Other necessities | $3,817 | $318 |
| **Total expenses** | **$37,602** | **$3,134** |

| ANNUAL INCOME | Earnings | Food stamps | School lunch | Net taxes† | TOTAL | SHORTFALL Annual | Monthly |
|---|---|---|---|---|---|---|---|
| Maid/housekeeper | $20,000 | $2,000 | $471 | $5,483 | $27,954 | $9,648 | $804 |
| Preschool/kindergarten teacher | $24,000 | — | $403 | $3,729 | $28,132 | $9,470 | $789 |
| Nursing aide | $25,000 | — | $403 | $3,413 | $28,816 | $8,786 | $732 |
| Food service manager | $36,000 | — | — | −$674 | $35,326 | $2,276 | $190 |

\* Three-year-old in licensed, home-based care, 6-year-old in family-based care.

† Taxes include state and federal income tax and payroll taxes; credits include federal child-care tax credit, federal child tax credit, federal Earned Income Tax Credit. If net taxes are greater than $0, she gets money back on her taxes.

*Source:* Budget and tax estimates are from the National Center for Children in Poverty (2014); earnings estimates are from the American Community Survey 2010 (American FactFinder 2014); the value of school lunches is from the U.S. Department of Agriculture (2013); Earned Income Tax Credit estimates are from the Internal Revenue Service (2012).

for children as they mature. One result is that single parents, and poor parents in general, rely more on "media time" as a parenting strategy than do higher-earning parents (see Changing Technology, "The Digital Divide").

· *Social capital.* Closely related to the time squeeze is the frequent scarcity of social capital in single-parent families (J. Coleman 1988). Often starting with a smaller family network, children in single-parent families may have access to fewer resources from adults—especially economically successful adults—who can support them in various ways as they grow up (Lin 1999).

Family structure clearly affects children's lives and their development in many ways. However, I should emphasize that the shape of one's family is not an share common experiences. Most teachers say that they want more parental involvement in the schools, and parents who are willing and able to provide that presence may improve their children's prospects in school (Langdon and Vesper 2000). At the college level, the cost of education and related expenses place an additional barrier to success before families and increasingly make completing college more difficult even for those who are able to attend. Of course, this barrier is much more difficult to overcome for students whose families are unable to help them cover the costs (Henretta et al. 2012).

For a variety of reasons, then, children from higher social classes advance further in school, on average. As the benefits of higher education have increased—and the penalties for *not* getting higher education have grown steeper—the achievement gap between those from rich families and those from poor families has actually been increasing (Reardon 2011).

The consequences are serious and have grown more so since the 1970s. As Figure 4.14 shows, since the 1970s, those with BAs and higher degrees have been pulling away from workers who only completed high school, so they now earn about 80 percent and 170 percent more, respectively. This growing inequality increases the pressure on parents to help their children succeed in school.

parents were less assertive, and they tended to defer to the decision making of the professionals.

All the parents Lareau studied wanted to help their children be happy and successful. But for adults in different social classes, their own background of experiences—the nature of their daily struggles and joys—gives them a different perspective, which influences how they try to promote their children toward adulthood and independence. Lareau believes that the strategy of concerted cultivation provides important benefits for middle-class children. They are more likely to grow up with a sense of confidence and entitlement and to feel empowered to stick up for themselves in school and the workplace. For example, they are better prepared to choose an appropriate college and figure out how to get admitted to it (Lareau and Conley 2008). On the flip side, poor and working-class parents are more concerned that their children have fun and enjoy childhood. That's not a minor issue: many children as young as their early teens report feeling stressed when they have multiple activities scheduled outside of school hours and wish they had more free time (S. Brown et al. 2011). But by not aggressively cultivating their children's skills and talents, poor and working-class parents may miss opportunities for them to move up in the class hierarchy.

When we see the important role of parenting in determining the future social class status of children—and how access to money and other resources affects the odds of success in that effort—it's clear that parenting is not just about love. It's also about the unpaid work that mothers and fathers do within the family. The nature of that work, and how it is divided between men and women, is one of the subjects of our next chapter.

## KEY TERMS:

division of labor     exploitation

life chances     social capital

class identity     Gini index

poverty line     social mobility

# Questions for Review

**1.** Using the issue of division of labor, explain how functionalist and conflict theorists differ on the topic of social class and families.

**2.** What is social capital, according to Pierre Bourdieu? How does social capital distinguish poor families from wealthy families?

**3.** How do marriage, social networks, and inherited wealth allow families to maintain or improve their social class position across generations? Why is this a disadvantage for working class American families?

**4.** Is inequality increasing in the United States? What evidence might you use to support your argument?

**5.** Why has poverty increased since 2000?

**6.** What are some of the social programs and policies enacted by U.S. lawmakers to help impoverished families?

**7.** What is the relationship between family structure and social mobility?

**8.** What is educational inequality? Why do students with wealthier socioeconomic backgrounds succeed in school at higher rates than children from less wealthy families?

**9.** What is class identity? What does class identity tell us about families that income does not?

Why do people create extreme sexual dimorphism in visual works? Can you think of any male-female pairings in creative visual works (such as movies, comics, or video games) in which the woman is an equal physical size or larger? Male and female humans are much more similar than are male and females elephant seals or ogres.

than 80 minutes ahead of the fastest female runners. It may have seemed that women were hopelessly weaker. But by 2010, the gap was down to less than 12 minutes, a mere 8 percent advantage for men (International Association of Athletics Federations 2014). Maybe the fastest man in the world will always be faster than the fastest woman, but this example shows that social intervention—such as the intensive training and encouragement of female athletes—can radically reduce such disparities. When feminist sociologists say that male domination is "neither natural nor inevitable" (see Chapter 1), they may be correct, even though some differences between the sexes are biological.

Height is one easily observable difference found in almost every family. The average American man in his 20s is about 6 inches taller than the average woman of the same age (McDowell et al. 2008). The average difference is substantial, but the overlap between the two groups is large as well. For example, the actor Michael J. Fox, at 5 feet 5 inches, is shorter than almost half of all U.S. women today; and at 5 feet 10 inches, Michelle Obama is taller than almost half of all American men. Figure 5.1 shows the height distributions of married men and women.

However, social behavior serves to enhance the difference in height between men and women rather than minimize it. The cultural expectation in Western countries is that men pair up with shorter women (Fink et al. 2007). With the rein in some of the more extreme forms of gender differentiation. For example, Abi and Emma Moore are sisters, each with their own children, who created an organization called Pink Stinks, which "confronts the damaging messages that bombard girls through toys, clothes and media." They write: "Girls' products overwhelmingly focus on being pretty, passive and obsessed with shopping, fashion and makeup—this promotes a dangerously narrow definition of what it means to be a girl. These 'Girly' products and concepts are marketed, for the most part, under the umbrella of pink" (Pink Stinks 2013).

The issue of gender identity in childhood is far from settled. When it comes to transsexual teenagers and adults, most mental health experts now believe they should be supported in attempting to achieve the gender identity they want. But for younger children who identify with the other sex, there is no consensus. Some believe that therapy to "normalize" children's gender identity is warranted, while others support the social transition to the other gender, possibly leading to hormonal or surgical intervention (D. Hill et al. 2010).

Far more common than transsexual identity is the routine adoption of androgynous styles and behaviors by children who are generally comfortable with their gender identity. Yet here again there are extremely different approaches. On the one hand, many parents routinely encourage children to bend gender stereotypes—like those children in the 1974 letter to Ann Landers. On the other hand, some parents (and authorities) enforce strict gender roles. For example, a school district in suburban Dallas suspended a 4-year-old boy from his prekindergarten class because he refused to cut his long hair and his parents wouldn't force him to. School officials said that the district's policy was meant to "reduce distractions" in the classroom (McKinley 2010).

Taylor Pugh, just 4 years old in 2009, was suspended from prekindergarten because his long hair violated his school's dress code. In the background are his brothers and best friend, whose short haircuts were allowed.

Finally, some feminists have also pursued psychoanalytic theory, inspired by work on childhood development that explores the emergence of male and female identity in families. In the tradition of Sigmund Freud and others, boys are seen as growing to reject their mothers and denying their own female nature, while girls emulate the nurturing behavior of their mothers (Chodorow 1978). In this view, the tendency of mothers to take primary responsibility for child rearing appears to be the basis of modern gender identities, since this relationship establishes the idea in children that women are emotional caretakers, while men are rational (though emotionally distant) leaders. Once that idea takes hold, it establishes the foundation for wider differences between men and women throughout society. And because these identities are developed at such a young age, people tend to think that gender differences are inherent to human nature rather than a product of social behavior (Brody 1999).

## Masculinity

As we have seen in our discussion of race in Chapter 3, close examination of the dominant racial group (Whites) has often been neglected in research that focuses on the trials and tribulations of subordinate groups, such as African Americans and Latinos. Similarly, much of the early research on gender was really about women. That made sense because studies of gender sought to expand the common perspective of men as representative of society as a whole.

However, in the last few decades, researchers have explored how rigid gender expectations take their own toll on men and male identity. It is now clear that masculinity also has its own history and development—that it, like femininity, is socially constructed (Connell and Messerschmidt 2005). Researchers in this tradition see multiple masculinities—that is, different constructions of what it means or requires to be a boy or man—in different cultural and historical settings. Because these ideas involve fatherhood, parenting, and relationships with women, they have become important to studies of the family (Doucet 2006).

Just as women's fashion permits more variation in choice of clothes than men's, expectations for men's behavior and identity in general are often more strictly enforced than are those for women. A narrow view of masculinity is perhaps hardest on gay men and others who do not fit the mold established by the dominant image. For example, among young people who identify as gay or bisexual, 43 percent of men report being bullied in the previous year, compared with 26 percent of women (Berlan et al. 2010).

## Symbolic Interaction

If gender identity and behavior are indeed socially constructed, how is this achieved? The theory of symbolic interactionism (see Chapter 1) argues that complex social systems are maintained through elaborate patterns of interpersonal interaction. Only by enacting our social roles and receiving feedback from others who understand their meaning can we build and maintain our identities.

Each of us faces the task of turning our membership in a sex category into the accomplishment of a complex gender identity, a process that has been called "doing gender" (West and Zimmerman 1987). One way we do this is by enhancing those aspects of our body and personality that conform to the common image of our gender and suppressing those parts of ourselves that don't fit. This theory is especially important for the study of families, because our performance of gender identity requires an audience, and the most important audience from an early age are the members of our own family.

I drew on this theory in my earlier discussion about the importance of height differences between men and women in marriage. The common practice of matching taller men with shorter women sets the stage for the performance of gender identities in which men are physically dominant over women. By application of this simple rule, lifelong patterns of interaction are replicated in almost every family home—which brings us to the issue of gender socialization.

# Gender Socialization

How different or similar boys and girls are, and how they get that way, is the subject of much research and debate (C. Martin and Ruble 2010). The nature and extent of our differences are crucial, because how we create, interpret, and act on those differences is ultimately what determines the patterns of behavior we see in society.

These patterns develop through **socialization**, the process by which individuals internalize elements of the social structure, making those elements part of their own personality. Many people think of gender socialization as simply teaching boys to be boys and girls to be girls. But the reality is more complex. It is not only something taught or done to people; it is also something people do to themselves. This includes learning the norms, rules, and beliefs of the culture around them as well as ways to adapt their behavior to get along in that environment.

Because gender is an important part of self-identity and behavior, the socialization process includes learning to adapt to the ways that gender is organized. This is not as simple as learning a particular "gender role," but rather requires developing the capacity to act and react to the actions and expectations of others. Thus, socialization is not like a computer program or brainwashing; people do not always follow the rules they learn through the socialization process, even if they have learned the rules well. And it is not something experienced only by children, but is a lifelong process by which people learn to act—and think—in consideration of what others do and expect.

Gender socialization is the outcome of countless interactions, starting with those between parents and children. At the youngest ages, of course, parents have the dominant influence over this process. But as children age, their socialization

**socialization**

The process by which individuals internalize elements of the social structure, making those elements part of their own personality.

# Siblings

Aside from parents, no one is closer to a young child than his or her siblings. The presence of an other-gender sibling fosters development of separate gender identities based on gender-typical behavior and is one way siblings differentiate themselves within the family. But when two siblings are of the same gender, one may adopt behaviors that are less gender typical as a way of building an individual identity. To further complicate matters, birth order matters as well, as brothers with younger sisters have been shown to hold more traditional attitudes about gender than other boys (McHale, Crouter, and Whiteman 2003). And when older siblings are charged with caring for younger siblings, which has been common especially among African-American families, sibling influences are even more pronounced (Whiteman, Bernard, and McHale 2010).

# Interactive Circles of Socialization

Moving beyond parents and siblings, we find that people internalize elements of gender through all their interactions in the wider world. After all, families do not exist in social isolation; their interactions always take place in a broader social context—within a community or a country, for example. Religion may be an especially important cultural influence (see Changing Culture, "Gender and Religion"). Another influence on children, naturally, is the way their own parents were socialized. Based on their own socialization, parents raise their children with an eye on how others see, or might see, their behavior. That includes people the parents respect, as well as those they compete with, fear, or even despise. Parents also use their own upbringing as a frame of reference, for better or worse. Thus, even the intimate behavior of parents is a pathway in which wider social influences affect children's development. (And remember, although this section focuses on children, socialization is a lifelong process, so parents are doing it, too.)

I have created a graphic representation of these wider social forces in Figure 5.5. We see individual family members interacting within a family, according to gender and family relationships. How those interactions play out also reflects influences from the local environment—for example, friendship circles, schoolmates, and people at work—as represented by the dark background color seeping into the lighter family circle. The process is repeated at the larger cultural level, where what I've labeled "cultural context" colors both local and family interactions.

In reality, the world around individuals and their families could be represented by any number of such circles and layers. It is up to researchers to find and explain the specific influences and how they work. And indeed, they have made many fascinating discoveries. To convey the flavor of that approach, I will describe some of their findings.

Figure 5.5 **Multiple levels of social context for gender socialization**

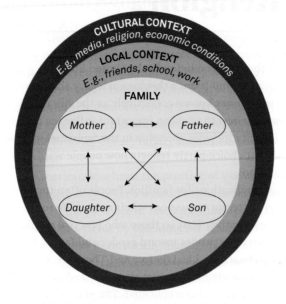

Individual interactions within families are influenced by the local content as well as by the larger culture around them.

# School

For children, the primary location for nonfamily social interaction is school, where they are exposed to both the formal content of the school's instruction and authority and the informal "curriculum" of teacher behavior and expectations. One set of gender interactions around school concerns clothing. Parents usually send young children to school dressed in more or less gender-typical clothing. Teachers, partly reacting to how the children are dressed and partly imposing their own ideas about how children should act, in turn often treat children differently according to gender. For example, wearing dresses limits the physical behavior girls can appropriately do, sometimes leading to embarrassment and a heightened level of self-awareness of their bodies and clothes, and teachers often remind children of these limits (K. Martin 1998). Over the years, we can expect such gender differences to be reinforced in the children's personalities.

For older children, gender differences in school may be less focused on boy-versus-girl identification, but the gender differences are no less crucial to the future of men and women as adults. One common observation is that boys are more likely to pursue education and careers in mathematics-related fields, something that may be traced to high school, where girls are much less likely to take advanced math courses (Ma 2001). Although some people believe that males have a biological advantage in math, this appears to be a case of strong influences from the social context. One study of 22 mostly wealthy countries found

# How does gender affect the workplace?

Some of the most common occupations in the United States—truck driving, construction work, secretarial work, and nursing, for example—are almost completely segregated by gender. The same is true among some professions that require college degrees, such as engineering and elementary education. One reason for this is that the occupations women dominate are often in some way similar to the work women historically have done without pay at home for their families (such as child care), while men are more likely to do jobs that are not closely associated with domestic work (such as driving trucks). Some of this segregation is the result of men and women choosing different kinds of jobs. For example, boys grow up cooking, cleaning, and babysitting their relatives less often than girls do, so they may not want jobs doing that kind of work. But there are also sexist decisions by employers, and sometimes male workers try to keep women out of well-paying jobs. As a result, job segregation is an important part of the story of gender inequality in society.

*Sources: U.S. Bureau of Labor Statistics (2013), Current Population Survey.*

**http://wwnpag.es/sbtn5**

Go to this link for an animation and additional information.

■ **Men (%)**  □ **Women (%)**

# Male-dominated fields

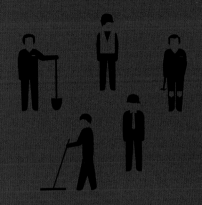

| | |
|---|---|
| 97% | Construction laborers |
| 98% | Electricians |
| 96% | Truck drivers |
| 96% | Groundskeepers |
| 92% | Construction managers |

# Relatively equal gender representation

| | |
|---|---|
| 43% | Retail supervisors |
| 48% | Food service managers |
| 46% | Postsecondary teachers |
| 55% | High school teachers |
| 55% | Financial managers |

# Female-dominated fields

| | |
|---|---|
| Registered nurses | 89% |
| Licensed practical nurses | 92% |
| Receptionists | 91% |
| Secretaries | 95% |
| Pre-K and K teachers | 98% |

especially true in middle-class occupations like real estate, bookkeeping, and high school teaching, where more than half the work is now done by women (Cotter, Hermsen, and Vanneman 2004). This change was possible partly because women devoted more of their lives to paid work and gained the experience and training they needed to move into new positions. But more important, the system of college education was increasingly open to women. Women with college degrees had the credentials—and the incentives—to pursue new careers (P. Cohen and Bianchi 1999). In the early 1970s, among young adults (ages 25 to 34), there were just 68 women for every 100 men with college degrees. Thirty years later, women substantially outnumbered men in that category: 114 women per 100 men (P. Cohen 2007).

Nevertheless, some of the most common occupations in the country—truck driving, construction work, secretarial work, and nursing, for example—are still almost completely segregated by gender, as you can see in the Story Behind the Numbers. And even in many professions that require a high level of education—such as engineering, law, and medicine—men still greatly outnumber women. There are several reasons for this persistent occupational segregation (see Chapter 11).

First, you will notice that the occupations women dominate are often in some way similar to the work women do—or did—without pay at home for their families. Child care, nursing, and teaching, for example, are jobs that were once done at home. On the other hand, men are more likely to do jobs that are not closely associated with domestic work, such as driving trucks and engineering (P. Cohen 2013b).

Do men and women simply choose different kinds of jobs? Yes and no. In some cases, job segregation does reflect worker preferences, based on likes, dislikes, and skills developed from childhood. For example, boys are less likely than girls to be called on to cook, clean house, and care for their younger siblings. But sometimes occupational segregation reflects the desire of employers, who have their own vision of what men and women should do, or of the male workers who dominate certain jobs and seek to protect them from what they see as women's encroachment.

One careful study tracked the hiring process in a single large corporation, a customer call center. The researchers wanted to see how employer decisions—those made in the human resources offices—affected the sorting of men and women applicants into different jobs. They found that job screeners, not just applicants' own choices, played a central role in the ultimate segregation of men and women in the company (Fernandez and Mors 2008). It is reasonable to believe that as women increased their presence in the ranks of managers and employers, such decision making would become more equitable. And that has happened, but the pace of change is slow, and in many workplaces women are absent from those decision-making positions (Huffman, Cohen, and Pearlman 2010).

The second source of continued segregation, which is more important for professional jobs, is the differences in what men and women study in college and graduate school. The same question applies to this process as to hiring: is it individual choices based on socialization or is it the decisions of those in positions of authority (such as teachers and admissions officers) that lead men and women into different fields of study? The answer is undoubtedly a combination of the two. But we do know that the level of segregation in education dropped rapidly in the 1970s and 1980s—that is, women entered fields they had traditionally been excluded from or steered clear of, such as math and science, business and law. However, after the mid-1980s, the pace of change slowed. Now, although men and women each account for about half of the PhD degrees awarded in the United States, the division into separate spheres remains pronounced. Women receive 70 percent of the psychology doctorates, for example, while men get more than 85 percent of those in engineering (P. England 2010). (In sociology, incidentally, women earn about 60 percent of the PhDs.)

## Gender, Status, and Pay

The question of who has which job is very important for the gender bottom line at work: who earns more? The short answer is that men do. Among full-time workers in all occupations in 2012, women's median earnings were just 81 percent of men's (see Figure 5.7). And the biggest reason for that disparity is that men and women work in different jobs. Within the same job at the same workplace, there is much less gender inequality, partly because it's illegal. However, laws requiring equal pay for equal work are notoriously difficult to enforce, and as recently as 2014, the U.S. Congress failed to pass a proposed Paycheck Fairness Act that would have strengthened protection for women in the workplace.

One important observation about change in the labor force in recent decades is that women have entered occupations formerly dominated by men much more

Figure 5.7 **The gender pay gap: women's weekly earnings as a percentage of men's, full-time workers, 1970–2012**

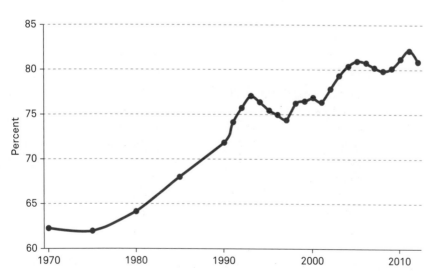

SOURCE: Hegewisch, Williams, and Edwards (2012).

# 6     **Sexuality**

Sex and sexuality are important elements of interaction within the institutional arena of the family. For adults, families are a place where sexual behavior between partners is socially acceptable and expected, part of the special kind of intimacy that sets family relationships apart from all others. For children, families are where sexual identity (see Chapter 5) is first learned and where many hold their darkest sexual secrets, including rape and abuse (to which we will return in Chapter 12). The fundamental question of who we are often begins with sex: in English, we usually describe people with gendered pronouns (he/she) and nouns (boy/girl, brother/sister, man/woman) rather than neutral terms, such as "child," "sibling," or "person." Those core identities have a biological basis and are rooted in the beginning of all human life, but they are also subject to social change.

As we saw in Chapter 5, sexual and gender identity are building blocks of social interaction. But sexuality plays an important role in self-identity as well, a role that has become increasingly visible and explicit since the sexual revolution of the 1960s. Today, the phenomenon of celebrities "coming out," or revealing their sexual orientations in public, is not sensational, but this wasn't the case as recently as two decades ago.

In 1997, Ellen DeGeneres was a successful comedian with her own sitcom on national television. However, her "all-pants wardrobe," the "awkward chemistry" she had with male characters on the show, and the conspicuous absence of a boyfriend generated Hollywood gossip that she was gay (Handy and Bland 1997). In the face of such career-threatening rumors, rather than concoct a straight persona or slide out of the spotlight, DeGeneres decided to embrace her sexual orientation publicly. After some delicate negotiations with Disney, which

When we are children, the family is where we first learn about sexual identity. When we are adults, sexual behavior between partners is socially acceptable and expected.

# Sexuality between the genders

## Women (%), ages 18 to 44

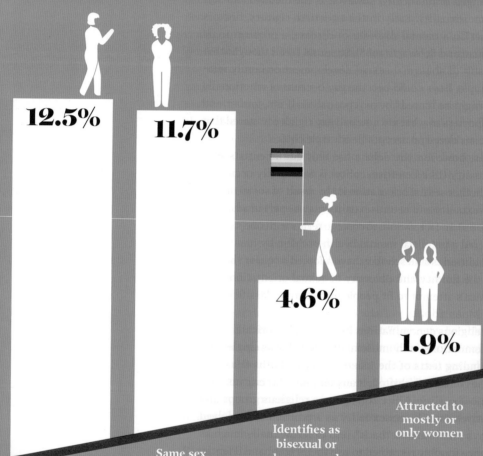

**12.5%**
Same sex behavior ever

**11.7%**
Same sex behavior in the last 12 months

**4.6%**
Identifies as bisexual or homosexual

**1.9%**
Attracted to mostly or only women

*Source: Chandra et al. (2011).*

In recent years social scientists have improved the research on sexual orientation. We can answer some basic questions confidently based on large federal surveys. First, same-sex sexual attraction and behavior occur more commonly among women than among men. Women are especially more likely to be exploratory than men, more frequently reporting isolated or past same-sex sexual experiences and romantic attractions. For example, women are almost three times as likely to have had a same-sex sexual partner in the past year. Second, exclusively homosexual behavior and identity are relatively rare, occurring in less than 5 percent of American adults. But the way we ask the question matters quite a bit— "have you ever had sex with a man?" is a very different question from "do you consider yourself gay?" This kind of complexity makes it hard to study human sexuality, but it is even harder because stigma and fear make the subject difficult for many people to talk about.

## Men (%), ages 18 to 44

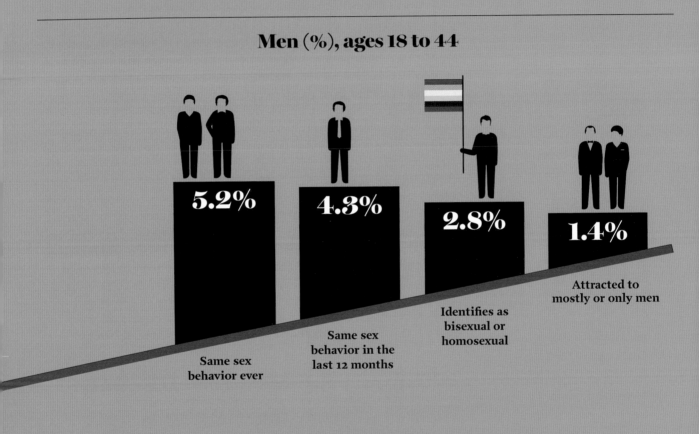

**5.2%** Same sex behavior ever

**4.3%** Same sex behavior in the last 12 months

**2.8%** Identifies as bisexual or homosexual

**1.4%** Attracted to mostly or only men

http://wwnpag.es/sbtn6

Go to this link for an animation and additional information.

for inflicting harm on gays and lesbians, some of whom committed suicide (Chambers 2013).

In the face of these countervailing scientific and ideological forces, the U.S. population is divided between those who think that homosexuality is wrong and those who don't. However, the proportion who feel that gay or lesbian relations are "morally wrong" has dropped rapidly in recent years and is now well below half, as Figure 6.1 shows. Homosexuality is seen as acceptable by more people than are extramarital affairs or teenage sex. But there is greater moral condemnation of homosexuality than there is of single parenthood, sex outside of marriage, or divorce.

It is worth noting that heterosexuality, the majority sexual orientation, is not usually studied or even discussed explicitly. It is as if there are "people" and then there are "gay people." For example, the great majority of mothers, when talking to their preschool-aged children, refer to adult relationships as if they are always heterosexual (K. Martin 2009). This reminds us of how Whites are ignored in studies about race (see Chapter 3), because what is seen as "normal" requires no explanation. In fact, that is part of the concept of stigma, the sense of being different rather than conforming. Taken together, the pressures to conform to the majority sexual orientation and the assumption that everyone is straight until proven otherwise have been referred to as *compulsory heterosexuality* (A. Rich 1980).

Interestingly, those who believe that homosexuality is something people are "born with," rather than a personal choice or an outcome of social environment, are much more likely to have positive feelings toward gay men and lesbians (Haider-Markel and Joslyn 2008). In this light, some researchers have examined early childhood experiences, looking for clues to the development of

Figure 6.1  **Percentage saying the particular behavior is "morally wrong"**

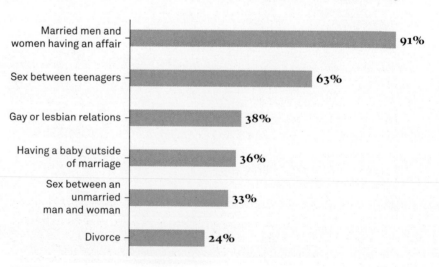

SOURCE: Newport and Himelfarb (2013).

sexual orientation—perhaps inspired by Freud's speculations—but no factors have emerged as pivotal to that development (Risman and Schwartz 1988). That leaves the field to those who consider biological factors more important, a question to which we will return shortly.

# Coming Out

The rapid pace of change in cultural attitudes toward homosexuality has left many families divided, with older generations holding more negative views than those who grew up in a more tolerant era. This generational clash has shaped many *coming out* experiences—so named in reference to the historical pattern of gays and lesbians keeping their sexual orientation "in the closet" before "coming out" to make their true identities known.

**Coming out** is the process of revealing one's gay sexual orientation to the significant people in one's life, a process that may unfold over years (Rust 1993). Consider the example of an anonymous woman who made her story public on the website gayfamilysupport.com. She had no ambition to shake up her family or take a political stand regarding her sexuality, even though her relationship, if exposed, could have put her girlfriend's career in jeopardy at a time before gays were permitted to serve openly in the U.S. military. (Under the policy known as "don't ask, don't tell," which lasted from 1993 to 2011, homosexual men and women could serve in the armed forces provided they kept their sexual orientation secret.) But eventually she felt she had to tell her parents. She related:

> So my family seems pretty normal, open-minded, relaxed. Then why did it take me until I was 22-years-old to tell my parents that I'm a lesbian? . . . I met someone. She is not just a girl, she is the love of my life. We've been "hiding" for over four years now. We live together, but because we are still young it still sounds OK for young girls to have roommates. . . . I finally said, "Well enough is enough." One day I sat down with her and said, "Baby we are in our twenties, we have a house, we have cars, jobs, dogs, we pay taxes, and neither of us has told our parents we love each other?" So I went first. I pulled my parents aside separately and told them I was in love. . . . My dad said, "Kinda' figured. I'm OK with it. I still love you just the same, but I do want grandkids." I assured him that we could still have kids, adoption probably. My mom, oh God. When I told her I started to cry immediately. . . . She blamed it on my friends, she said it was a choice. . . . She said she never really wanted to talk about it again. Meaning she was just going to pretend like I never told her. Pretty harsh, could've been worse.

This coming out story—posted online by a noncelebrity, involving only her own family—is a far cry from the Hollywood stardom version exhibited by Ellen DeGeneres. But both represent the reality that sexuality forms a core of the modern identity. Family relationships are often where such identities are formed and expressed. And when social change occurs, such as the increasing acceptance of

**coming out**

The process of revealing one's gay sexual orientation to the significant people in one's life.

efforts cover subjects other than sexual behavior, collectively they have served to follow up and extend the original Kinsey Reports with more sound scientific methods and data.

# Sex before Marriage

As marriages were increasingly judged on the basis of their sexual qualities, extramarital sex also grew more common and acceptable. Research in the last generation has established some common patterns of this behavior. Here are a few generalizations that serve to anchor our more detailed investigation:

- *Sex comes before marriage.* Beginning with the generation born in the 1960s, almost everyone—95 percent of Americans—has had sexual intercourse before marriage (Finer 2007). That is not so much because people are having sex at younger ages, but because they get married at older ages after having sex in their teens and early 20s. (Of course, some of these people are merely having sex with the partner they will eventually marry.)

- *Men have more partners than women.* The average age for first intercourse is about 17 for both men and women, but men on average increase their number of partners more rapidly through young adulthood. By the time they reach their late 30s, most men have had about seven sexual partners, compared with four or fewer partners for women (Figure 6.2).

- *Having many partners is relatively uncommon.* Despite the greater acceptance of sexual freedom, only 10 percent of men and 7 percent of women ages 15 to 44 report having three or more sexual partners in the previous year. Among adults in the age range 25 to 44, 29 percent of men and 11 percent of women report having a total of 15 or more sexual partners in their lifetime (Chandra et al. 2011).

- *Sex without consent is relatively common.* Ten percent of women and 5 percent of men, asked about their first intercourse, report that they "really didn't want it to happen at the time," and that is especially likely when it occurred at a young age (Abma, Martinez, and Copen 2010). Among women ages 15 to 44, almost a quarter—23 percent—report that they have been forced to have intercourse (Chandra et al. 2005). As we will see in Chapter 12, rape occurs most often within families or between dating partners.

Although one of the major changes in sexual behavior has been the growth of extramarital sex, most sexual activity still takes place between people who are in long-term relationships with an expectation of fidelity. People in married, cohabiting, or long-term dating relationships generally expect to have sex only with their long-term partner and expect the same commitment from him or her (Treas 2004). Before discussing such relationships, however, we will pause to

## Figure 6.2 **Median number of lifetime sexual partners**

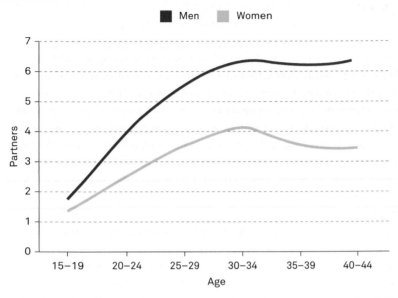

Data are for opposite-sex partners only and include oral sex, anal sex, and vaginal intercourse.

SOURCE: Chandra et al. (2011).

consider how men and women are treated differently in the moral standards for sexual behavior.

**The Sexual Double Standard** A common assumption in our society is that women are more passive and inhibited sexually, while men are more performance and achievement oriented (taking pride in having a large number of sexual partners, for example). That fits with the pattern of men having more sexual partners than women. However, because this belief is so culturally ingrained, it's hard to know the origins or causes of the pattern. As noted earlier, some believe that it is traceable to evolution; but its persistence today is surely the outcome of social forces.

Consider our language regarding sexual intercourse. Most of the popular terms refer to things men *do to* women, not the other way around. One of the milder of these terms—amazingly—is "hit." In R. Kelly's song "Sex Weed," for example, he tells his sex partner, "Girl I want your sex weed. I just want to hit it all the time." It seems strange that an explicitly violent word such as "hit" would seem less offensive than the other terms available. (Referring to a woman as "it" is also worth questioning.)

That onesidedness—in which men are perceived as doing sex to women—contributes to a moral standard that punishes women for going against the norm of passivity. The **sexual double standard** refers to the practice of applying stricter moral or legal controls to women's sexual behavior than to men's. Historically, this meant that women must not only refrain from initiating sex, but

**sexual double standard**

The practice of applying stricter moral or legal controls to women's sexual behavior than to men's.

# Your Sex Education(s)

Where do young people get the information they need about sex? A recent survey investigated how old children were when their parents broached various sex-related topics with them (Beckett et al. 2010). The study made headlines because it revealed that a number of "advanced" topics—such as how to use specific forms of birth control and how to handle the social pressure of a boyfriend who won't use a condom—were never discussed until after the teenagers had already had intercourse. Those in favor of comprehensive sex education in school took the results to mean that schools have to step in because parents often don't get the job done.

Of course, young people learn about sex—and other topics—not just from parents and schools, but from other sources as well, especially media of all kinds and their peers. In fact, one study that compared local TV ratings and birth rates provided evidence that the MTV reality series *16 and Pregnant* itself may have contributed to the drop in teen birthrates, presumably by portraying a negative example of teen parents (Kearney and Levine 2014). There are many different paths to similar information, but sometimes the source makes all the difference.

This exercise aims to take advantage of the diversity of educational policies and practices experienced by today's college students. It can be done individually, in small groups, or as a classroom exercise. Using the following table to jog your memory, try to recall where and when you first learned about these topics (if you did). Then, in a short essay or group discussion, relate the content of the lessons. Consider these possible questions for starters:

- Did different sources or authorities give you different information? If so, whom did you believe, and why?

- Were you in a school that taught "abstinence-only" sex education, comprehensive sex education, or something else? What difference did that make to you?

- Which lessons were most important to you, and how did the source of the information matter to you?

- Was the education you received effective overall? Why or why not?

| Topic | Age at first introduction | Source of information | | |
| --- | --- | --- | --- | --- |
| | | Parent | School | Media | Peers/ other |
| Body development | | | | | |
| How babies are made | | | | | |
| Sexual orientations | | | | | |
| How sex spreads disease | | | | | |
| How birth control works | | | | | |
| How to use birth control | | | | | |
| Using condoms against STDs | | | | | |
| How to refuse sex | | | | | |
| Abstinence until marriage | | | | | |

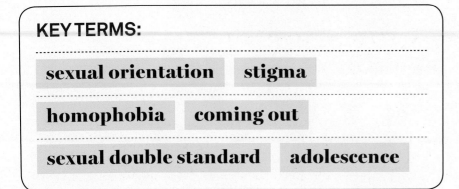

**KEY TERMS:**

sexual orientation    stigma

homophobia    coming out

sexual double standard    adolescence

# Questions for Review

**1.** What is sexual orientation? How have attitudes toward homosexuality changed in the medical and scientific community?

**2.** According to researchers, what is the role of genetics, evolution, and social environment in determining human sexual orientation?

**3.** What did masturbation mean to moral authorities in the nineteenth century?

**4.** What is the sexual double standard? What events, social movements, and technological innovations have challenged this attitude? Why?

**5.** Who has sexual intercourse more often and with higher levels of satisfaction: married couples or single people? Why?

**6.** How has technology exacerbated the generation gap in perceptions of adolescent sexuality? Why is this gap in understanding a problem for policymakers, parents, and teenagers?

**7.** Why have teenage pregnancy rates declined in the last twenty years?

**8.** Who is most at risk for HIV/AIDS infections? Why?

**9.** What does social network analysis reveal about the spread of sexually transmitted diseases? Why might sociologists find this data useful?

# 7

# Love and Romantic Relationships

The night Jason first met Liz—they were in their mid-20s—he was immediately impressed. "Liz was tall, beautiful, and I could tell right away she was an unusual person who had her act together," he remembered. "And she made me laugh." A childhood friend had invited Jason to a party at Liz's apartment; he was looking for a job and later emailed Liz for contacts. What were the odds they would begin to date, hit it off, move in together, and marry three years later? On their first date, according to the *New York Times* wedding page, "they discovered they shared more than a sense of humor. He had played soccer at Princeton; she was on the water polo team at Penn." They were also both going to be doctors.

Was it a mysterious romantic spark that set off their relationship, beginning with her beauty and propelled by their joint passion for "helping others"? Or was it two young, White, single-and-looking, athletic Ivy League graduates with successful professional careers ahead of them, meeting at a party of people with similar backgrounds, and taking the obvious next step? We can't know for sure what attracted Liz and Jason to each other, but these questions highlight the sociological approach to love and relationships.

We are individuals, with our own experiences and outlooks on life. At the same time, we are embedded in a social world that shapes what goes on around us—and within us—in ways that we often don't recognize. The dynamic of that interaction, between self and society—or, to put it another way, between biography and history—is the heart of sociology. As the sociologist C. Wright Mills famously put it, "No social study that does not come back to the problems of biography, of history, and of their intersections within a society has completed its intellectual journey" (1959/2000:6). There may be no better subject for which to learn this lesson than one as apparently intimate, personal, and individual as love itself.

Online dating services promise perfect matches among millions of users via statistical algorithms, but are also hedging their bets by hosting face-to-face events that are more reminiscent of pre–Internet Age dating.

# Scripting Diversity

As we saw in Chapter 2, family structures have become more diverse over the past century. Similarly, the ways couples meet, form relationships, and build families have become more diverse as well. Rather than a change from one style of family formation to another, modern societies have moved from a dominant style to an abundance of approaches from which to choose. This freedom of choice—and the resulting pressure to choose—are prevalent features of our era, as discussed in Chapter 1.

Sociologists sometimes use the concept of scripts as a metaphor for the way people know how to interact in their differing roles (Simon and Gagnon 1984). A **social script** is a commonly understood pattern of interaction that serves as a model of behavior in familiar situations. Just as language has to exist before we can speak to each other, we often need scripts to at least get us going in a new social relationship (Laner and Ventrone 2000).

Recall a key insight from symbolic interaction theory: To interact successfully, people need to be able to see themselves through the eyes of others (see Chapter 1). For that reason, social scripts are a source of reassurance, letting people act on the assumption that their behavior is understandable and acceptable to others, without having to invent every situation from scratch. Naturally, scripts aren't step-by-step instructions that people follow to the letter. Rather, they serve to anchor or orient behavior—to help people locate their behavior in a social setting. And the *absence* of scripts can create a feeling of disorientation and confusion that may be quite powerful. Before you know how to act, in other words, you need to know what scene you're in and what role you're playing.

An example from TV may help illustrate the point. In a classic episode of the sitcom *Frasier*, Frasier attempts to set up his new boss with his single friend Daphne, but the boss (a gay man) thinks he's been invited to a date with Frasier. "That's a hell of a view," says the boss as he walks into Frasier's apartment and looks out the window, to which Frasier replies, "It's even better from the bedroom." What, seen from one perspective, is a casual comment with no sexual overtones—two straight male coworkers discussing an apartment—becomes an overt sexual approach when seen as the opening line of a date. The humor in the rest of the show stems from the repeated failure of the different characters to perform according to the scripts others are attempting to follow. (The episode, called "The Matchmaker," also won a special award from the Gay and Lesbian Alliance Against Defamation for its treatment of gay dating as noncontroversial.)

By the mid-1990s, when *Frasier* aired that episode, the "dating system" already had been declared dead (B. Bailey 1988). That doesn't mean people didn't go on dates anymore. In fact, most people still agreed on what a first date should be like—its appropriate script (Rose and Frieze 1993). But the rules were looking less clear.

By now it is safe to say that diversity reigns over conformity in how relationships are begun and built. As the TV show demonstrated, there are still scripts, but it's harder to know which one we're supposed to be following. Four specific developments underscore this overall change:

---

**social script**

A commonly understood pattern of interaction that serves as a model of behavior in familiar situations.

- The demise of the dating system as the dominant mode of relationship formation. Without a commonly understood series of stages from introduction to commitment—including the timing of sexual interaction—developing a relationship has become more variable and individualized.

- The increasing acceptance of living together as a common stage in relationships (see Chapter 8). With cohabitation now lasting anywhere from a short engagement to a lifetime, decisions about when, whether, and how to live together are a source of further uncertainty.

- The incorporation of divorced and older singles (many with children) into the mix of those looking for new relationships. This trend introduces still more variation in the assumptions and expectations for relationship behavior.

- The continual adaptation of communication technology to relationship dynamics, increasing the immediacy of interaction (M. Rosenfeld and Thomas 2012). The Internet has broadened the social world for many people, even as it has made it possible to meet and communicate with people based on very narrow specifications (for example, "29-year-old, tall, computer programmer Muslim male who likes cats but not dogs—and watching sports except football; willing to move to the West Coast").

You may be surprised that I did not include more sexual freedom or less relationship commitment in that list of trends. That's because, despite the perpetual concern that "kids these days" are leading the culture astray—a complaint that goes back at least to the Puritans of seventeenth-century New England—there isn't much evidence that young people exert that kind of influence in contemporary American society. While people born before the 1980s may be at a loss to understand "sexting" or "hooking up," these relative geezers (my age) are also pushing the dating scene in new directions, especially with sophisticated matching systems, and bringing apparently ever-more-complicated relationship histories and desires to that virtual first date.

Some people see a cultural landscape in crisis, in which "living by traditional moral virtues" has become an "alternative lifestyle," as two conservative professors complained (George and Londregan 2009). But I don't think the facts support the idea that American society has recently been dragged down the tubes by declining sexual morality and collapsing relationship commitments. As noted in Chapter 6, the proportion of high school students having intercourse has declined over the last few decades. As far back as 1976, 70 percent of 21-year-olds were no longer virgins. That seems similar to the late 2000s, when about three-quarters of college seniors reported having at least one hookup (Armstrong, England, and Fogarty 2010).

More than 20 years ago, an interviewer asked a sexually active 16-year-old about the future of her relationship: "Are we going to get married?" the teenager said. "The answer is no. Or will we be together next year? I don't know about that; that's a long time from now. But we won't date anyone else as long as we're together. That's a commitment, isn't it?" (Giddens 1992:10). Going back further,

The couple at left may be the ideal image of romantic love, but the family at right is probably more common.

almost 100 years, a poet wrote, "Then should our love last but an hour / Need we turn from each other in shame?" (Hoyt 1923). The answer to that question probably depends on what one means by "love."

# Love

Some scientists believe that humans developed the capacity—and the need—for love as part of the evolutionary apparatus of survival early in our development. Because human children require hands-on care for years, unlike most animals, children who were loved by their parents were more likely to survive. Because it made survival more likely, loving behavior became part of human nature (Lampert 1997). In fact, as we saw in Chapter 2, a broader sense of caring was necessary for human society to survive, as parents needed help from other adults to provide care for their offspring.

In a general sense of the term, **love** is a deep affection and concern for another, with whom one feels a strong emotional bond. However, that definition is not quite enough to answer the poet's question, "What is love more than a flame?" (Hoyt 1923). In the "flame" sense, we usually mean **romantic love**, which is the passionate devotion and attraction one person feels for another. According to sociologist Ann Swidler (2001), the modern version of romantic love is "mythical" because it involves an imaginary perfection. People elevate the idea of romantic love in their minds even if they know it is not always (or even often) attainable. That's why "the image of a couple walking hand-in-hand along the sea [is] more prevalent than the image of a man and a woman casually watching television" (Illouz 1997:5).

Swidler (2001) details four qualities of this romantic ideal. First, love is unambiguous and clear, as in "love at first sight." Second, love is unique, so there is "one true love" to be found for each person. Third, individuals seek both

**love**

A deep affection and concern for another, with whom one feels a strong emotional bond.

**romantic love**

The passionate devotion and attraction one person feels for another.

to prove and to demonstrate their true character by overcoming obstacles in the quest for love. These obstacles may be social, such as the barrier between the feuding families in *Romeo and Juliet*. Or the obstacles may be personal, as when a man gives up smoking or drinking to win over the object of his love. Finally, love is permanent, and a truly loving relationship is therefore eternal.

Clearly, this version of romantic love is an ideal, but it serves to animate and motivate many people in their search for happiness and satisfaction. And when real-life love falls too far short of the ideal—maybe just because a relationship has gone on for a few years and the "passion" is diminished—it may be doomed. Interestingly, as we will see in Chapter 8, the modern structure of marriage reinforces the ideal of romantic love by institutionalizing some of its elements. That is because adults, usually at a relatively young age, see themselves making a single, fateful choice to marry the one person who will be their partner in loving harmony forever.

The expectation that spouses would actually *love* each other was not common in Europe before the 1600s, but since then it has come to dominate the idea of marriage (Coontz 2005). In recent times, anthropological research has found that some version of romantic love exists in virtually all existing cultures (Jankowiak and Fischer 1992). This supports the notion that love is inherent in our species, but we also know that the expression and interpretation of this ideal are culturally and historically specific.

Romantic love carries its own social scripts, which are useful for applying labels to our emotions in ways that help us decide how to act. For example, when (if) a couple reaches the moment in their relationship when one says to the other, "I love you," it is commonly understood to be a turning point. If the sentiment is reciprocated, the relationship is assumed to be going "to the next level." However, the meaning of such a moment has been subject to increasing uncertainty in recent times. Does it mean that the relationship is heading toward marriage? The moment still carries emotional weight—and demands a response one way or the other—but the next steps are often not clear, requiring further negotiation.

# Making It Work

The negotiation and communication of modern relationships naturally take some of the romance out of romantic love. The spontaneous, irrational, passionate image of love weakens when people get out their calendars to schedule dates or compare prices for different brands of condoms. But that doesn't seem to weaken the idea of love, which remains central in modern relationships.

How is that possible? Swidler (2001) explains that there are actually two "cultures of love" in the United States, which exist side by side. Next to mythical, romantic love is a realistic or **utilitarian love**, which is the practical, rational dedication of one person to another based on shared understanding and emotional commitment. This version of love drives people to carefully consider the pros and cons of different partners and to look within themselves and try to

**utilitarian love**

The practical, rational dedication of one person to another based on shared understanding and emotional commitment.

identify what they really want from a relationship. People "work" on their relationships—often with the help of professional therapists or books by experts—to build love over time and maintain it through ongoing effort. The watchword of utilitarian love is probably "communication."

Because utilitarian love is more rational, and romantic love is more spontaneous, some social theorists believe that utilitarian love is a reflection of modern culture. In that view, the shift from romantic love to utilitarian love parallels, for example, the growth of rational science replacing irrational religion as a way of explaining the world or the spread of democracy replacing monarchy (Lindholm 1998).

**romantic relationships**

Mutually acknowledged, ongoing interactions featuring heightened affection and intensity.

In this chapter, we are investigating love and **romantic relationships**, a general term that refers to mutually acknowledged, ongoing interactions featuring heightened affection and intensity (W. Collins, Welsh, and Furman 2009). Although romantic relationships need not be sexual, they usually include at least anticipated sexual interaction. Unfortunately, this definition can't be any more precise than the relationships themselves, which often have no fixed beginning or end and may not even be called the same thing by both partners.

Part of the uncertainty of modern romantic relationships stems from the coexistence of romantic and utilitarian love in many people's minds. As they move back and forth between these two ideals, people may start or end relationships—making demands on their partners or resisting them—based on whether they meet the criteria of either ideal of love. Because relationships are not as strictly regulated by family elders and other authorities as they once were, individuals no longer commit to relationships based on the expectations of others. Of course, the perceptions of other people—including family members, peers, friends, and employers—are still relevant. But our choices are now perceived as individual. If maintaining a relationship is a daily choice, love is one of the criteria people evaluate in making that choice.

As Anthony Giddens (1992) or other modernity theorists might say (see Chapter 1), the newfound freedoms of the late modern era set people up as lone individuals, without fixed directions to follow. If the love that results feels fragile—partly because it *is* more fragile and the underlying romantic relationships less stable than they once were—then its success should be all the more rewarding because it is based on personal choice and commitment. In that theory, such "pure" relationships are a hallmark of modern independence, along with all the uncertainties that it entails.

# Relationship Rituals

In Chapter 2, we saw that the path to marriage evolved from the courtship system of the nineteenth century to dating in the twentieth. Since then, the dating system has become much less dominant (B. Bailey 1988). Although most people still date—and often use that term—it is not a clear and commonplace pathway from meeting to marriage.

We will begin by describing the form and function of dating. Then we will turn to the hookup scene, which causes part of the confusion over relationship-building scripts. As we will see, the bigger story is not hooking up per se, but instead the diversity of scripts available to follow (or create). That diversity is made more complicated by online dating, the increasing presence of older adults in the dating scene, and unique experiences for gay and lesbian couples, all of which I will address in this section.

# Dating

To some students, it seems old-fashioned even to discuss dating in a college textbook today. "No one dates anymore" is a common refrain. But most people do still date, or do something similar to what used to be called dating. So despite changes in terminology, this remains an important area of study for sociology of the family.

When the dating system emerged in the early twentieth century, part of what made it so different from the older rituals of courtship was its widespread acceptance of overlapping relationships without commitment. It may be hard to understand how rapid and dramatic that change seemed to people at the time. For example, as late as 1948, an academic article reviewing college textbooks on marriage and the family complained that they didn't cover dating. "Today in most of the country," the author wrote, "especially in towns and cities, much dating goes on with no suggestion of marriage, either immediate or remote" (Lowrie 1948:90). He recommended that students take a course on the subject of dating in the last year of high school or the beginning of college.

On the other hand, it is also remarkable that the new system, in which young people met and socialized—sometimes sexually—with multiple potential partners, away from parental supervision, was so readily accepted (after a few decades of grumbling by the older generation). Rather than condemning the practice, Lowrie (1948) pointed out that dating seemed to improve young people's personality, life experience, personal poise, socialization skills, and preparation for marriage.

Dating was so accepted by the middle class that a 1956 survey of women entering college showed that they went on an average of about 12 dates per month (or 3 per week) with an average of about five different men (Kanin 1957). In fact, dating came to be seen as the "traditional," more formal system of getting to marriage. The dating system helped guide the transition from passionate romantic attraction—including lust—to the stable, mature love idealized in the established view of marriage. The social scripts associated with dating also served to regulate the acceptable timing of sexual intimacy.

By the time the rules of the dating system started to lose their grip on popular behavior, around 1965, its demise provoked fears of the "death of romance." Concerned elders now fretted that "in our search for freedom, honesty, love, and equality...we have found only meaningless sex, loneliness, and lack of commitment" (B. Bailey 1988:2). They were especially troubled by uncommitted more than 90 percent of students said they had been on at least one date, however they defined it (McClintock 2010). As an important exception, however, college students who commute to campus or attend part time often do not participate as readily in the campus dating scene (Risman and Allison 2014).

We have also learned that despite the spread of egalitarian beliefs—which promote equality between men and women—the majority of college students expect men to take the lead in formal date situations. That is especially the case for first dates. For example, most men as well as women believe that the man should extend the invitation, provide the transportation, open doors, cover expenses for the first date—and make the first sexual move if there is one (Laner and Ventrone 2000). Of course, their hopes for the outcome of dates are often different. Research consistently shows that men in college are more likely than women to have a sexual goal, while women more often want a developing romantic relationship (Mongeau, Jacobsen, and Donnerstein 2007). (As we will see in Chapter 12, rape and sexual violence perpetrated by men are also most likely to occur in dating and romantic relationships.)

Ironically, because of the gains women have made in access to higher education—they significantly outnumber men on many campuses today—men benefit from being in short supply (Bogle 2008). According to informal accounts, the relative scarcity of men increases their bargaining power in the dating scene, both in terms of getting dates and in determining their outcome (A. Williams 2010). That is a stark contrast to previous generations, when men far outnumbered women. A study of students in 1950, at a school where men outnumbered women more than 3 to 1, found that women were twice as likely as men to go on multiple dates per week (W. Smith 1952).

On many college campuses in the United States, there are more female than male students. The rapid rise of women attending college is an impressive achievement; however, a potential unexpected effect of the gender imbalance could mean male students have more leverage when dating.

# Hooking Up

Given the hookup scene's reputation for casual sex and noncommitment, it might seem odd to discuss it in a chapter on love and romantic relationships. Yet, as people move through the stages of their lives—whatever course they follow—these uncommitted sexual encounters are part of the basis for their later experiences and decisions. They help form the relationship history people bring from one encounter to the next, usually including dating, longer-term relationships, and marriage.

Without a fixed definition of **hooking up**, it is difficult to know how common it is. Even among a sample of White, heterosexual college students at two East Coast colleges, researchers found competing definitions of hooking up, depending on where students had gone to high school. Still, it is safe to say that the term usually implies something casual rather than prearranged and without explicit commitment or exclusivity. Some people include all forms of sexual interaction, while others specifically exclude intercourse (Bogle 2008).

A survey of Ohio students in Grades 7 to 11 found that 31 percent reported having had sexual intercourse with someone they did not consider a "boyfriend," "girlfriend," or someone they were "dating or going out with." Yet these hookups—if we call them that—most often involved people the students considered friends, ex-boyfriends, or ex-girlfriends. In other words, more than half of those who had ever had intercourse had done it outside of what the researchers considered a "romantic relationship" (W. Manning, Giordano, and Longmore 2006).

In college, a large study of students at 17 universities found that about three-quarters reported ever "hooking up" (Figure 7.1). (In this survey, the students used their own definition.) In follow-up questions, the researchers learned that many people had multiple hookups with the same person—which starts to look more like what might have been called a relationship at one time (Armstrong, England, and Fogarty 2010). In that case, the idea of hookups rather than dating seems to reflect a recognition that the relationships are not long-lasting or exclusively committed, and it might not be all that different from the era in which college students dated multiple partners in overlapping sequences.

I should stress that such general descriptions of sexual and romantic behavior, especially among young people, cannot capture the full range of emotional interactions that people experience. For example, although many men embrace the idea of casual sex with no strings attached, especially at a certain time in their lives, there are also a substantial number who are looking for, or at least open to, lasting relationships and emotional connections with

**hooking up**

A casual sexual or romantic encounter without explicit commitment or exclusivity.

Figure 7.1 **Number of hookups reported by college students**

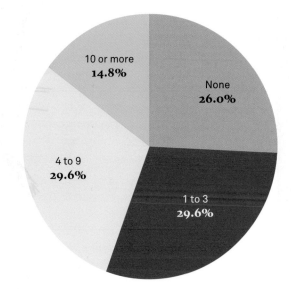

SOURCE: Armstrong, England, and Fogarty (2010).

are not subject to antisegregation laws. But the private proms are supported by the schools' decisions not to hold official proms, decisions prompted by court orders to desegregate the student body (Harrison 2007).

The White prom in Montgomery County, Georgia, for example, cost more than $200 per ticket, and the White parents made sure it was a segregated affair (Doyle 2009). In some cases, such as in Randolph County, Alabama, in 1994, the principal canceled the prom only after learning that mixed-race couples were planning to attend (*Lee v. Randolph County Board of Education* 1995).

## Sexual Orientation

The conflict over race looks a lot like the conflict over sexual orientation. When senior Constance McMillen asked the principal of her high school in Fulton, Mississippi, whether she could bring her girlfriend as a date to the 2010 prom—and wear a tuxedo—the answer was no: no girlfriend, no same-sex slow dancing, and no girl wearing a tuxedo would be permitted.

After McMillen protested, with the help of the American Civil Liberties Union, the district canceled the prom. A federal court reviewed the complaints and held that the district had violated McMillen's rights by canceling the prom. However, the court let stand the district's decision to defer to a private prom. Later, the parents who planned the private prom ended up discouraging McMillen and her date from attending anyway (*McMillen v. Itawamba County School District* 2010).

Although it was 30 years later, the McMillen case in Mississippi actually mirrored one from Rhode Island in 1980. In Cumberland High School, a gay male student was denied permission to bring his boyfriend to the prom, only to have the decision overturned by the courts. That decision, *Fricke v. Lynch* (1980), was the basis for Constance McMillen's case in 2010. As already noted, some social practices change more slowly than others in different parts of society.

## Lines in the Sand

The symbolic power of the prom is sometimes confusing, especially in the case of race. Black and White students at some of the schools in question appear to socialize and especially play sports together with relatively little conflict (Lange 2003). The dispute over proms occurs because parents and school authorities recognize it as an important stepping stone in what might be a long-term mate selection process. These older people are drawing from their own histories and recalling the prom scripts of their own youths, when prom dates often led to steady relationships and potential marriage.

One White high school senior in rural Georgia said, "I wanted to go to the Black prom, but my mom wouldn't pay. She doesn't like me talking to Black people anyway" (Doyle 2009). Parents may have trouble controlling the dating behavior of their children and whom they socialize with, but when it comes to an event with a formal role in relationship scripts, like a prom or marriage, those resistant to change are more likely to dig in their heels.

Among teenagers, those who are gay, lesbian, or bisexual tend to have their first "serious" relationships at older ages and are less likely to have active dating lives, especially in areas where few other people are visibly out (W. Collins, Welsh, and Furman 2009), partly because they have more difficulty meeting and identifying appropriate romantic partners. But they also may be bullied or harassed by peers or singled out for punishment by authorities. These risks lead many people to conceal their sexual orientation (Mohr and Daly 2008). However, there are a variety of coping strategies, especially among teenagers, including staying in romantic relationships longer to avoid painful transitions or pursuing heterosexual relationships as a way of conforming (Glover, Galliher, and Lamere 2009).

Daily discrimination can take a psychological or even physical health toll (Pascoe and Richman 2009). When it comes from people in positions of authority, it is especially threatening. Such discrimination has been shown to contribute to depression and suicidal thoughts, which are much more common among gay, lesbian, bisexual, and transgender high school students (Almeida et al. 2009).

# Mate Selection

In Shakespeare's play *The Merchant of Venice*, Jessica says to her lover, Lorenzo, "Love is blind, and lovers cannot see." But while it may be true that lovers act impulsively, to the coldhearted social scientist, the patterns of human behavior suggest that even love is anything but random—and truly blind love is rare. (Although Shakespeare was fond of the idea of love at first sight, I should point out that Lorenzo had already judged Jessica to be "wise," seen her to be "fair," and knew that she had proved herself "true"—so he wasn't really blind, either.)

In fact, how and why people choose each other or end up together are central to our understanding of families and society and to broader questions of social change. Sociologists call this process **mate selection**. Understanding these first steps—some of which form a path to family formation—is necessary for explaining at least three ways families influence the broader society.

**mate selection**

The process by which people choose each other for sexual or romantic relationships.

- *Inequality.* If pairs of rich people form some families and pairs of poor people form other families, then there will be a very strong tendency for the lines of wealth and poverty to remain fixed through the generations. On the other hand, if people get together at random or actually seek each other out across the lines of social class or other divides, then inequality will be reduced over time. (Notice that this assumes that people transmit their social class background to their children, which we discussed in Chapter 4.)

- *Inclusion versus exclusion.* I concluded Chapter 3 with a discussion of "social distance," as reflected in the rates of intermarriage between Whites and members of minority groups. Although a growing proportion of Americans tell survey takers that they do not object to romantic relationships between people of differing race or ethnicity, U.S. society remains far from color blind in this regard (J. Lee and Bean 2010). Patterns of attraction and family formation are still gauges of the level of social inclusion or exclusion for members of different groups.

- *Family dynamics.* How families work together is partly the result of how couples choose each other and how those choices affect their relationships throughout adulthood. The stability of marriages, caring for children and other family members in need, and the health and happiness of family members—all these issues are related to the issue of mate selection.

In this section, we will discuss attraction and attractiveness, especially in relation to gender. Beyond physical attraction, of course, romantic relationships emerge from emotional connections and common bonds that come from various sources. Finally, we will investigate how social boundaries between groups help to shape people's choices between partners.

# Evolution

Interestingly, some of the research on the evolution of human sexual attraction has involved such cultural innovations as Barbie dolls, *Playboy* centerfolds, and the Miss America pageants—and ancient art and literature as well (Singh, Renn, and Singh 2007).

Scientists have attempted to piece together the evolution story by studying the historical record, by comparing people and tastes in different cultures, by studying the behavior and characteristics of nonhuman animals, and—more recently—by studying genes and their expression directly. Experts have different opinions, but my assessment of the evidence so far is that evolutionary forces operate in the background, while our preferences and actions flexibly adapt around, or even against, the forces of "nature" through social interaction. With regard to families in particular, of course, sexual attraction is only part of what holds people together. The utilitarian aspects of couple relationships today are more important than any primal attraction in creating and maintaining real families.

There are complicated and sometimes conflicting forces at work in the process of natural selection, and social behavior is especially difficult to puzzle out. We know that specific traits might have emerged through evolution if they (a) increased the odds of survival, like resistance to disease; (b) increased reproductive ability, like healthy ovaries; (c) increased success in competition with other potential mates, like big muscles (or good aim); or (d) presented some gimmick that fools potential mates into thinking one of the other good traits is present. Attraction to a particular feature of humans might have made evolutionary sense at one time, but we can't tell which attractions are evolutionary as opposed to cultural or a combination of the two. For example, it is common to assume that attractive features are those that are healthy, since mating with healthy people is good for survival. However, many of the traits considered attractive in modern Western societies bear no connection to health or reproductive fitness. For example, men with big chest muscles and thin waists aren't generally healthier than men who are thin all over (though they might win more fights). In women's case, some "attractive" features are related to good health, such as relatively low body fat and slim waists, but the overall connection between beauty and health is not strong (Weeden and Sabini 2005).

Consider that last example related to female attractiveness: a slim waist, usually measured by the waist-to-hip ratio. Some scientists believe that when this ratio is low (that is, the waist is slimmer than the hips), it sends a signal to men that a woman is fit for childbearing. Over time, then, men who were attracted to that quality would be more likely to survive and reproduce successfully (Barber 1995). Some studies have found that men in different cultures are attracted to this quality in a woman (Singh, Renn, and Singh 2007). And several researchers have analyzed *Playboy* magazine centerfold models and Miss America pageant winners (which list women's body measurements), finding that their average waist-to-hip ratio has been about 0.7, which is quite low.

However, a common beauty characteristic by itself isn't proof that the attraction to it has evolved biologically. And several pieces of evidence point in the other direction. First, there are considerable differences in what is considered attractive. The centerfolds and pageant winners actually vary substantially above or below this supposed ideal waist-to-hip ratio (Freese and Meland 2002). Similarly, although ancient poetry and literature often mentioned slim waists as attractive, many writers didn't mention waists at all and focused their attention on other body parts (Singh, Renn, and Singh 2007). And of course, evolution has also produced homosexual men, who might not be attracted one way or the other to women's waists.

A second piece of evidence is the trend in the last 60 years among pornography and fashion models toward unhealthy levels of thinness. From 1985 to 1997, for example, more than three-quarters of the women who posed in centerfolds were severely underweight by medical standards (P. Owen and Laurel-Seller 2000). That trend has continued, as typical models are now taller but their body weight is about the same (Seifert 2005). It seems implausible that evolution would drive men's attraction toward women who are so thin that they don't menstruate and are unable to conceive children. From these conflicting streams of theory and evidence, I conclude that although evolution played a role in developing human beauty standards, these forces today are just some influences among many.

As an aside, when it comes to waist-to-hip ratio, no one beats Barbie. Well, almost no one: about 1 in 100,000 women matches her waist-to-hip ratio of 0.56 (Norton et al. 1996). Thus, Barbie might seem beautiful or attractive in some cultures, but it's not because she's a "natural" beauty. Still, more than 50 years since her creation in 1960, if we are to believe the doll's manufacturer, Mattel, 90 percent of young girls in the United States have at least one Barbie doll (Vaidyanathan 2009). Given the nature of "pretend play," it is obvious that many of these girls identify with Barbie at least in some ways. And that returns us to the gender issues we introduced in Chapter 5.

From 1950 (left) to 1980 (right) to 1990 (middle), Barbie's body hasn't changed much.

# Gender

This discussion of women's body parts may seem unbalanced, or even sexist. But research on the evolution of sexual attraction has focused much more on women—assuming, perhaps, that the most powerful men (rich, strong, well armed) will "choose" the women they want, rather than the other way around. From a sociological point of view, this raises other questions. We ask not only why people want what they want, but also how people with power maintain their power. In other words, who gets to choose? Both questions are relevant to the issue of mate selection.

To address why people want what they want, remember that in Chapter 5 we defined *socialization* as the process by which individuals internalize elements of the social structure, making those elements part of their own personality. In the case of gender socialization, one of the most important outcomes is simply the differentiation of men from women. The low waist-to-hip ratio of a Barbie doll or *Playboy* model is a prime example of exaggerating a difference between the bodies of men and women; and marking that trait as "beautiful" underscores the social value we place on such differences. If beauty is in the eye of the beholder, then the cultural beauty standard is a way of getting our heads to tell our eyes what beauty is.

Enhancing the difference between men and women doesn't just take place in our heads, of course. In Chapter 5 we examined cosmetic surgery. But one less dramatic social practice related to waists and hips is the wearing of high-heeled shoes, which most Americans seem to agree has a positive effect on women's sexual appeal. These shoes change a woman's posture to accentuate the movement of her pelvis, hips, and abdomen, thus calling attention to her waist-to-hip ratio (E. Smith and Helms 1999). In the process, unfortunately, high heels also undermine the basic functions of the foot's arch and cause all kinds of damage to the woman's body (Linder and Saltzman 1998).

From a socialization point of view, since almost everyone who wears them is a woman, high heels help establish the difference between men and women in the minds of children and reinforce it at all ages. And from the perspective of symbolic interaction, high heels help women "do gender" (West and Zimmerman 1987). They enhance those aspects of women's bodies that conform to the common image of gender and do so in view of the daily audiences that observe their bodies.

Feminist sociologists also are concerned with the high-heeled shoe question, but from their perspective the question is: Why does it fall to women to alter *their* bodies to enhance gender differences, often risking their health and mobility in the process? One feminist answer is that men's power—political, economic, and cultural—affords them the leverage to demand submissive behavior from women. In fact, from this point of view, women's subordination is actually part of what men find attractive. High heels, then, don't just accentuate the hips; they also make women less powerful physically, which many men find attractive (MacKinnon 1991). To support this argument, I will mention a more extreme example related to feet: foot binding.

For about 1,000 years, some families in China—mostly wealthier families—bound the feet of their young girls, repeatedly tying them up as they grew and never releasing them as they aged. The bones of their feet became deformed,

 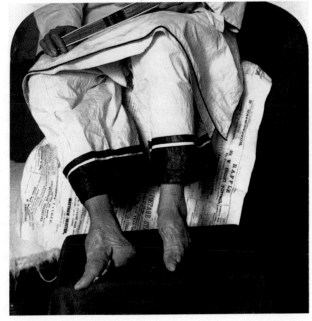

*Left:* American women in high-heeled shoes. *Right:* A Chinese woman with bound feet. Does manipulation of women's feet enhance their attractiveness or limit their physical mobility—or both?

shorter and downward-pointing, causing permanent harm to their physical mobility (Cummings, Ling, and Stone 1997). The look was considered attractive, apparently, partly because it accentuated a family's class status (showing that their women didn't have to do manual labor) and partly because it conformed to a beauty standard of women as docile and weak. Also, it caused women to take short, wobbly steps that were considered feminine (resembling at least distantly the gait of women wearing high-heeled shoes). The practice grew less common in the early twentieth century before finally being banned by the Communists, who took power in 1949.

It might seem that foot binding and high heels have only a superficial resemblance, both involving women walking on their toes. After all, high heels are women's choice, not forced on them by men. But "choice" can be complicated. It was mothers, not fathers, who were responsible for binding the feet of their daughters, so although the girls themselves had no choice, the practice was enforced by women. And even in the case of high heels, some feminists would argue that the choice is only as "free" as women are in male-dominated society. Conforming to the dominant beauty standard is learned at an early age, and most women perceive it as necessary for success in love, marriage, and careers.

## Race/Ethnicity

So far, we have only scratched the surface of questions related to romantic attraction. What if every person on earth could meet every other person on earth and freely choose a partner among them? Besides the obvious practical problems with this premise, there are two types of obstacles to achieving perfect choice. First, there are internal obstacles, which you may think of as mental or cognitive barriers to romantic attraction. Second, there are social and cultural boundaries that divide groups from each other. Of course, these types of obstacles may be closely related, so that social divisions in practice create the barriers in our minds.

To understand the relationship between cognitive and social mechanisms for attraction and division, we will need a few more terms. Sociologists use the term **homophily** to describe the principle by which similar people have more of a given kind of contact than dissimilar people. Although its linguistic origin means "love of the same"—an ideal as old as the ancient Greek philosophers—we use the term for all kinds of interactions in which "birds of a feather flock together" (McPherson, Smith-Loven, and Cook 2001). Homophily may be found, for example, in patterns of casual contact, friendship, and worker collaboration as well as romantic relationships.

One useful feature of this broader concept is that it frees us to think of homophily as not just a question of personal preference, but also one of practical limits. In the case of race, for example, one reason that "birds of a feather flock together" is that they tend to live in the same neighborhoods and attend the same schools, so they meet each other more and share common experiences.

Homophily may act in ways that are quite invisible to us. Returning to the example at the beginning of the chapter, Jason remembers being attracted to Liz

**homophily**

The principle by which similar people have more of a given kind of contact than dissimilar people.

because she was tall, beautiful, and had her act together. Was he also attracted to her because they were both White and had other similarities in their upbringing, perhaps so obvious as to go without comment? Or did the similarities in their background merely bring them together at the moment in which they were looking to make a match?

**Endogamy** In Chapter 3, we defined *endogamy* as marriage and reproduction within a distinct group. The most obvious case of this in U.S. society today occurs along the lines of race and ethnicity. However, various systems of endogamy have been practiced in all societies along the most important dividing lines of the day. In prehistoric times, exogamy—the opposite of endogamy—was an important means by which small bands of humans built connections between groups and extended their influence (as well as preventing the health problems associated with inbreeding, or breeding within small groups).

The ideal of utilitarian love, as we have defined it here, often reinforces endogamy, because forming families within a given group may reduce family complications and increase access to systems of social support (such as friends and extended family members). Romantic love, on the other hand, because it is based on individual desire rather than group affinity, challenges such a rational basis for love and has the potential to ruffle feathers between groups (Illouz 1997). For example, when family inheritance and status are at stake, people in positions of authority are usually more concerned with controlling the matching process, and they use that control to maintain the boundaries of their groups (Goode 1959). On the other hand, ruling classes throughout history have used exogamous "dynastic marriages" as a means of forging alliances between countries, families, and political regimes with competing interests.

To see how homophily and endogamy play out among young people today, we will return to the often-studied population of American college students. In Chapter 3, we saw that there has been a dramatic increase in the rates of racial-ethnic intermarriage in recent decades. During that time, the proportion of high school graduates moving on to college has grown, especially for African Americans. This has increased the rate at which Blacks and Whites meet and socialize together, especially in the more liberal environment of college campuses, where the stigma of interracial dating and relationships is less pronounced.

On the other hand, it is certainly not the case that bringing members of two groups together in one social space is all it takes to remove the barriers between them. When there is diversity in the backgrounds of students on campus, the dating system is selective—that is, romantic relationships are not assigned at random across the population. In fact, this is one of the earliest observations to emerge from studies of mate selection on American campuses. Going back to the 1920s, we know that students in high-status positions in the Greek (fraternity/sorority) system and with fathers in high-status occupations are more likely to be in relationships with those of similar status positions (Reiss 1965).

In the survey of Stanford University students mentioned earlier, researchers found that African Americans are the most isolated group in the dating scene (McClintock 2010). Asked about their most recent date (however each person

# Race and ethnicity divides college students' dating lives.

Person going on date is:
## White

Person going on date is:
## Black

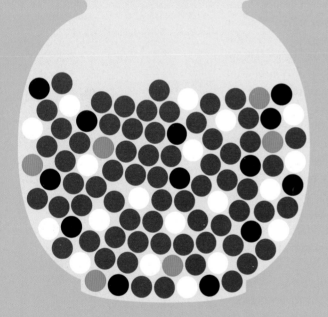

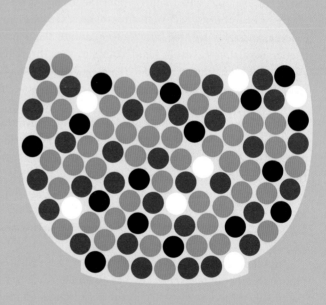

### Chance of dating someone who is:

White: **61%**     Black: **6%**

Hispanic: **13%**     Asian: **20%**

### Chance of dating someone who is:

White: **31%**     Black: **46%**

Hispanic: **17%**     Asian: **7%**

*Source: Author's calculations from McClintock (2010).*

You might think that at an elite school such as Stanford University, where all students are expected to emerge as highly paid professionals, race and ethnicity wouldn't be a major force in their love lives. But a survey of roughly 500 recent dates showed a strong tendency for the students to date within their own group. The illustrations show the breakdown of dates for each group. For example, if people dated at random, 11 percent of dates would have involved one Black student. But Black students dated each other 46 percent of the time. Hispanics and Asians dated within their own groups about twice as often as they would have if dates were randomized. This segregation is all the more striking given that the students are mostly young, geographically concentrated, and often far from the eyes of their parents.

**In a totally random scenario the % chance of dating:**

White: **55%**        Black: **11%**

Hispanic: **14%**        Asian: **20%**

Person going on date is:

# Hispanic

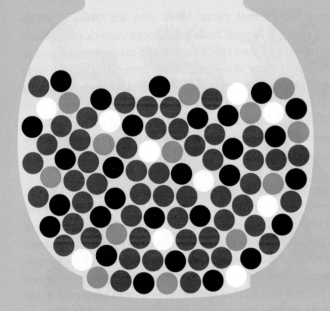

Chance of dating someone who is:

White: **50%**        Black: **13%**

Hispanic: **28%**        Asian: **10%**

Person going on date is:

# Asian

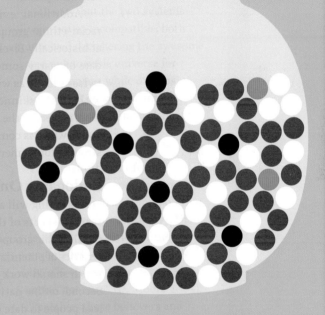

Chance of dating someone who is:

White: **54%**        Black: **4%**

Hispanic: **7%**        Asian: **35%**

http://wwnpag.es/sbtn7

Go to this link for an animation and additional information.

# Relationship Scripts

About 20 years ago, two researchers published the results of a survey of mostly White, straight, traditional-aged college undergraduates about dating scripts (Rose and Frieze 1993). They asked students to identify elements of both a hypothetical first date and an actual first date between a man and a woman. They also asked who would perform each action, the man or the woman. The results showed a fair degree of consistency in the expectations among men and women, with an especially strong agreement that men should take the initiative on most aspects of the date. I created the simplified list below based on their findings.

Either alone, in small groups, or as a class, compare this list with your own ideas of what you would expect on a first date and what you expect others would expect.

Before you say, "No one dates anymore," look over the list. If you don't call it "dating," do you or your friends do something that includes these activities or others like them? What about the gender balance? Would you expect a man to take the initiative on these or other aspects of a date? Why or why not?

Feel free to modify this activity, to include same-gender dates—whether or not you think this would lead to a different script—or to develop scripts for other stages or types of a relationship, such as online dating, group dating, or hooking up.

Finally, in class discussion, small groups, or independent writing, interpret your lists. What makes yours different from the list below? Consider the historical period and the social context (type of school, age or race/ethnicity of students, and so on). Is such a script useful, harmful, or even relevant today?

## College Student First-Date Script, circa 1993

- Pick up date*
- Leave together
- Confirm plans
- Talk/joke/laugh
- Go to movie/show/party
- Eat

- Drink alcohol
- Take date home*
- Ask for another date*
- Kiss goodnight*
- Go home

*Items expected to be done by the man.

## KEY TERMS:

social script    love

romantic love    utilitarian love

romantic relationships

hooking up    mate selection

homophily

# Questions for Review

**1.** Explain how social scripts (or their absence) affect our interactions with others.

**2.** Contrast the dating experiences of men and women at various ages: younger teenagers, college students, and older adults.

**3.** How do you define "hooking up"? How do your friends and classmates define it? Does the definition vary by age, regional background, or other life factors?

**4.** How do same-gender couples negotiate dating and relationship scripts differently from different-gender couples?

**5.** Describe three groups of singles that have become more prevalent recently.

**6.** Explain how schools and parents work around antidiscrimination laws to hold segregated proms.

**7.** Why might societal ideals of physical attractiveness no longer be related to health or reproductive fitness?

**8.** Can you see patterns of homophily in your friends and romantic partners?

# 8 Marriage and Cohabitation

Kristin Perry had a problem: she couldn't legally marry her long-time partner, Sandra Stier. "I'm a 45-year-old woman," she said. "I have been in love with a woman for 10 years and I don't have a word to tell anybody about that. [Marriage would tell] our friends, our family, our society, our community, our parents . . . and each other that this is a lifetime commitment . . . we are not girlfriends. We are not partners. We are married" (*Perry v. Schwarzenegger* 2010:12–13). It seems that the symbolic power of marriage is so great that without the recognition it provides, Perry and Stier couldn't express the true meaning of their relationship *even to each other.*

Perry's story, which she told during a federal lawsuit for same-sex marriage rights, illustrates the social value of marriage in American society. But it also shows the power of the government in bestowing that benefit through its legal recognition. (Recall our discussion of the legal definition of marriage in Chapter 1.) That sense of acceptance is one of the central motivations behind the drive to legalize marriage between people of the same gender. Paradoxically, many people who do have the legal right to marry don't seem to appreciate the weight it carries, treating the distinction almost casually. One man in a long-term, live-in relationship with a woman told an interviewer, "For credit card applications or for medical, we wouldn't say we're married. But to get a reservation at a restaurant, or if someone were to ask me at work if I was married, I would say yes. . . . Everyone at work thinks we're married" (P. Cohen 2010b).

This contrast in attitudes illustrates an important feature of marriage. On the one hand, it is a *symbolic* status, with emotional value, that sends a strong signal to others about our relationships. On the other hand, it is a *legal* status, which brings tangible benefits and protections to those who receive it. Together, these two features of marriage contribute to the culturally and politically charged nature of the debates over marriage; and the value placed on marriage contributes to the notion that its perceived decline represents a cultural crisis.

Sandra Stier (left) and Kristin Perry (right) taking their case to court. The institution of marriage and the "married" label carry enormous power in society.

# Are people getting married later, or not at all?

http://wwnpag.es/sbtn8

Go to this link for an animation and additional information.

## Men

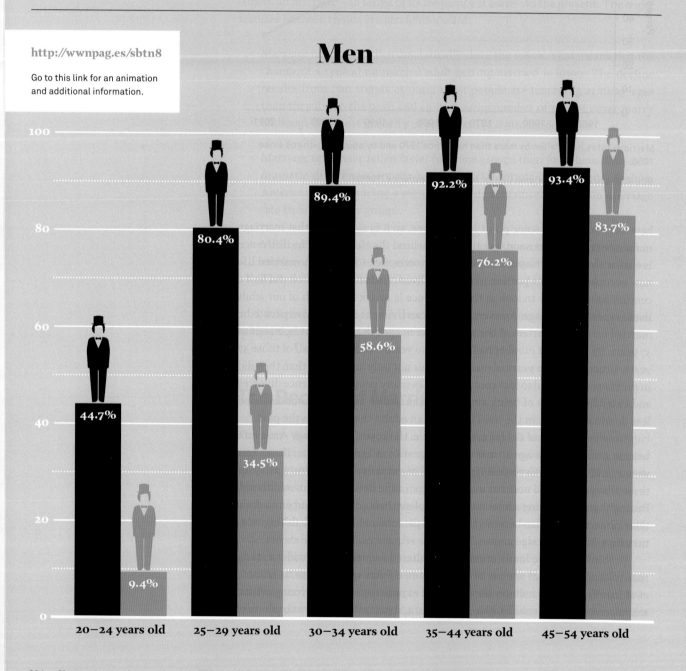

| | 20–24 years old | 25–29 years old | 30–34 years old | 35–44 years old | 45–54 years old |
|---|---|---|---|---|---|
| Black | 44.7% | 80.4% | 89.4% | 92.2% | 93.4% |
| Gray | 9.4% | 34.5% | 58.6% | 76.2% | 83.7% |

In the U.S. in 1970, 45 percent of men and 64 percent of women married in their early 20s. Those numbers have now plummeted to 9 percent and 16 percent, respectively. Despite the decline in marriage, most people still get married eventually. More than 80 percent of people have been married (at least once) by the time they reach their fifties.

*Source: Author's tabulation of U.S. census data.*

**Percentage of Americans ever married, by age**

■ 1970 ▦ 2011

# Women

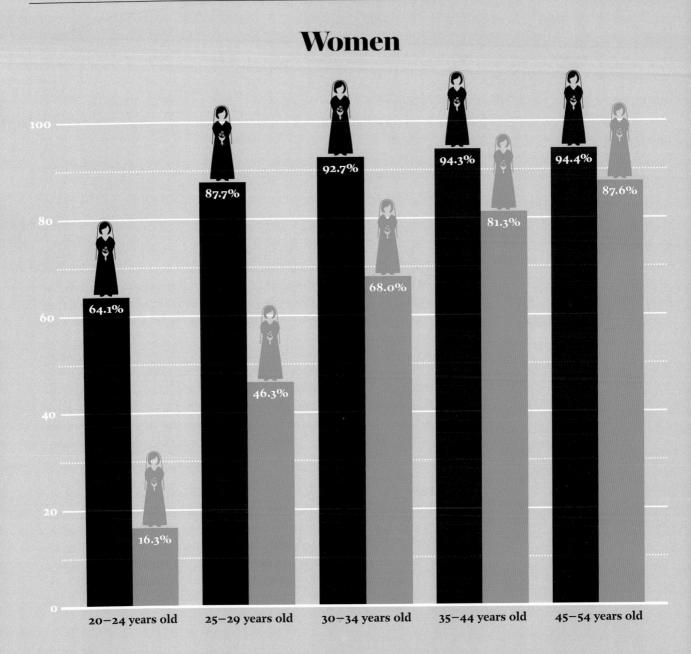

| | 20–24 years old | 25–29 years old | 30–34 years old | 35–44 years old | 45–54 years old |
|---|---|---|---|---|---|
| 1970 | 64.1% | 87.7% | 92.7% | 94.3% | 94.4% |
| 2011 | 16.3% | 46.3% | 68.0% | 81.3% | 87.6% |

## Figure 8.2 Women's experience in young adulthood, by age

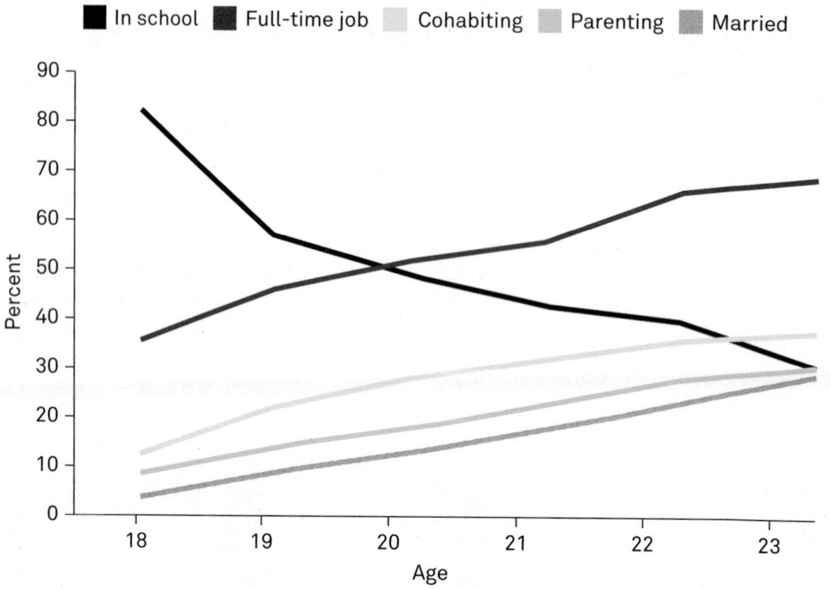

■ In school  ■ Full-time job  ■ Cohabiting  ■ Parenting  ■ Married

From age 18 to age 23, more young women experience school, full-time employment, cohabitation, and parenting than marriage.

SOURCE: Amato et al. (2008).

which may be occurring at a time). At the end of the teen years, not surprisingly, school is the most common commitment. But by age 23, more young women are engaged in full-time employment, cohabiting relationships, and parenting than are married. Even assuming that most of them eventually do get married, their adulthood will have been heavily influenced by a range of adult experiences outside of marriage.

There is no single reason for such a complex and far-reaching change as the decline in marriage (Smock 2004). However, by comparing people who marry with those who don't, by studying how the behavior of married and single people has changed, and by comparing different societies at different times, social scientists have been able to sketch the broad outlines of this story (G. Lee and Payne 2010). I will break the types of explanation into three categories: culture, economics, and demography.

**Culture** The worry that people in modern American society are excessively individualistic, or self-oriented, is very old (Baumeister 1986). Recently, some social critics have argued that individualism is the underlying cause of decaying American institutions, weakening the bonds that hold people together (Putnam 2000). With the rapid decline of marriage in the late twentieth century, that argument took on new urgency, especially for those who believe that a cultural change lies behind the "retreat from marriage." For example, the sociologist

David Popenoe famously concluded more than 20 years ago: "Quite clearly, in this age of the 'me-generation,' the individual rather than the family increasingly comes first" (1993:538). In this view, the fact that young people today are less likely to marry implies that they simply care more about themselves—and less about others—than they did in the past.

But is a change in young people's attitudes toward marriage and family—and especially a growing devotion to self-interest—really behind the decline in marriage? Yes and no. Marriage does seem less important to many people than it once was. For example, a growing number of Americans—36 percent in 2010—agree with the statement, "The present institution of marriage is becoming obsolete" (Pew Research Center 2010). One middle-aged African-American woman recently expressed this ambivalence on a social networking website, writing, "If I ever get married, fine. If not, I will not spend one day trying to get a ring from every guy I meet and miss out on enjoying each day."

However, in many ways, marriage appears to be as important as ever. In fact, some researchers suggest that Americans hold marriage in such high esteem that they feel that neither their lives nor their potential spouses can meet their ideal of marriage. So they postpone marriage not because they don't *want* to marry, but because they want a *better* marriage than they feel they can achieve. That ideal may include the wedding day itself, which most people consider a once-in-a-lifetime affair worthy of great expense (see Changing Culture, "Weddings—And the Price of Perfection"). One 20-something single mother told an interviewer, regarding her boyfriend, "Right now we're getting our credit straightened out, paying off any debts. . . . Then we'll start saving money for the wedding" (Edin and Kefalas 2005:115).

Especially among the poor and working class, however, wedding bells may be postponed by a sense of economic insecurity that undermines the notion of marriage itself (Edin and Nelson 2013). A young man living with his pregnant girlfriend told researchers that instead of getting married right away, "I'd rather get engaged for two years, save money, get a house, make sure . . . the baby's got a bedroom" (Edin and Kefalas 2005:106). Before the 1960s, the social pressure on such a couple to get married would have been much stronger.

Ironically, there probably has been both a falling appreciation for marriage among some people and a rising ideal of marriage among others, with both contributing to declining marriage rates. As marriage has become less of a requirement for many aspects of adulthood—including intimacy, sex, living together, and becoming a parent—it appears to have become more of a symbolic achievement rather than a practical necessity (Edin and Reed 2005). And if marriage is a status symbol, then it makes sense that many people set a higher standard for what makes an acceptable spouse. That raises the importance of economic factors, as we will see.

**Economics** If changes in the culture seem to be contradictory, with some people discounting marriage and others elevating it to an unrealistic standard, economic factors are also complex. There are at least two major issues to consider: how economic independence frees people from a need to marry and how

# Weddings—And the Price of Perfection

How much do you think a perfect wedding would cost? $5,000? $20,000? $50,000? More? What does the price of a wedding tell you about the value of marriage?

A wedding may be a religious or civil ceremony, marked by a consumer spending binge, or just a party with friends and family. Even if it is preceded by weeks or months of planning and followed by a honeymoon, it might not seem obvious that it changes people and their social roles fundamentally. But the interactions during this intense sequence of events carry the kind of symbolic weight that helps people recognize and adjust to a new, married identity.

The new practices begun after a wedding, as apparently trivial as starting to use a complete set of dishes for the first time, beginning to use married names, or sleeping in the same room while visiting relatives, may help create a new conception of oneself as a married person. They also reinforce the idea in others that the couple's relationship is different, that their family is undergoing a transformation. In short, weddings are part of how people *socialize* themselves into their new roles (Kalmijn 2004). All this may help explain why weddings remain so important for so many people. In fact, their social significance may have increased even as the marriage rate declines (Cherlin 2004).

The cost of hosting an ideal wedding is itself a barrier to many people considering marriage, especially those who will be covering the costs themselves. In one study, a 36-year-old carpenter who lived with his girlfriend said they had discussed getting married at the courthouse instead of having a church wedding, but his girlfriend wanted a "big ceremony with my mother by my side." His response was, "We just can't afford it, your mother doesn't have any money. It's not like she's going to pay for anything. I'm going to pay for this and we can't afford it. . . . So, no, we can't do it" (Smock 2004:969). As marriage rates diverge between rich and poor, it's worth considering how every lavish wedding seen on screen or in the neighborhood reinforces the difference between those who can and those who cannot afford one.

Figure 8.3 **The cost of a wedding with all the trimmings: $44,798**

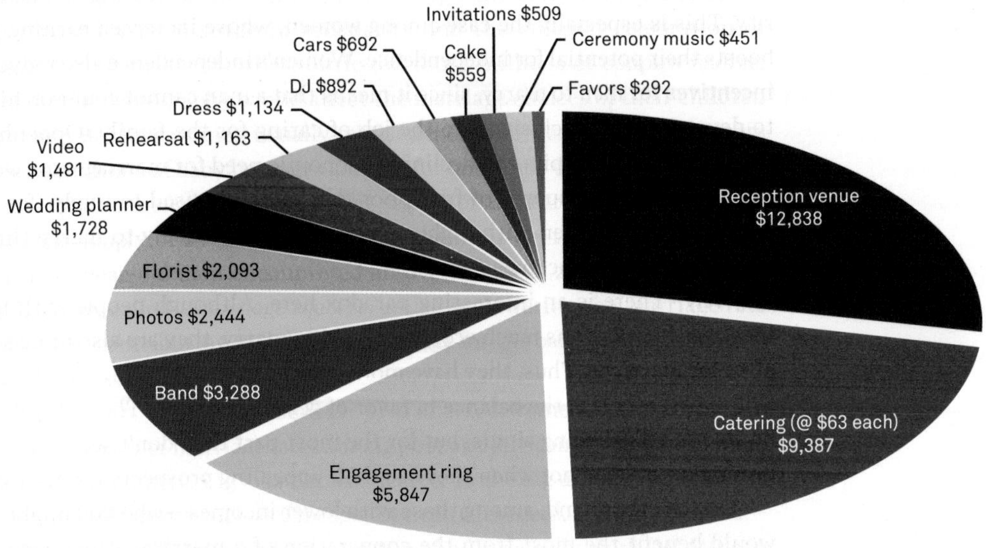

Invitations $509
Cars $692
Cake $559
Ceremony music $451
DJ $892
Favors $292
Dress $1,134
Video $1,481
Rehearsal $1,163
Wedding planner $1,728
Florist $2,093
Photos $2,444
Band $3,288
Engagement ring $5,847
Reception venue $12,838
Catering (@ $63 each) $9,387

These are the average amounts spent on each item by those who bought them.

SOURCE: The Knot (2010).

And the cost of weddings seems to have increased over the past century. Industry groups put the cost of an average wedding at $28,000 in 2009 (The Knot 2010). For comparison, the *Saturday Evening Post* in 1945 featured a detailed account of one man's daughter's wedding and how much "the whole shebang...set him back." Remarkably, his expenses—when you adjust them for inflation to today's dollars—were just about $28,000, very close to today's average. But his family was quite rich: for example, the champagne he served cost $67 per bottle in today's money, and the reception was at their country club. So if today's average couple spends as much as Horace W. Osborne did in 1945, it is probably safe to say that weddings have grown more expensive. Further, the Osborne family had no DJ, rehearsal dinner, wedding planner, or videographer. According to The Knot, a wedding today with all the trimmings, at the national average size of 149 guests, costs about $45,000—but it's $692 less if you drive yourselves instead of hiring limos (Figure 8.3).

Of course, some people are critical of what Chrys Ingraham calls the "wedding industrial complex" (2008). Maybe they prefer a simple wedding. Or they just don't want to spend their money to support the advertising, jewelry, and fashion industries—all while reinforcing traditional notions of marriage to which they might not subscribe.

On the other hand, the "wedding industrial complex" can serve the needs of modern families in many ways. For example, in some circles, both partners in an engaged couple now wear engagement rings, to express their love and their equality—and maybe to flaunt their ability to buy rings (Shattuck 2010). Once again, the shape of the wedding, like the shape of the marriage itself, is up for negotiation. And the choices we make about this present an image of ourselves and our families to the people we know, and even to ourselves.

But the reason for the change among those with less education shows that their situation is quite different. Economic insecurity has become pronounced for young adults without college degrees, especially men. To get a foothold in a good job as a young man has increasingly required a college education. And in addition to low wages, a lack of job security plagues those at the low end of the job market (Danziger and Ratner 2010). As a result, young adults face what researchers call the "transition to adulthood" with increasing uncertainty. One outcome of this uncertainty has been a tendency to delay marriage, perhaps in favor of a less committed nonmarital cohabitation relationship. By the time they are in their late 30s, people with more education and better job prospects may finally be ready to marry, even as those in poorer situations find their marriage opportunities growing bleaker.

The disparity in marriage patterns between those with more education and those with less affects several important aspects of inequality. First, by the simple math of adding incomes together, the growth of the double-income married couple—juxtaposed to the lower levels of marriage among the poor—increases the income gap between rich and poor families (McLanahan and Percheski 2008). Second, there is a more subtle aspect of inequality at work here. The great majority of adults want to be happily married eventually, but those with higher education are more likely to achieve that goal. That is a different kind of inequality—the inequality between those who have the ability and means to achieve their family ideals and those who do not.

## Why Do People Still Get Married?

After several pages devoted to a discussion of the decline of marriage, it is worth noting that there remain a variety of compelling reasons *for* people to get married. True, some of the reasons have eroded in recent decades. For example, most Americans do not feel they need to get married before having sex, living with a partner, or even raising children. And because so many marriages end in divorce, a wedding does not necessarily signify a lifelong commitment either. All of this contributes to what sociologist Andrew Cherlin (2004) refers to as the "deinstitutionalization of marriage." By that he means that the formal and informal rules of marriage—its social *norms*—have become weaker, leaving marriage itself more optional and behavior within marriage more negotiable.

And yet the great majority of Americans end up getting married. Why? One way to answer that is to use Cherlin's concept of the marriage institution. Although the institution is weaker, it still provides reasons to marry (Lauer and Yodanis 2010). We can put the reasons to marry in three categories:

- *Incentives.* A variety of rewards steer people toward marriage (or penalize them, relatively speaking, for *not* marrying). For example, state and federal governments offer rights and benefits to married couples. These include social protections, such as parental rights over their children and access to immigration for a spouse, and financial benefits, such as tax breaks and

Social Security pension funds. Market actors also contribute incentives, such as employers and insurance companies that offer insurance benefits for married couples.

- *Social pressure*. Because many people are aware of the real (or perceived) benefits that marriage provides, young couples often encounter advice and pressure to marry. Some advice comes from the media's packaging of social science research, which is generally positive about the benefits of marriage (Parker-Pope 2010). Or it may come directly from family experts and professionals, such as counselors and social workers. Other sources of pressure to marry include family members and religious leaders, although these have weakened in recent decades (Tucker 2000).

- *Imitation*. As noted in Chapter 2, modern society offers many more choices about family life now than it did decades ago. Because choice also implies responsibility, however, we feel we have only ourselves to blame if something goes wrong. In that situation, the "crowd" can serve as a reassuring presence in support of our decisions. Ironically, then, the more choices people have, the more they may seek to imitate others around them as a way of narrowing their options. That might affect smaller decisions, such as naming one's child after a celebrity, but it also helps lead people into marriage. Thus, although young adults may delay or experiment with alternatives (such as cohabitation), in the end most people choose to conform to common behavior patterns.

Clearly, with the pronounced decline in the frequency of marriage we have observed, these various reasons to marry are not as persuasive as they once were. Nevertheless, marriage remains one of the dominant experiences in the lives of most adults. The desire to marry, however, can only be realized if people can find suitable partners. And as with any of the family choices we discuss in this book, what seems most personal is often shaped by forces that are larger than any one person.

# Who Marries Whom

In the previous chapter, I mentioned that I don't frequently pry into strangers' relationships. But there are two specific examples I would like to focus on for illustration—famous people whose stories are already well documented (or exploited) by others.

When Barack Obama and Michelle Robinson met, they may have been the only two Black lawyers at their firm in Chicago (Remnick 2010). They were also both Harvard Law School graduates, both tall and athletic, and as a couple they had the usual height and age spreads—he being a little taller and a little older than she. So in some ways they were even more similar than the couple I described

Is marriage a market? What can we learn from Barack Obama and Michelle Robinson (top) and J. Howard Marshall and Anna Nicole Smith (bottom)?

in Chapter 7. However, the fact that she was a successful professional—and even his superior at the law firm—is a sign of how standards have changed as well.

Compare the future First Couple with an extremely different couple: J. Howard Marshall and Anna Nicole Smith. When their brief marriage began in 1994, he was an 89-year-old oil tycoon worth hundreds of millions of dollars, and she was a 26-year-old model who had dropped out of ninth grade before achieving fame—or notoriety— as *Playboy*'s 1993 "Playmate of the Year" (Goodnough and Fox 2007). The age and income difference between them was extreme compared with the Obamas, but in some ways their marriage conformed more closely to the traditional breadwinner-homemaker model. Is there a sociological story here?

Some researchers conceive of the spouse-matching process as a marketplace, in which people offer something of value for sale while they shop for what they like (and can afford). This concept was advanced by the economist Gary Becker (1973), whom we met in our discussion of exchange theory in Chapter 1. To define marriage as a market, like the market for cars or bubble gum, he made two assumptions. First, marriage must be *voluntary*, meaning people only marry if and when they think it will improve their lives (like buying bubble gum). And second, there must be *competition* for spouses (like shopping around for the right price on the right car). If those basic conditions exist, Becker theorized, then we can think of marriage as a market process.

The market concept fits with a long-standing popular view of certain patterns, or stereotypes, that people observe in American marriages (M. Rosenfeld 2005). For example:

- Rich men marry women who are poorer, yet beautiful (like Marshall and Smith).

- Men choose wives based on their potential as mothers, while women choose husbands for their potential earnings (something Smith vehemently denied doing).

- Members of lower-status groups (such as Black men) marry members of higher-status groups (such as White women) when the latter have less money or education than themselves.

In each case, people are seen to be using the assets they have to win the qualities they want in a marriage partner. Put another way, those with higher status in one respect, such as education, exchange that with a partner who has a higher status in a different realm, such as race.

Many sociologists find Becker's notion of market principles in marriage to be naive or idealistic. To us, social life seems more chaotic and conflict ridden than Becker's tidy supply-and-demand formulas imply, as if buyers line up for spouses who are auctioned off in order from best to worst, according to careful assessments of their "quality." Specifically, sociologists have described three problems with the idea (Illouz and Finkelman 2009). First, people making marriage decisions have desires that may be in conflict, such as sexual attraction and economic potential. Second, people often make bad decisions, especially in the realm of love and romance, so we cannot assume that marriage choices are "rational." And third, in real life, people shopping for a spouse do not have as many choices as, say, someone shopping for a car or bubble gum, so it's not reasonable to assume that spouses reflect a conscious choice from among many alternatives.

Despite such sociological skepticism, however, the marriage market concept has been very influential, and the term is widely used in research (Kalmijn 2010). Without accepting all the assumptions of exchange theory, in this book I use **marriage market** to mean the social space in which people search for potential marriage partners. Often we think of that space as simply the local area—the neighborhood, campus, or city, for example—but it need not be strictly geographical. With online dating, for example, the social space may be a group with some common interest or quality (for example, Christian vegetarians). In the study of marriage markets, we do consider economic factors. But sociologists focus further on two related sociological issues: the construction of personal preferences and the drawing of boundaries between groups.

> **marriage market**
>
> The social space in which people search for potential marriage partners.

Returning to the Obamas: First, why would two African-American, Harvard-educated lawyers have a *preference* to marry each other? Maybe rather than making an exchange to get something they don't have, perhaps their common experience growing up to become liberal Black students at elite universities, exceeding expectations, and becoming highly successful in the face of long odds, all the while learning—being trained—to see the world in a similar way, made them susceptible to each other's charms and ways of thinking.

That interpretation calls to mind the discussion of socialization in Chapter 5. If socialization is a way to internalize elements of the social structure into our own personality, then it makes sense that our choice of a marriage partner might reflect that process. In other words, people bring their life stories—embedded in their personalities—to the marriage market. Note also that the Obamas' story follows the description in Chapter 7 of homophily ("birds of a feather flock together"). Such patterns, in which similar people end up together, are caused by both personal preferences and practical limits.

And that brings us to the second sociological aspect of marriage markets: *boundaries*. As we will see, race, education, and religion are the most resilient boundaries carving up today's U.S. marriage market. Those divisions are created by cultural or traditional practices (such as attitudes against interracial marriage) as well as more structural barriers (such as residential segregation).

How did preferences and boundaries shape the Obamas' market of potential matches? We cannot know the intimate details, but here is a suggestive fact:

# Cohabitation

While we study changes in marriage patterns—who gets married and who marries whom—it's ironic that one of the biggest changes in marriage in recent decades has been something that happens *outside* of marriage. Defined as living together as a sexual or romantic couple without being married, **cohabitation** has rapidly become an expected stage in relationships for the majority of couples. Cohabiting couples may have a strong informal commitment to their relationship, and they may or may not be engaged to marry, have children, or be sexually exclusive. Naturally, in modern societies, all of that is up for negotiation.

As you can see in Figure 8.7, cohabitation has become much more common in the past several decades for Americans at all levels of education. Overall, by 2007, almost 60 percent of women under age 45 had cohabited with a man at some point in their lives. And among all couples living together, 1 in 5 are not married (National Center for Family and Marriage Research 2010). By changing the pathway to marriage, the experience before marriage, and the alternatives to marriage, cohabitation has radically changed the experience of marriage itself (Smock 2000).

**cohabitation**

Living together as a sexual or romantic couple without being married.

Figure 8.7 **Percentage of women ages 19 to 44 who have ever cohabited, by education, 1987–2007**

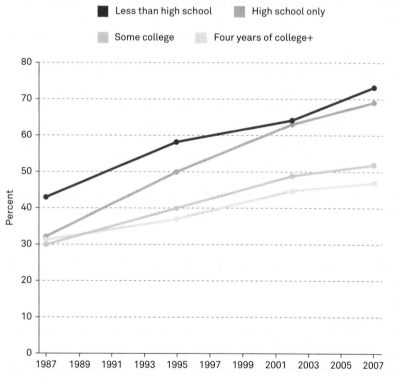

Cohabitation rates have increased rapidly, but the increase is fastest, and the levels are highest, for those with less education.

SOURCE: National Center for Family and Marriage Research (2010).

Although the increase in cohabitation is broad, as Figure 8.7 shows, we also see that cohabitation is more common—and has increased faster—among women with less education (these figures are for women because they were originally collected in a government survey about women's health and family planning). Combined with what we have learned about marriage patterns, we now see that cohabitation is part of the social class divide in family experience. Those with less education are less likely to marry, but more likely to live together. Thus, we should not conclude that they have no partners, but rather that their relationships are less stable and committed, on average, than those who have a higher level of education and therefore more economic security.

Unfortunately for researchers, cohabitation is not always a clearly defined status (W. Manning and Smock 2005). First, some people live together only some days of the week or some weeks of the year—or "off and on," depending on the ups and downs of the relationship. So "living together" may be hard to pin down. And second, informal romantic or sexual relationships—without marriage or some other legal recognition—do not have clear start and end dates. The individuals involved sometimes do not even agree between themselves on the nature of their relationship. All of that makes cohabitation difficult to study—but does not make it less important to try.

Although most Americans will experience cohabitation at some point in their lives, it occurs at different ages, under many different circumstances, and for different lengths of time. On average, however, cohabitation is not a long-lasting relationship. As Figure 8.8 shows, only 61 percent of couples are still unmarried and living together after one year, and only 15 percent after five years. By the fifth year, about 40 percent have married (and some of those have already divorced) and about half separate. Clearly, there are very different outcomes for these relationships.

Family instability among cohabiting families has been especially worrying to those concerned with children in low-income families (Graefe and Lichter 1999). More than one-third of all cohabitors live with children, and those families often are poor (Artis 2007). For children whose mothers live with several men over a period of years, a series of changes in family structure—with the conflict those changes may entail—is a source of stress in their development (Fomby and Osborne 2010).

When we think about these experiences of cohabitation, it is helpful to break them into three conceptual categories: before marriage, instead of marriage, and after marriage. I say "conceptual" categories because we cannot cleanly separate couples into these three groups. But the elements of each kind of relationship— the people involved, their motivations, and the consequences for them—are worth examining.

# Before Marriage

Living together before marrying is the most common form of cohabitation among younger adults. For these couples, cohabitation is a proving ground for the relationship—a chance to experience living as a couple without making a

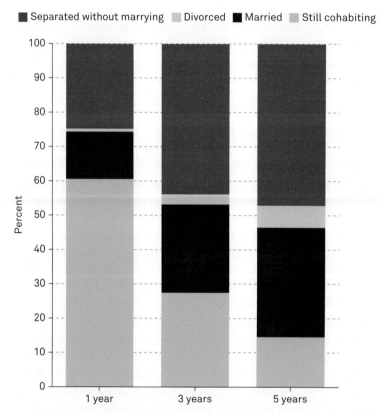

Figure 8.8 **Relationship status 1, 3, and 5 years from the start of a first cohabitation**

■ Separated without marrying ■ Divorced ■ Married ■ Still cohabiting

A quarter of cohabitors separate within a year, while 14 percent get married. After 5 years, about 40 percent have married (some of whom have already divorced), and about half have broken up.

SOURCE: Adapted from Goodwin, Mosher, and Chandra (2010).

public, legal, or religious commitment. In the past 40 years, living together has gone from something 1 in 10 American couples did before marriage to the experience of 2 out of 3 couples (National Center for Family and Marriage Research 2010). Cohabitation is now a widely expected stage in the relationship process (W. Manning, Longmore, and Giordano 2007). And most people believe that this arrangement—once commonly known as "living in sin"—is the right thing for a couple to do.

But living together without marrying—even with the expectation of marrying—is not just an experiment in a vacuum; it has effects on the relationship that may be permanent. These may be positive, such as the tendency to share housework more equally (Batalova and Cohen 2002). But there are also risks. Ironically, one risk is that couples who move in together may get married out of "relationship inertia"—the momentum of a lesser decision (moving in together) making a more important decision (marrying) easier to fall into carelessly (Stanley, Rhoades, and Markman 2006). Couples may end up living together under imperfect conditions, without making clear or informed decisions that take into account the long-term consequences of their actions (W. Manning and Smock 2005).

Among poor and working-class couples, cohabiting often reflects a plan to marry once they have more money (Smock, Manning, and Porter 2005). For example, one 28-year-old fast-food manager, already living with a woman and their child, told researchers, "We need to be financially secure [before we can marry]. We need to be able to support ourselves, you know?" If that doesn't happen, such couples may never marry, or financial strain may break up the relationship along the way. In other words, they may view their cohabitation as a step toward marriage, but economic reality often intervenes to block their desire from being realized (Gibson-Davis, Edin, and McLanahan 2005).

Financial pressures also drive some people into living together in the first place. For example, during the recession in the late 2000s, there was a large increase in the number of younger, low-income cohabiting couples, with many moving into already crowded households, suggesting that their decision to move in together was motivated more by a financial crunch than by a romantic ideal (Kreider 2010).

# Instead of Marriage

A smaller group—not as well understood by researchers at this point—chooses cohabitation instead of marriage (Thornton, Axinn, and Xie 2007). Some of these couples are ideologically opposed to marriage, with its traditional image and expectations, but this is relatively rare (Rhoades, Stanley, and Markman 2009). Others make their relationship commitments without the help of religious or civil authorities, choosing to express their bonds independently (Elizabeth 2003).

But the choice is not always freely made. Nontraditional couples face obstacles to marriage even if they desire to marry. For example, their families may oppose the marriage, their religion might frown on it (in the case of interfaith couples), or they may face condemnation on the basis of race/ethnicity, age, or social class differences. In such cases, couples often end up cohabiting to avoid the choice between confronting that opposition and ending their relationship. As a result, cohabiting couples are more likely to include partners with bigger differences in educational attainment or different racial-ethnic backgrounds (Blackwell and Lichter 2000).

Finally, we should not assume that both parties in a couple see things the same way. When one partner wants to marry and the other doesn't, cohabitation may be a compromise. And some cohabiting relationships do not result in marriage because the couple can't make it work. For example, among women with a history of being abused as children, the difficulty in forming or maintaining intimate relationships may translate into a series of unstable cohabiting relationships without a marriage (Cherlin et al. 2004). For a minority of cohabitors—about 1 in 5—living together with a series of partners is an alternative to marriage, voluntary or not. This pattern is most common among the economically disadvantaged (Lichter and Qian 2008).

These responses are mostly individualistic in that they are benefits for the men themselves. But they also imply mutuality. How could these men expect to continue receiving these benefits if they were not returning the favor to their wives? The theme of mutual support is one of several that run through studies of marriage's benefits and (less often) its costs—to which we now turn.

# The Benefits of Marriage

People rarely explain their reasons for marriage by describing how it will save them money on rent or taxes or make them look good to their bosses at work or to their parents. And they don't usually say that they might need someone to help them get to the bathroom in the middle of the night when they are old and sick. But when sociologists study the benefits and costs of marriage, these are some of the issues they investigate. I will return to those bread-and-butter issues, but first, the not-so-simple question of happiness.

## Happiness

There are two kinds of studies of marriage and happiness. The first kind asks whether people are in happy marriages—that is, whether the marriage is emotionally healthy. The second is about whether people who are married are emotionally happy in general. Naturally, these issues are linked.

With regard to happy marriages, the tendency of married people to describe their marriages as "very happy" has not changed much since the 1970s, although there has been an improvement since 2006. It is surprising that they haven't grown even happier, because fewer people are married now, and it has become much easier (and more acceptable) to leave an unhappy marriage. So we might expect the *remaining* marriages to be happier. In fact, because marital satisfaction tends to decline over the life of a marriage, we might expect marriages to be getting happier simply because there are more short-term marriages now (Lavner and Bradbury 2010). But Figure 8.9 shows only a slight decline in happiness after the 1970s, and a slight improvement again in the 2010s. However, the total numbers mask two important differences. First, Whites describe their marriages as happier than Blacks and others. Second, men say their marriages are happier than women do (Corra et al. 2009).

If you have ever been caught in the middle of a conflict between spouses, you probably won't be surprised to learn that men and women often describe the same marriages differently. In fact, many couples do have significant differences of opinion over how happy the marriage is—and it is usually the wife who has the more negative view (Schumm, Webb, and Bollman 1998). These gender differences fit with the long-standing view that marriage is more beneficial for men than for women, which led one sociologist to declare that every marriage is

Figure 8.9 **Percentage describing their marriage as "very happy,"**
**1973–2012**

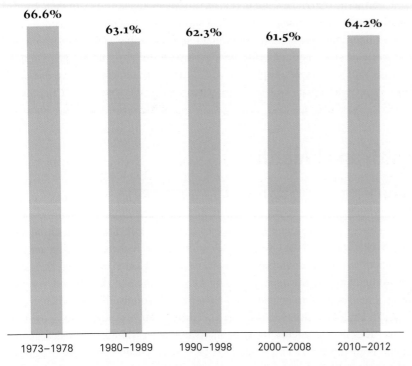

The question was, "Taking all things together, how would you describe your marriage:
very happy, pretty happy, or not too happy?"

SOURCE: Author's calculations from the General Social Surveys, 1972–2012 (Smith
et al. 2014).

really two marriages—his and hers—that are often worlds apart (Bernard 1982).
However, the differences overall are not as great as that statement implies. Probably more important is the simple fact that richer people are happier in their
relationships, whether they are married or cohabiting, because they have less
stress over economic insecurity (Hardie and Lucas 2010).

Unfortunately, we do not have comparable studies of gay and lesbian couples
(Biblarz and Savci 2010). There have been some attempts to compare happiness and satisfaction in straight versus gay/lesbian couples (usually focusing on
cohabiting rather than married couples). And the evidence so far suggests that
cohabiting gays and lesbians are about as happy as cohabiting straight people
(Wienke and Hill 2009). But these are mostly small studies that can reach only
tentative conclusions (for example, Schumm, Akagi, and Bosch 2008). When we
have enough information to make those comparisons, we might learn more about
the nature of relationships between men and women as well.

With regard to the happiness of married people, there is enough research to
say that, on average, married people are happier than those who are not married—
and this applies to both men and women (Wienke and Hill 2009). However, there

also are good reasons to suspect that happiness makes people get and stay married as much as marriage makes people happier. That is, happier people may be more attractive as marriage partners, better at developing relationships, and better at keeping the marriage from breaking up (Mastekaasa 1994). In fact, careful research that tracks people over time has shown that getting married does lead to greater happiness on average (H. K. Kim and McKenry 2002). An important caveat to these conclusions is that people in very unhappy marriages are usually not as happy as single people. We will return to the question of what makes relationships more happy or less happy when we discuss divorce in Chapter 10.

## Health and Wealth

If happier people are more likely to get married, so are richer people, as we have seen in this chapter. So it is not surprising that married people—and married couples—have more income, more property, and more education than unmarried people. When we study the effect of one condition (such as marriage) on another (such as wealth), social scientists say there is a **selection effect** when the cause being studied has already been determined by the outcome that is under investigation. The best way to solve such puzzles is with longitudinal studies, to see the sequencing of events (see Chapter 1). Through such studies, we know that marriage does bring benefits to its participants, even though privileged people are more likely to marry in the first place. I see marriage benefits stemming from three sources: behavioral changes or responsibility, cooperation, and social status.

**selection effect**

The problem that occurs when the cause being studied has already been determined by the outcome that is under investigation.

**Responsibility** More than 100 years ago, Émile Durkheim (1897/1951) argued that married men were less likely to commit suicide because of their strong social ties and the people who depended on them (J. Smith, Mercy, and Conn 1988). This is borne out by evidence that married women have lower suicide rates, made even lower the more children they have (Høyer and Lund 1993). In fact, married people are less likely to die from a variety of causes, even when we compare people at the same level of income and education (N. Johnson et al. 2000; Manzoli et al. 2007).

Most young adults see marriage as a sign of greater responsibility, which leads them to behave more cautiously (with less binge drinking and marijuana smoking, for example). The close presence of a spouse who depends on them (or keeps an eye on them) also encourages this development (Duncan, Wilkerson, and England 2006). In general, the productive routine, sense of responsibility, and obligations that people take on when they are married seem to promote healthier (and more lucrative) behavior (Umberson, Crosnoe, and Reczek 2010).

**Cooperation** Families can save money and effort by sharing their assets and abilities. Extra hands—and minds—working and living together can increase the efficiency of everything from paying rent and buying food to managing child-care arrangements and taking care of sick relatives. In economic theory, these benefits are maximized when the two spouses bring different skills and assets to the marriage (Becker 1981). For example, one of the reasons married men earn more than single men is that some of them have wives at home lightening their housework and child-care burdens, which economists call "specialization" (Bardasi and Taylor 2008). However, even though husbands and wives have grown more similar in terms of their skills and work behaviors, cooperation itself brings benefits. This surely contributes to the health advantage of married people noted earlier, as well as to differences in income and wealth accumulation. For example, 80 percent of married-couple households own (or are buying) their homes, compared with 65 percent of households in general (U.S. Census Bureau 2013c).

**Status** Although less tangible than health and wealth, social status is also a reward for marriage. For example, a classic study of professional workers concluded that married men received higher salaries because their managers thought they deserved to be paid more (Osterman 1979). The flip side of that is that even though married women—especially mothers—are celebrated by their peers and popular media, they may find that employers believe that they "deserve" lower wages (Correll, Benard, and Paik 2007). Even worse, some women who have not married feel a stigma from others in their social circles or a feeling of failure and loss that takes a toll on their happiness and even their mental health (Sharp and Ganong 2007).

## Religion

One clear difference that sets married couples apart is their tendency to participate in religious observances and practices. Married people attend religious services more often than singles, as you can see in Figure 8.10. When husbands and wives share the same religious beliefs and attend religious services together, this tendency is associated with greater marital happiness. However, while religious beliefs remain common and strong among Americans, the institutional authority of religious leadership has declined. Even religious people are now more likely to pursue the individualistic goals of self-fulfillment and self-determination than they were in the past. The growing independence of spouses and especially the trend toward equality in men's and women's employment have weakened the traditional religious presence within marriage (Myers 2006).

It is perhaps no wonder that marriage is so advantageous. Why else would rich, healthy, well-educated, and powerful people be more likely to get married? However, should this be taken to mean that marriage is *inherently* good? Not necessarily. Rather, given our current society and its cultural expectations, marriage is a means to social

Figure 8.10 **How often adults attend religious services**

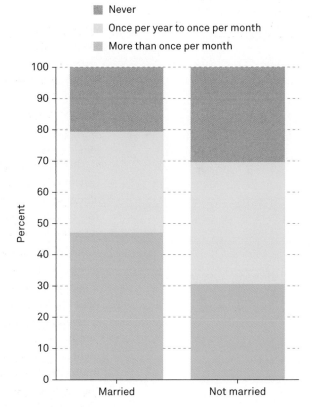

Married people attend religious services much more than unmarried people.

SOURCE: Author's calculations from the General Social Surveys, 1972–2012 (Smith et al. 2014).

advantage. Consider the findings from a study of 30 different countries. Overall, married people are happier and more satisfied with their lives than cohabitors, and both groups are happier than single people. However, the "marriage advantage" is smaller in countries where cohabitation is more common (Soons and Kalmijn 2009). If American society did not structure its rewards around the ideal of married family life, as we'll see in the next section, then perhaps the disadvantages of *not* being married would be reduced.

# The Politics of Marriage

Marriage has not historically had a merely symbolic role in society. In her review of the place of marriage in many different cultures, Stephanie Coontz (2005) points out that whether, and to whom, people were married have determined everything from the "legitimacy" of children and the mutual obligations of husbands and wives to the orderly distribution of property from one generation to the next. In premodern Europe, marriage also served to bind families to the church, since Christian authorities regulated marriages. And in the United States, it brought families under the jurisdiction of the state. The historical decline of marriage, then, has brought about a lack of formal regulation over couple relationships.

Of course, in modern society, many aspects of individuals' lives—including things they are required to do (for example, care for their children) and are prohibited from doing (for example, commit violence)—are regulated outside the realm of legal marriage. And that is what makes marriage seem more symbolic now. But rather than cooling the debate, this symbolic character seems to heighten the emotions in the politics of marriage and its future.

In the sweep of history, some aspects of the decline of marriage clearly are beneficial. For most people, especially women, individual freedom has increased while repressive authority has weakened. Even married people are made more free by the loosening of restrictions on marriage and the right to divorce. Consider the practice of women taking their husband's family name, as most still do (Gooding and Kreider 2010). Few people realize it is a remnant of an older system in which women became the property of their husband's family upon marriage. That legacy is still visible in the traditional practice of the bride's father "giving" her away at the wedding (Coontz 2005:76).

Maybe the growth of individual freedom in the institutional arena of the family inevitably led to fewer marriages or to more divorces. But this development has been—and remains—highly contentious. We conclude this chapter by discussing two political movements on behalf of marriage in society. The first is the effort to encourage marriage among poor people—especially parents—based on the reasoning that children benefit from the care of married, preferably biological parents. The second is the legal and political campaign to extend marriage rights to same-sex couples, based on the demand for equal access to the symbolic and practical benefits of marriage for gay and lesbian couples and their families.

The state-run Oklahoma Marriage Initiative has spent millions of dollars to promote marriage and reduce the divorce rate—one of the highest in the nation—including marriage workshops for prisoners.

# Marriage Promotion

In the 1990s, the majority of legislators in the U.S. Congress believed that the federal welfare program in effect since the 1960s, known as Aid to Families with Dependent Children, was not working (Sidel 1998). Although it cost only a tiny share of the federal budget, conservative political activists had argued that the program—designed to help support families without breadwinner husbands—wasted money by essentially paying poor women to remain single (Murray 1984). When the welfare system was reformed in 1996, Congress created the Temporary Assistance to Needy Families (TANF) program. TANF established two major goals: to provide assistance to poor families (although less than in the past) and to "encourage the formation and maintenance of two-parent families" (Bush 2004).

With the Personal Responsibility and Work Opportunity Act of 1996, the federal government entered a new era of marriage promotion. TANF was designed to promote the well-being of children under the assumption that they would be better off living with married parents. The opening passage of the legislation declared, "Marriage is the foundation of a successful society" (P. Cohen 2014a). To further this goal, the law essentially gave poor mothers a stark choice: get a job or get married. Cash assistance was made temporary, and recipients were expected to have or seek a job. And, using funds from that welfare program, the federal government spent hundreds of millions of dollars—most of it distributed to state agencies and nonprofit groups—to encourage poor people to get married and to help them make their marriages more successful (Heath 2012).

For example, the Oklahoma Marriage Initiative received millions of federal dollars for "marriage and relationship training." It held thousands of workshops and counseling sessions and also trained people to repeat the training program elsewhere (Bush 2004). Supported in part by federal welfare grants, religious organizations, marriage counselors, and family advocates of various stripes have operated programs to promote and strengthen marriages (Nock 2005). In another example, the U.S. Conference of Catholic Bishops offers a website called ForYourMarriage.com, with "bite-sized pieces of inspiration to make your marriage the absolute best it can be," including common advice about communication and commitment, as well as tips such as: "Although being a person of faith is not essential to making your marriage work, it's a bonus."

From the beginning, however, there were serious concerns about marriage promotion. First, some experts immediately were concerned that government money would be used to encourage people in abusive or unhealthy relationships to stay together, creating even greater harm than not marrying in the first place. The federal program showed its awareness of this concern by referring to itself as the *Healthy* Marriage Initiative, with the goal of "increasing the percentage of children who are raised by two parents in a *healthy* marriage" (emphasis added).

Second, because the "retreat from marriage" has been the result of widespread cultural, economic, and demographic changes, marriage experts were skeptical that the trend could be reversed by simply teaching individual behavior changes to poor people. This objection also reflects a basic concern that poverty and economic insecurity are the main problem for children, as these conditions deter marriage (rather than single parenthood creating poverty). Critics argued that rather than promote marriage through training, counseling, and other programs championed by "family-values" conservatives, the federal government should pursue broader policies that make employment more rewarding for the poor, such as tax law changes, an increase in the minimum wage, and child-care support (Coontz and Folbre 2010).

Whether or not we like the idea of the federal government promoting marriage, it does not appear to have worked (M. D. Johnson 2012). One large evaluation of the Building Strong Families project in eight states compared the relationship status of about 5,000 couples before and after half of them received an extensive array of support services intended to strengthen their relationships. After 15 months, there was no difference between the two groups—those who received the services and those who did not—in terms of their relationship quality or whether they were still together (Wood et al. 2010). More broadly, in the decade of the 2000s, while the program was in place and operating in every state, the percentage of young adults (ages 25 to 34) without college degrees who were married fell by 10 points, from 54 percent to 44 percent—much faster than it fell in the previous decade (Mather and Lavery 2010). At least among those with less education and lower incomes, the retreat from marriage continues.

## Marriage Rights

Meanwhile, the political movement for gay and lesbian rights was not retreating, but rather advancing toward legal marriage. Before the 1970s, there was no

# Same-Sex Marriage

The federal government provides many benefits to married people. However, after the late nineteenth century, when the federal government intervened to regulate marriage among American Indians and Mormons (see Chapter 2), it has mostly been up to individual states to decide who is legally married. A crucial exception occurred when the U.S. Supreme Court ruled in *Loving v. Virginia* (1967) that state laws prohibiting interracial marriage were unconstitutional. Now that some states provide for legal same-sex marriage and others legally forbid it, the issue of which marriages to recognize has become a federal one once again, and the right to equal treatment under the law is at stake.

Starting in 2004 some states began changing their laws to permit same-sex marriage (see Figure 8.11). The first of these changes were made by state judges. Then several state legislatures voted to permit same-sex marriage. Finally, starting in 2012, a series of states passed same-sex marriage referendums by popular vote, representing the clearest expression of majority support for broadening marriage rights. As of April 2014, 17 states and the District of Columbia permitted same-sex marriage. In contrast, in 35 states where support for same-sex marriage is much weaker, state laws specifically prohibit same-sex marriage (National Conference of State Legislatures 2013).

The federal court case *Perry v. Schwarzenegger* (2010), with which this chapter opened, proved to be an important step in the legal march toward gay and lesbian marriage rights. The decision by the U.S. district court in that case overturned California's voter-approved ban on gay marriage. The judge writing the decision, Vaughn Walker, ruled that the state had no legitimate reason to deny marriage rights to couples of the same sex. Because the law no longer differentiates between the male and female partners in a marriage, he reasoned, the state could not justifiably require one partner to be male and the other female. Instead, given the benefits of marriage—both symbolic and practical—he determined that denying gays and lesbians access to those benefits was a form of discrimination that was not justified. (Some forms of discrimination are legally justified, such as denying blind people drivers' licenses or denying gun permits to convicted felons.)

As the *Perry* case was making its way through the courts, eventually becoming the U.S. Supreme Court case known as *Hollingsworth v. Perry* (2013), so, too, was a case involving the federal government's Defense of Marriage Act, or DOMA. That law, passed by Congress in 1996 and signed by President Bill Clinton, forbade the federal government from recognizing the marriages of same-sex couples, even if they were legal in a specific state. And it released states from their obligation to recognize same-sex marriages performed in states that allow them. The federal aspect of that law—by which the government would not honor the marriages of some states in such policy areas as the tax code, Social Security, and military benefits—led to a U.S. Supreme Court challenge in the case *United States v. Windsor* (2013). The Supreme Court decided both cases in the summer of 2013, in the process almost, but not quite, creating a constitutional right to legal marriage regardless of sex.

Figure 8.11 **Percentage of U.S. population living in states where same-sex marriage is legal, by date the new laws took effect**

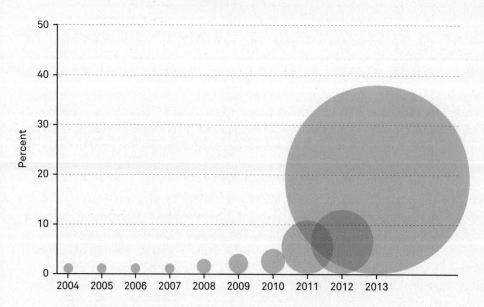

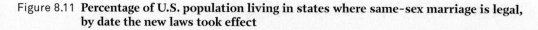 2004 – Massachusetts, by state supreme judicial court decision

2008 – Connecticut, by state supreme court decision

2009 – Iowa, by state supreme court decision;
Vermont, by vote of the state legislature (overriding the governor's veto)

2010 – New Hampshire, by vote of the state legislature;
Washington, D.C., by vote of the city council

2011 – New York, by vote of the state legislature

2012 – Washington, Maine, Maryland, all by majority of voters in
state referendums

2013 – Delaware, Rhode Island, Minnesota, Illinois, and Hawaii, all by vote of their
state legislatures; New Jersey and New Mexico, by state supreme court
decision; California, by U.S. Supreme Court, which let stand a lower court
ruling that the state's ban on same-sex marriage was unconstitutional

SOURCE: Author's calculations from Census Bureau data and various sources, as of December 2013.

In *United States v. Windsor,* Edith Windsor, who married her wife, Thea Spyer, in Canada in 1997 after a 40-year engagement, protested the federal government's refusal to recognize their marriage. The cost of that refusal was tangible: Windsor had to pay more than $600,000 in taxes when Spyer died (Applebome 2012). The estate would not have been taxed if Spyer or Windsor were male and the marriage was considered valid by the federal government. In the decision, Justice Anthony Kennedy wrote that denying legally married couples federal benefits harmed those couples without any justification. He declared that denying federal recognition to married couples creates a system of "second-class marriages" for no other reason than to "impose inequality," that it "humiliates tens of thousands of children now being raised by same-sex couples," and "makes it even more difficult for the children to understand the integrity and closeness of their own family and its concord with other families in their community and in their daily lives." At the same time, the U.S. Supreme Court let stand Judge Walker's decision allowing same-sex marriage in California on technical grounds.

The result of the two court cases was to shift the national balance in favor of same-sex marriage. The court did not go so far as to overturn the state bans on same-sex marriage that remained in effect. But in very clear language, the court cast legal suspicion on those bans, and a new round of legal challenges seeks to bring those laws under scrutiny in the hope of creating a national right to marriage for same-sex couples, like the right to interracial marriage established in *Loving v. Virginia*. In fact, by the end of 2013 a federal judge—using the precedent set in the Windsor decision—overturned the state of Utah's ban on same-sex marriage, which had been approved by the conservative majority of its voters (Eckholm 2013). The decision was immediately appealed.

After the *Windsor* decision, President Obama directed the federal government to start writing new rules for married couples. The Internal Revenue Service (IRS), Defense Department, Department of Veterans Affairs, Department of State, and other federal agencies have new regulations to grant federal benefits to same-sex couples with valid state marriages (Savage 2013). The IRS rule is especially interesting, because the agency now allows people to file tax returns as a married couple if they were married in a state that allows same-sex marriage, such as Maryland, even if they live in a state that does not, such as neighboring Virginia (Lowrey 2013).

The conflict over same-sex marriage in the United States is part of a global debate. As of 2013, same-sex marriage is legal in 16 countries besides the United States, the largest of which are Brazil, France, England, South Africa, Spain, and Argentina. However, along with those U.S. states that permit same-sex marriage, these countries have a population of about only 650 million, just 8.6 percent of the world's population.

major controversy over the gender of people getting married (Eskridge 1993). But in that decade, the gay population became more visible and, eventually, politically organized. The movement was energized by police crackdowns on gay bars (since homosexuality was illegal). The most famous occurred at New York City's Stonewall Inn in 1969, which resulted in a riot as the bar's patrons fought back (Armstrong and Crage 2006).

In 1988, the General Social Survey asked U.S. adults whether they agreed with the statement, "Homosexual couples should have the right to marry one another." Seventy-three percent disagreed and only 12 percent agreed (the rest were unsure). But marriage was not a prominent issue in the gay rights movement until the 1990s. Originally, most members of the gay and lesbian community were not interested in marriage rights, and some feminists joined them, arguing

# 9 Families and Children

In Chapter 6, we saw celebrity Ellen DeGeneres make her sexual orientation part of her public image on national TV. Later, Ellen married the actress Portia de Rossi. As a married couple, it might seem obvious that the two had become a family. Rossi even legally changed her last name to DeGeneres. And yet when rumors spread that they were going to have a child, the headlines were all about whether they were ready to "start a family" (Berman 2009). And that's not just because they're a lesbian couple; the phrase "start a family" is commonly used to refer to couples that are having a first child. The often unspoken assumption is that childless couples somehow add up to less than a family.

As we learned in Chapter 1, Americans have long debated which biological, legal, and emotional connections create families. That debate has intensified as family patterns have become more diverse. Most of the concern focuses on whether *other* people's situations really count as families. For example, it might seem obvious to the people involved that "two women living together as a couple with one or more of their children" constitute a family. But when that description was read to Americans in a national survey, only 55 percent of respondents agreed that such a group should be considered a family (Powell et al. 2010). The persistence of the common euphemism "start a family" shows that children are a vital part of the cultural image of family life. But the fact that a lesbian couple with children might not be considered a family shows that the context in which families raise children is also part of that popular image.

Another example helps illustrate the way that having children completes the picture of a family for so many people. In an interview with researcher Diana Parry (2005:281), a woman named Heidi explained why she and her longtime boyfriend got married only after they decided to have children: "We probably wouldn't have gotten married if we hadn't decided to have kids. We had a great relationship, we'd been together for six years, we had owned a house together

Do you consider Specialist Alexis Hutchinson and her son, Kamani, a family? Her childcare plans fell through just before deployment, and she chose her son over her military commitment, for which the Army arrested and later discharged her.

for three years, everything was going fine and there was no real reason to make that next step except kids." Before having children, in other words, Heidi and her boyfriend were not a family, even though they lived together for years in a committed relationship. But having children called for a more complete family identity, one that included marriage.

In this chapter, we will investigate who has children and who doesn't as well as how the children are raised, or—as many Americans now might say—how they are "parented."

# Childbearing

A glance at national statistics tells us that most American families have one to three children, with two being the most common. This is much lower than in the distant past, as family sizes declined for most of the twentieth century. (The exception was the baby boom period of 1946–1964, when most families had three or four children; see Chapter 2.) But that simple history glosses over a vast and growing diversity of family experiences. In the last few decades, several changes in particular have complicated this picture. Probably most important, more children now are born to parents who are not married. In 2011, a record high of 41 percent of births were to unmarried women (J. Martin et al. 2013). The trend toward single motherhood is commonly recognized, but some other recent changes are less so:

- About a third of unmarried parents are actually living together (cohabiting) at the time of the birth (U.S. Census Bureau 2011d).

- While fewer parents are married now than in the past, ironically, many children are involved with *more* than two parents. That is because a growing number of families include stepparents and siblings from parents' previous relationships. In fact, more than one-quarter of those parents with two or more children have had children with two partners or more (Dorius 2011).

- The number of women reaching age 45 without having any children has doubled since the 1980s. And because more families are having their first children at older ages, there are more adults—singles and couples—spending much of their lives without children (Abma and Martinez 2006).

Each of these facts suggests that the organization of American family life is changing markedly in ways that increase the diversity of family experiences (Smock and Greenland 2010). For those who have children, the structure of their families and the relationships around them reflect a broadening range of practices. And the growth of childless families—and families with fewer children, born later—has moved children out of the center of family life, at least for some adults.

Before we delve into these patterns, we will need to establish some terms and concepts for the study of families and children. I will use the informal expression "have children" to mean either biologically producing or adopting children. When someone "has" a child in either of these ways, he or she becomes a **parent**, an adult intimately responsible for the care and rearing of a child. We may identify **biological parents** as the adults whose bodies produce a child, including the father's sperm and the mother's egg. (If a different woman carries the fetus to term before it is born, as in the case of surrogate parenting, she is not considered a biological parent.) **Adoptive parents**, on the other hand, are parents to a child they did not produce biologically. In the United States today, adoption is usually a legal arrangement, with rights and obligations enforced by government authorities; but it may be informal as well, as with some stepparents or partners of a biological parent.

You may notice that this definition of parents is not restricted to a mother-father couple; in fact, it does not include either a specific number of parents or their genders. In many families, the parenting roles are more fluid than that, especially when the law does not set the rules, as in the case of same-sex parents in some places (which is one reason many same-sex couples want to make their marriages legal). The most common example of this ambiguity occurs in the case of stepparents interacting with biological parents and their children—the "blended family" situation to which we will return in Chapter 10. And it is even more complicated when the adults involved are not married but have only informal relationships (Edin, Tach, and Mincy 2009).

Individuals who are able to produce children biologically are commonly described as "fertile" (as opposed to those who experience infertility). But when I speak of **fertility**, I use it in the sense of the number of children born in a society or among a particular group. There are several ways of quantifying fertility, which we need not describe in detail here (Weeks 2011). When possible, I use a number that is simple to grasp: the **total fertility rate**, which is the number of children born to the average woman in her lifetime. For example, the U.S. total fertility rate in 2012 was 1.9. That means that the average woman would have almost two children over the course of her reproductive years if birth rates stayed the same.

Fertility rates are generally measured for women—mothers—rather than men because the information comes from birth certificates, which do not always specify the father (even though fathers remain legally responsible as parents). This social science custom is unfortunate because it neglects the importance of fathers (Guzzo and Furstenberg 2007).

Besides being relatively easy to understand, the total fertility rate is also useful for thinking about populations as a whole, such as countries or ethnic groups. If a country has a total fertility rate of more than 2.1 or so, the population will usually grow; if the rate is lower than that, it will eventually start to shrink. That is because if each woman bears two children, they "replace" herself and her partner in the population. Because some people don't survive to produce children or choose not to produce children, demographers refer to a total fertility rate of 2.1—rather than exactly 2.0—as "replacement fertility."

As mentioned earlier, the most common number of children for American women to have is currently two; and as Figure 9.1 shows, about one-third of women have borne two children by the time they turn 45 years old. Still,

**parent**

An adult intimately responsible for the care and rearing of a child.

**biological parents**

The adults whose bodies—including the father's sperm and the mother's egg—produce a child.

**adoptive parents**

Parents to a child they did not produce biologically.

**fertility**

The number of children born in a society or among a particular group.

**total fertility rate**

The number of children born to the average woman in her lifetime.

Figure 9.1 **Number of children born by the time a woman reaches age 45**

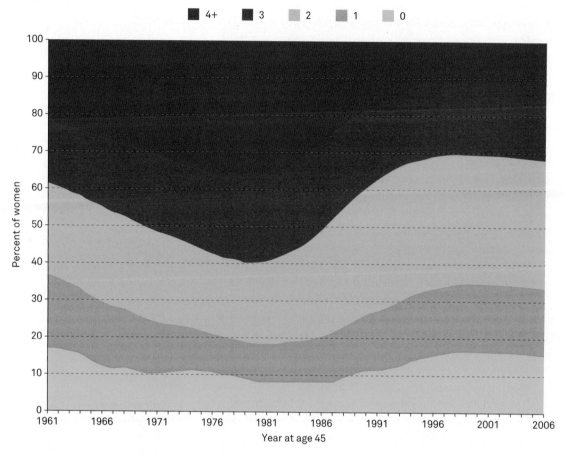

SOURCE: National Center for Health Statistics (2010).

one-third have had three or more children and one-third have had only one or none by the time they turn 45. And as recently as the 1980s, as the parents of the baby boom were reaching the end of their childbearing years, the most common number of children was four. More than a third of baby boom mothers had four children each. By 2006, only about 12 percent of women turning 45 had that number of children. In the remainder of this section, I will discuss some recent patterns of childbearing relating to marital status, race/ethnicity, and education.

## Unmarried Parents

As noted earlier, 41 percent of all children born in the United States are born to parents who aren't married, up from 28 percent in 1990 (see Figure 9.2). This trend is closely related to the decline of marriage that we observed in Chapter 8. That is, since the 1980s, marriage has declined more than childbearing, causing an increase in the number of unmarried parents. However, within this trend, there are people who become single parents in different ways:

- Young adults, either alone or with a partner they are not ready or willing to marry. These families are more likely to be poor than most other families (McKeever and Wolfinger 2011).

- Older women who are single—by chance or by choice—who decide to have children as single parents even though they might have preferred to be married first. Rather than wait for a marriage that might not occur, they adopt a child, use a sperm donor, or get pregnant with a man they're not planning to parent with (maybe even a man they live with). These families are less likely to be poor (Hertz 2006).

- Divorced people who are in serious relationships but not remarried. About 1 in 5 of them are living with a partner. They may eventually marry, but for some the divorce experience and the complications of the previous marriage are holding them back (S. Brown 2000).

- Finally, gay and lesbian couples who aren't married, either because they choose not to marry or because the law prohibits their marriage (Gates et al. 2007).

## Race and Ethnicity

We saw in Chapter 3 that single parenthood is much more common in some groups than in others. This is especially true among American Indian, Black, and Puerto Rican families, for whom more than half of all children are born to parents who are not married. However, there also are differences in how many children members of the major racial and ethnic groups have, as Figure 9.3 shows. The total fertility rates indicate that Latina women on average have almost 2.5 children, African Americans have about 2, while Whites, Asians, and American Indians have the fewest.

The relatively high fertility rate among Latinos partly explains the growth of their population in the country as a whole, although immigration plays a major role as well (see Chapter 3). There are several reasons for this pattern (Landale and Oropesa 2007). First, most Latinos are descended from relatively recent immigrants—people who came from Latin American countries where fertility rates are higher than they are here. In their communities, having more children is a cultural expectation, and it's encouraged by the Catholic Church (Cutright, Hout, and Johnson 1976). (Catholic authorities actually prohibit the use of birth control, and although most Catholics today do not follow that rule, they still tend to have more children than average.) Not surprisingly, therefore, first-generation immigrants tend to have more children than those whose families immigrated in earlier generations. Second, groups with lower levels of education, such as

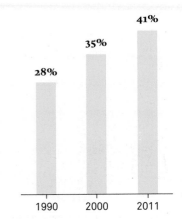

Figure 9.2 **Percentage of births to unmarried women**

SOURCE: U.S. Census Bureau (2011d); J. Martin et al. (2013).

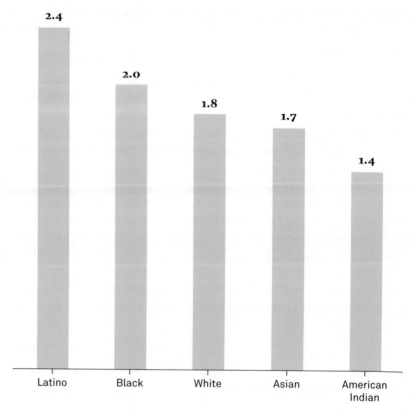

Figure 9.3  **Total fertility rates, by race/ethnicity: expected lifetime births per woman, 2010**

SOURCE: Martin et al. (2012).

Latinos, usually have higher fertility rates. And third, the immigrant Latino population includes many young, healthy adults—those who were most ready and able to move to a new country in search of better employment opportunities—who also tend to have large families.

# Education

Education is the final fertility pattern in this overview. The long-standing pattern, not just in the United States but around the world, is that women with lower levels of education have more children (Kravdal and Rindfuss 2008). If you check the number of children for women in their 40s, when most are done with childbearing, the difference is substantial. Women who did not finish high school have an average of 2.6 children, compared with 1.8 or fewer among those with bachelor's degrees (see Figure 9.4). This is partly because some women stop their education after they have children—whether out of choice or necessity—while others postpone childbearing until they have finished school. As a result, those with higher education have children later in life (when they have fewer remaining childbearing years), while those with less education start having children younger and end up having more. Perhaps more important, however, once they have higher education, women face the prospect of giving up higher incomes and career status if they decide to have more children. This is known as an **opportunity cost**, the price one pays for choosing the less lucrative of the available options. In contrast, those whose lives are more devoted to child rearing in young adulthood—rather than advanced education—have less to lose (financially, at least) by having additional children.

If we link education patterns in childbearing to the economic costs and benefits experienced by the parents, it might imply that people carefully plan out their childbearing and educational careers. In fact, clear evidence of conscious birth planning emerged during the recession of the late 2000s, when birth rates fell sharply for women of all ages—except those age 40 and over (Sutton, Hamilton, and Mathews 2011). It appears that many younger women deliberately postponed having children because of economic hardship or uncertainty, while women who were nearing the end of their childbearing years had no such luxury, deciding to have children even though it might mean difficult economic sacrifices. That pattern shows the extent to which many couples plan their births around their economic circumstances.

Clearly, however, careful planning is not always the rule. Half of all pregnancies are identified as "unintended," meaning the woman was not trying to

**opportunity cost**

The price one pays for choosing the less lucrative of the available options.

Figure 9.4 **Average number of children ever born to women ages 40 to 44, by educational level, 2010**

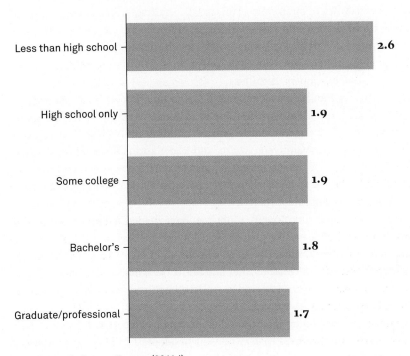

SOURCE: U.S. Census Bureau (2011d).

get pregnant at the time, though she may have wanted to at some later time (Finer and Henshaw 2006). An especially large portion of births among people with less education are unintended. In fact, if we only count those women who had children only when they fully intended to, the education differences in the number of children mostly disappear (Musick et al. 2009). The high frequency of unintended births, especially among women or couples with less education or economic resources, partly results from their lack of access to good quality medical care, including contraception and health education.

# Adoption

Half a century ago, most adoptions were secretive. Private agencies tried to match adoptive parents with children who were as similar to them as possible—especially racially. And children with medical or developmental problems were almost always shunned in the process (Herman 2008). Most parents did not want their adopted children to know of their origins, and there was little or no contact between the adoptive family and the birth family (usually a poor single mother). Since then, adoption has become much less common, but it is so much more open and acceptable that we probably discuss it more (Fisher 2003).

The main reason adoption became less common after the 1960s is the falling number of babies relinquished by birth parents. Because the stigma associated with unmarried motherhood has declined, unmarried young women are more willing and able to parent their own children. At the same time, with the growing availability of birth control (discussed in Chapter 6) and the legality of abortion, those women who are not willing or able to be parents are less likely to bear children. And fertility treatments offer an alternative to more parents who can't conceive on their own. Currently, only 2.1 percent of U.S. children—about 1.5 million—live in adoptive families.

On the other hand, adoptions have become much more open. Almost all adopted children now know that they live in an adoptive family. And most adoptions today include an agreement to put the children in touch with their birth family at some point (Vandivere, Malm, and Radel 2009). Research shows that by the time they reach adolescence, the great majority of adopted children say they are glad they got to know their birth parents. Child development experts believe that this is helpful for their sense of identity and security. One teenager's story illustrates how such "open" adoptions have helped reduce the stigma of adoption: "I remember in, like fifth grade, this one girl was like, 'I feel so sorry for you because your parents, like, gave you up,' and I'm just like, 'You know it's not like that. I've met my birthmother and know the whole story, and she loved me and still does and did me a favor letting me be raised, you know, in a better situation'" (Berge et al. 2006:1024).

Adopted children today can be divided into three categories. A national survey in the mid-2000s found that 37 percent of adopted children were adopted through the foster care system, which provides temporary care of children whose parents or other family members are unable to care for them. Another 38 percent were born in the United States and adopted through private services, usually as newborns. Finally, 25 percent were internationally adopted—that is, born in other countries and adopted by American parents (Vandivere, Malm, and Radel 2009).

International adoption is a complicated and sometimes contentious issue. And it has a high public profile, partly due to adoptions by celebrities such as Madonna and Angelina Jolie. But these adoptions also attract attention because they usually create multiracial families, which are easily noticeable in the American social environment (Kreider 2007). From the early 1990s to the mid-2000s, it appeared that there was an ever-increasing flow of children adopted into the United States to be the children of American parents. At the peak in 2004, when almost 23,000 children were adopted abroad, the largest numbers were coming from China, Russia, South Korea, and Guatemala (see Figure 9.5). However, in the nine years that followed, the number dropped dramatically, as the flow of children from each of those countries shrank. The decline was part of a worldwide trend in which international adoption was more closely scrutinized for ethical and legal violations. In the case of Guatemala, for example, adoptions to the United States were halted entirely when the U.S. government decided that the legal system in that country was not adequately safeguarding the poor women and their children who were entering the system.

Figure 9.5 **Children adopted into the United States from other countries, 1990–2013**

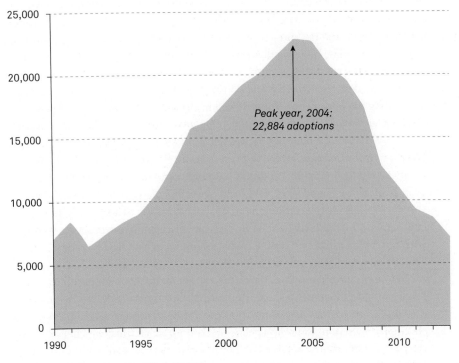

SOURCE: U.S. Department of State (2014).

To facilitate the complicated legal relationships involved in international adoptions, many countries, including the United States, have joined the Hague Adoption Convention (Bureau of Consular Affairs 2011). The convention is an international agreement that seeks to facilitate adoptions in the best interests of children who need families. One of its goals is to ensure that efforts are made to find adoptive families in a child's home country before placing the child into an international adoption. And it attempts to strengthen protections against the sale or trafficking of children. In fact, one consequence of this international effort appears to be a decline in the number of international adoptions, but advocates hope it will also improve adoption practices around the world.

Although adoption generally has become more open and less stigmatized, most couples experiencing infertility do not try to adopt children. That suggests that they do not consider adoption as valuable or rewarding as having a child through infertility treatments or deciding not to have children at all (Fisher 2003). On the other hand, research shows that those parents who do adopt make unusually large investments in their children's well-being, in terms of both time and money, even after accounting for their relatively high levels of economic resources (Hamilton, Cheng, and Powell 2007).

# Why (Not) Have Children?

It would be useful to be able to characterize neatly the reasons people have children. Unfortunately, parents and potential parents are usually quite vague in their explanations. Consider Jack, a White 33-year-old who was living with his girlfriend when she became pregnant (Augustine, Nelson, and Edin 2009:110). Age 19 at the time, he remembered: "I was young, but I was ready. I thought I was okay, 'Let's start this family.' I was excited. I was a little scared. I loved her. She was my best friend. We could do this together."

Among the poor people interviewed in that study, the majority of pregnancies were not planned, but not completely unexpected either. More than having a reason *to* have children, they lacked the motivation to *prevent* it. In hindsight, however, the event takes on the full meaning of a life story. A 48-year-old Puerto Rican named Carlos said, "If I didn't have kids right now, I probably would have been dead. I have friends that died from overdoses of drugs, AIDS, alcoholic seizures and all kinds of stuff and most of those guys were those that didn't have children and I would have ended up like one of them, like a bachelor type guy with no kids and a heavy kind of addiction problem and dead by now" (Augustine, Nelson, and Edin 2009:110).

Before the development of a social safety net for old people—pensions, Social Security, and government-subsidized health care for the elderly—having children was an important part of most people's long-term survival plan. Even after children's labor stopped being a prime motivation for fertility, which was mostly the case in agricultural settings, parents hoped that their adult children would care for them in their retiring years. Now, however, raising children is a major expense, an investment that is expected to pay off not so much economically as emotionally and symbolically (Schoen et al. 1997).

Among the well-off, parents hope that their children will be a source of pride and achievement, bringing them happiness and satisfaction—and maybe showing off the family's successes to the wider community. And among the poor, having children serves as an important source of meaning and accomplishment that is not possible through economic means. In a stressful, unstable world of economic uncertainty, many poor people—especially women—hope that their children will provide a loving center to their lives (Edin and Kefalas 2005).

On the other hand, there are plenty of good reasons why people *don't* have children. In some cases, this reflects a deliberate choice on the part of the couple. In other cases, the decision is forced on them by circumstances or by nature. But whether voluntary or involuntary, the decision not to have children can be as life changing as the decision to "start a family."

# Abortion

Approximately 1.2 million abortions were performed in the United States in 2008, each reflecting the decision of a woman (and perhaps her partner) who was not ready, willing, or able to bear a child at the time of her pregnancy (Ventura et al. 2012). This represents 18 percent of the pregnancies in that year (another 17 percent resulted in miscarriage). The vast majority of these abortions (92 percent) take place in the first three months, or trimester, of pregnancy (Pazol et al. 2012). The reasons for terminating a pregnancy may be as complicated as those for having a baby. Sometimes, of course, the pregnancy must be terminated for medical reasons related to either the fetus or the mother. But the most common reasons offered refer to time and resource constraints, such as the need to finish school, the costs of caring for a child, or the need to care for other family members, including older children (Finer et al. 2005). As noted in Chapter 5, there are some sex-selecting abortions in the United States, but this practice remains quite rare in this country.

Not surprisingly, the groups of women more likely to have unintended pregnancies—single women, those with low incomes or education, and Black women—are also more likely to have abortions (R. Jones, Finer, and Singh 2010). The breakdown of pregnancy outcomes by marital status clearly shows the difference in abortions (see Figure 9.6). Among women who aren't married, 32 percent of pregnancies are terminated by abortion, compared with just 6 percent among married women.

Despite the Supreme Court's ruling, in the 1973 case known as *Roe v. Wade*, that a woman's right to abortion is protected as a private decision under the Constitution, the issue remains a divisive one in American politics (Luker 1984). The Gallup poll, which since the early 1990s has been asking Americans whether they consider themselves "pro-choice" (in favor of abortion rights) or "pro-life," has tracked a shift against abortion rights. In 2009, for the first time, the "pro-life" respondents reached a majority, and as of 2013, "pro-life"

Figure 9.6 **Pregnancy outcomes, by marital status (percentage of pregnancies)**

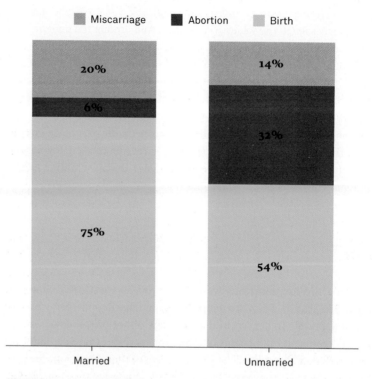

SOURCE: Ventura et al. (2012).

outnumbered "pro-choice" by a slim 48 percent to 45 percent. However, only 20 percent agree with the statement that abortion should be "illegal under all circumstances" (Gallup 2013).

With the right to abortion protected at the federal level by the courts, opposition has taken a variety of forms (McBride 2008). Rather than challenge the Supreme Court's decision directly, opponents have worked successfully to prohibit the government from spending public money on abortions for poor women and to restrict the practice as much as possible at the state level. For example, states have limited insurance coverage for abortions, imposed waiting periods before an abortion can be obtained, required women to view antiabortion pamphlets—or even an ultrasound image of their own fetus—and required parental involvement when the woman is below a certain age (Eckholm 2014). At the extreme, some abortion providers have been attacked, and several have even been murdered. Needless to say, no other medical procedure has been subjected to such a degree of political scrutiny.

This political campaign may have contributed to a downward trend in abortions, as the rate at which American women obtain abortions has fallen for several decades. At the peak of abortion rates, in 1990, there were 17.4 abortions for every 1,000 women of childbearing age. By 2007, that number had fallen to 16.0, a drop of 8 percent (Pazol et al. 2011). The decline is partly the result of couples' increased use of contraception, but it also reflects reduced access to abortion services. For example, one study found that one-third of women live in a county with no abortion service provider (R. Jones et al. 2008).

# Infertility

The flip side of unintended pregnancies is unsuccessful ones, as reflected in the experience of infertility. The usual definition of **infertility** is the failure of a couple to have a successful pregnancy despite deliberately having sex without contraception. Although the time frame for the definition is arbitrary, demographers use a period of 12 months of sex without contraception to define the condition. Such a general description is much easier to apply than a determination of the cause for a given couple, which may be the quality and quantity of their reproductive gametes (eggs and sperm), the physical and hormonal characteristics of the woman's body, and so on. Using this rather crude definition, we can say that worldwide, about 9 percent of couples experience infertility in a given year (Boivin et al. 2007). In the United States, the rate of infertility is lower, around 7 percent.

The causes of infertility are many. People who are older and in poorer overall health are more likely to experience infertility. Smoking, obesity, and a history of sexually transmitted infections also increase the problem. But a certain incidence of infertility appears to be inevitable even among people who are young and healthy. In the United States, the pattern of infertility is consistent with other kinds of inequality: White women are the least likely to experience infertility, followed by Hispanic and Black women; and women with higher levels of education have lower rates than those with less education (see Figure 9.7). We assume that these patterns are the result of better overall health among White women and those with more education.

Historically, failure to produce children cast shame on the wife. As far back as the stories in the Jewish Torah (Old Testament), both Abraham's and Jacob's wives, after years of infertility, offered up their maidservants to produce children (Genesis 16:1; 28:30). Infertility, in other words, justified infidelity. It was the woman's failure to reproduce that was to be overcome, and no one blamed the husband for having sex with the maidservant. Today, we know that male or female medical conditions are equally likely to cause infertility (so perhaps Abraham and Jacob could have tried providing their wives with a manservant instead).

With medical advances, infertility has come to be seen as a treatable problem, and an expanding number of methods are available. Treatment is something of a mixed blessing, however. For some families, the path of medical treatment draws them into a long, expensive, physically taxing process that keeps the spotlight on their intimate lives and puts pressure on their mental health, their finances, and their marriages (Whiteford and Gonzalez 1995). Because most treatments are more invasive to the woman than to the man, the burden that women historically felt in some ways persists. In fact, the stress associated with the infertility treatment itself—especially for the woman—is a growing area of concern among psychologists (Cousineau and Domar 2007).

**infertility**

The failure of a couple to have a successful pregnancy despite deliberately having sex without contraception.

Figure 9.10 **Percentage of all children living in the home of a grandparent**

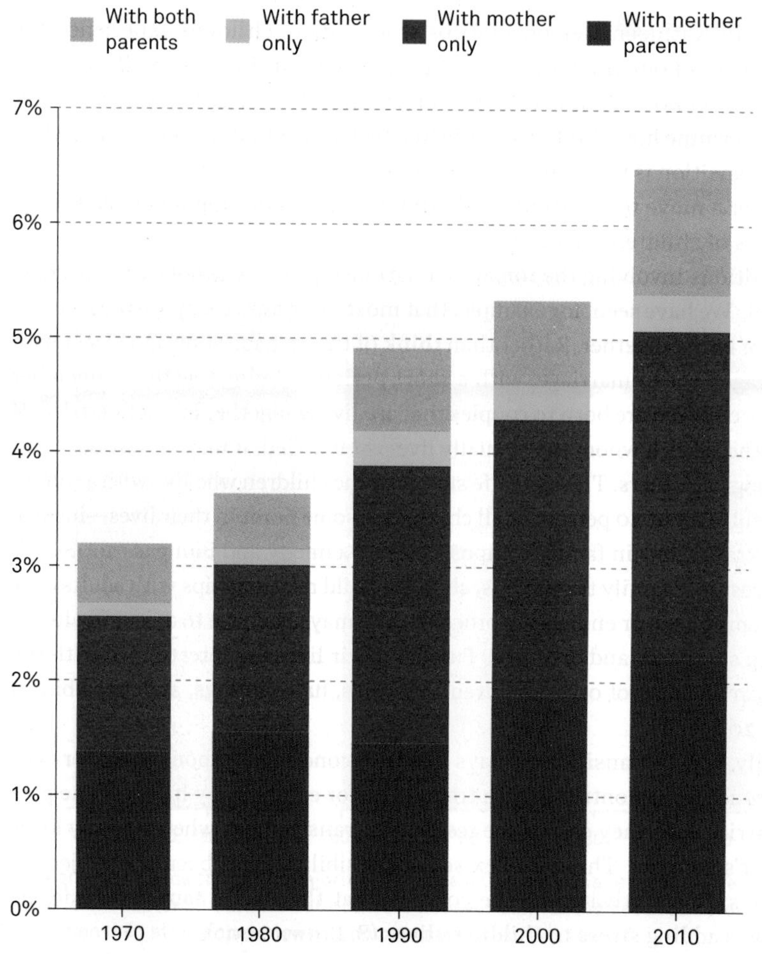
With both parents
With father only
With mother only
With neither parent
7%
6%
5%
4%
3%
2%
1%
0%
1970
1980
1990
2000
2010

SOURCE: U.S. Census Bureau (2013g).

the better, however, remember that a child moving into her or his grandparents' house because the family has trouble paying the rent is experiencing a transition that may add stress to the child's development.

# Parenting

**parenting**

The activity of raising a child.

Simply put, **parenting** is the activity of raising a child. Although the term is less than 100 years old in English, the idea of discussing how best to care for and manage the lives of children is not new. Nevertheless, the term *parenting* exploded into common use in the 1970s, along with a crush of popular books and magazines peddling all kinds of advice to all kinds of parents (P. Cohen 2010a).

As we move into a discussion of parenting, let's pause to ask what parents are attempting to accomplish with their children—and what children get from parents. I will skip over money and financial resources for the moment, though we will return to that issue in more depth later. In terms of parental behavior, we might say that parents provide—or try to provide—three broad categories of skills or resources to their children (Lewis 2012):

- *Socialization.* As defined in Chapter 5, socialization allows individuals to internalize elements of the social structure into their own personality. Successful socialization is not just turning children into mimics of the culture around them. Rather, it prepares them for what they will encounter in social interactions and allows them to see how they fit in social situations with less confusion and stress.

- *Social bonds.* As we saw in Chapter 2, parents are the first people with whom children build the stable bonds they need as a foundation of learning and development. Without early, strong emotional bonds with adults, children have difficulty establishing secure relationships with others as they grow and mature.

- *Social networks.* An obvious example of social networks is parents helping their children get a job with a friend or colleague. But the networking that parents do with their children is much more extensive and subtle than that, and it starts much earlier. Deliberately or not, parents usually facilitate an entire web of friends and neighbors, relatives, potential mentors, teachers, and peers that shapes the social environment of their children. Naturally,

A deluge of parenting books that both reflects and exacerbates parental anxiety.

such a network provides a mixture of positive and negative influences, so that maintaining and supervising it is a central part of parenting.

Parenting, then, is made up of many different parts and many relationships that all take place in a changing social environment that varies greatly from place to place. As parents develop a mental map of their goals and resources, they start with an image of childhood—who children are and what they need and deserve. As we will see, that mental image is a product of the historical moment.

## The Meaning of Childhood

Before thinking about today's American children, consider briefly their ancestors in two historical periods. First consider the chimney sweeps of the early industrial cities in the United States, United Kingdom, and elsewhere. Orphans—children whose parents were either dead or too ill or too poor to care for them—worked as "apprentices" to thousands of chimney sweeps. Their masters would send the (mostly) boys as young as 4 years old into the long, hot, narrow shafts to sweep out soot left behind by burning coal (Mukherjee 2010:237–239). This was necessary to prevent the soot from catching fire. In the United States, the masters were usually African Americans, both slave and free (Gilje and Rock 1994). The children suffered egregiously from this practice, sometimes becoming trapped and either getting burned or suffocating, sometimes contracting various illnesses, including cancer. Over the course of 100 years, a series of laws raised the minimum age at which children could work in chimneys, until the practice eventually died out. What had once seemed an acceptable practice to most people in the cities eventually looked like an appalling abuse of innocent children.

Decades later, in the American cities of a century ago, children appeared to be everywhere. They roamed the streets as delivery boys and girls, vendors, or shoe shiners. In the afternoons and evenings they played in the streets by the thousands—not in the parks, ball fields, playgrounds, malls, gymnastics studios, or playrooms where many play today. In the structure of urban life—the streets, buildings, workplaces, and even homes—children seemed to be an afterthought; except for the schools, there was no place for them. Even their bedrooms were often shared with adults, some of whom were unrelated renters.

On January 4, 1911, the *New York Times* reported that almost 200 children had been killed in street accidents in the city the previous year by cars, trolleys, and wagons. Not only were children killed by street vehicles, they also were routinely crushed by freight trains that passed through the poor neighborhoods of the city. One official said, "Something will have to be done here soon to force tenement mothers to keep their children off the streets and on the sidewalks" ("Killed in Streets," 1911).

The uproar that followed these deaths, which included protests and marches, reflected the growing clash between old and new visions of childhood. Following the laws prohibiting children being sent up chimneys, the city eventually implemented traffic safety laws and regulations and went on to expand public

### KILLED IN STREETS OF THE CITY IN 1910

**Death Toll of Vehicular Traffic Was 376, While 930 Persons Were Injured.**

**MORE THAN HALF CHILDREN**

**Highways Protective Association Gives Statistics and Makes Plans to Safeguard the Public.**

Headlines like this, in the *New York Times*, January 4, 1911, called attention to the perils of modern urban life for children.

parks and playgrounds, the infrastructure of modern childhood we know so well today (Frost 2010). What happened? In 2009 there were only 14 children killed in motor vehicle accidents in New York City (including those inside and outside of vehicles)—even though the city's population has grown more than 70 percent (J. Kennedy 2011).

As we saw in Chapter 2, the number of children surviving to adulthood increased dramatically over the nineteenth century, and partly for that reason, parents started having fewer children. Children's usefulness as laborers also decreased. From farm labor to chimney sweeping to factory work, children's labor was once everywhere. But as the new industrial workplace increasingly demanded workers with higher skills and at least a minimal education, a 17-year-old who could read and write was eventually much more useful than an uneducated 10-year-old. And growing concern with child safety contributed to a period of vigorous policy reform during the Progressive Era of the early twentieth century (Hindman 2002). According to sociologist Viviana Zelizer (1985), American children—fewer of them and more precious—were in the midst of a transformation, losing their *economic* value while achieving a newfound *emotional* value that was considered "priceless."

That development was apparent in the treatment of children without families. In the nineteenth century, if such children could be sold to foster families, they might escape the dangerous and miserable life of an orphanage. This system was not based on the need for children to be cared for, but on the premise that children should work for their upkeep—which is what they did for their foster families (who paid for them). Only toward the end of the century did advocates for children start asserting their rights to have a loving family free from exploitation. By the early twentieth century, public policy had shifted to favor foster care or adoption whenever possible—not so the children could work for their foster families, but so they could have something like a family life. The moral ideal of families and childhood had shifted.

The paradox of priceless childhood is how expensive it is. Setting aside all the public costs associated with raising children—education, medical care, product safety inspectors, and so on—the costs for a family are daunting. The parents of a typical family with two children today can expect to spend between $160,000 and $370,000 to raise each child up to age 17, depending on how rich the family is (see Story Behind the Numbers). Those are not just the costs of food, clothing, or even private schools. People with children also spend more on things like housing—like extra bedrooms, bathrooms, or a yard—translating into a cost of more than $125,000 per child for families in the high-income group. Much of this spending represents a desire on the part of today's parents to give their children whatever it takes to stay ahead in a world filled with uncertainty.

## Competition and Insecurity

In the last few years, child well-being experts have found it necessary to advise parents to let their children *play* more. It might seem odd that such experts are

# The high, and highly unequal, cost of raising children

Low Family Income (<$57,000)

High Family Income (>$98,000)

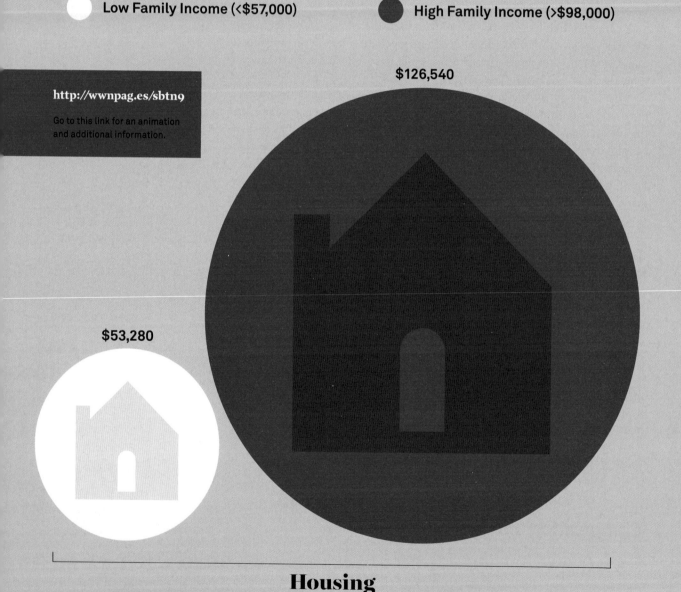

http://wwnpag.es/sbtn9

Go to this link for an animation and additional information.

$126,540

$53,280

**Housing**

Children are so precious that they are priceless. At the same time, of course, they are also very expensive. For a family with an income of less than $57,000 per year, a married couple with two children can expect to spend about $160,000 to raise each child up through age 17. A family with an income over $98,000 can expect to spend much more— up to $370,000. Expenses for those whose children go to college — or continue living in the family home after age 18 — add even more to that bill.

People with children spend more on food, clothing, and education, but they also spend more on amenities like extra bedrooms and bathrooms, or a yard. Rich parents spend more, which means rich children cost more. It also means more consumption by children of the rich, and that illustrates how much inequality is experienced by children.

*Source: Lino (2010).*

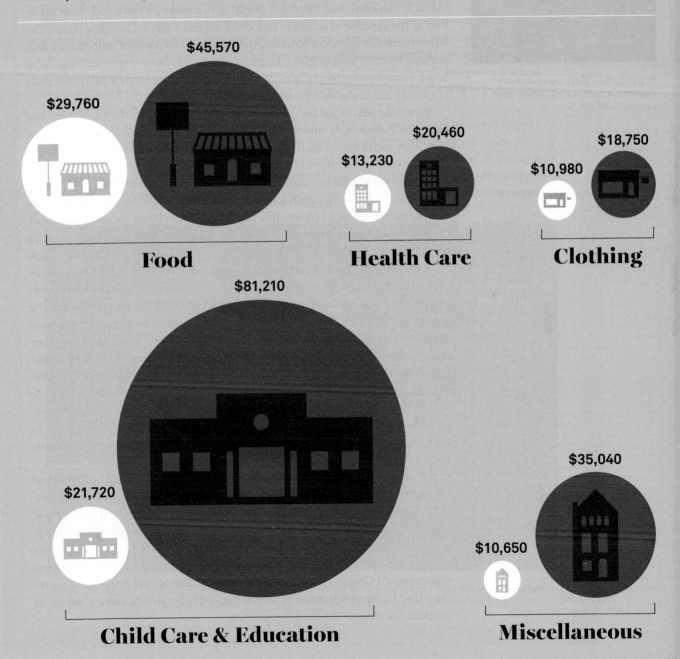

$29,760

$45,570

**Food**

$13,230

$20,460

**Health Care**

$10,980

$18,750

**Clothing**

$81,210

$21,720

**Child Care & Education**

$35,040

$10,650

**Miscellaneous**

The involved father ideal is now nearly universally accepted, and when men are asked to describe a father's responsibilities, their answers match this ideal quite closely. Research shows that most new fathers embrace the involved father ideal completely: they reject the suggestion that their economic role is more important than spending time with their children, and they believe that fathers must be as involved as mothers in their children's development (Lewis 2012). And despite the middle-class provider image that many people hold up as a model, many poor fathers have eagerly embraced the involved father ideal (Edin and Nelson 2013). Asked to choose the most important task for a father, almost two-thirds choose "show the child love and affection," while only 6 percent cite financial provision (see Figure 9.16).

Of course, the answers to a survey asked of men with newborn babies might not be the best indicator of their actual behavior over the lifetime of their children. And in fact, men's involvement on average remains much lower than women's, at least in terms of time spent on caring work. Nevertheless, the shift toward more intensive parenting has not been limited to mothers. Since the 1960s, married fathers have doubled the amount of time they spend one-on-one with their kids (Bianchi 2000). The involved father—as an ideal and as an incipient reality at least—has become a prominent feature of the American family's cultural landscape. As we will see, however, another important aspect of that tableau—divorce and remarriage—has played an important part as well.

# Parenting Advice

Sociologists who study the way people raise their children have often turned to published parenting advice as a source of information. For example, when the question is historical, it may be easier to find published advice than to figure out what parents really did. But advice isn't the same as parenting behavior. How might they differ?

Here's one example of parenting advice gone very wrong, as told by the women's rights activist Elizabeth Cady Stanton (1898[1993]). In the mid-nineteenth century, she decided to read up on parenting, because, as she remembered, "having gone through the ordeal of bearing a child, I was determined, if possible, to keep him." Some friends of hers, however, had a terrible experience at the hands of an "expert":

> They had been so misled by one author, who assured them that the stomach of a child could only hold one tablespoonful [of milk], that they nearly starved their firstborn to death. Though the child dwindled, day by day, and, at the end of a month, looked like a little old man, yet they still stood by the distinguished author. Fortunately, they both went off, one day, and left the child with [his aunt], who thought she would make an experiment and see what a child's stomach could hold.... To her surprise the baby took a pint bottle full of milk, and had the sweetest sleep thereon he had known in his earthly career.

For this workshop, let's consider the pros and cons of expert advice and the source of that advice for parents.

First, select a parenting topic to research. Examples include spanking, TV, exercise, diet and nutrition, potty training, and gender and play. The possibilities are endless. If you are working in groups, each group can take a different subject.

Second, develop a list of three or four advice sources. These could be from a simple Internet search, from a parenting book, or from a historical source in the library.

Third, compare the advice received. Consider these questions:

- What is the original source of the information? For example, was it a research study, personal experience, or a doctor?

- Whom is the advice aimed at? Does it seek to advise mothers, fathers, people with higher or lower levels of education, or a particular racial-ethnic group?

- How effective is it likely to be, and for whom? Can anyone follow the advice, or only some parents—such as those with jobs, lots of money, or helpful relatives?

- What are the motives of the group or individual offering the advice? Are they selling a product, book, or service? Promoting a particular ideology?

Finally, in your group, individual report, or class discussion, consider the outcomes that you think might result from people following—or not following—this advice. If the advice is helpful, what might be done to expand on its approach? If it is not helpful, how can we improve the method used or information presented?

European settlers who encountered them (Queen 1985). Likewise, ancient Jewish laws permitted divorce. Divorce was quite common among upper-class couples in the Roman Empire. But by the time of early Christianity, religious authorities introduced strong rules against divorce, with the Bible intoning, "what therefore God hath joined together, let not man put asunder" (Coontz 2005:86). In practice, however, the Catholic Church did not begin to enforce strict limits on divorce for common people until the eighth century. By the twelfth century, divorce was virtually impossible under Church doctrine. People could separate by mutual agreement (or, more often, one could desert the other), but they couldn't legitimately remarry unless they were granted an annulment, which was almost unheard of.

That history is what makes annulment important to understand. **Annulment of marriage** is a legal or religious determination that the marriage was never valid. After an annulment, the marriage is treated as if it never occurred. The logical distinction between annulment and divorce is what made it possible historically to prohibit divorce but still let some people (usually powerful men) take spouses. Because divorce is much simpler and easier to arrange today, there is little reason for people to try to have their marriages annulled legally. However, religious annulment remains an important issue, mostly for Catholics. Under the doctrine of the Catholic Church, remarriage is permitted only if the marriage is annulled by the Church—that is, judged to have been invalid and therefore not binding on the spouses. Some famous politicians, including presidential candidates John Kerry (a Democrat) and Rudy Giuliani (a Republican), have had marriages annulled by the Church before remarriage, partly to preserve their reputations with Catholic voters (Quaid 2007). As a legal procedure, annulment exists in the United States today but is very rare. It occurs only in cases of deliberate fraud at the time of the marriage, when one of the spouses was unable to consent to the marriage, or if it is discovered that the spouses were too closely related to be permitted to marry (Abrams 2013).

As the issue of annulment suggests, the controversy around divorce has always involved the issue of remarriage. Ending a marriage has never been as controversial as remarrying afterward and especially producing "legitimate" children—those whose parents are legally married—in a subsequent marriage. This tension is one source of the historical conflict between religious and state authorities, which long competed for the power to regulate marriage and divorce. This tension exploded in the sixteenth century, when England's King Henry VIII wanted an annulment so that he could take a new wife. The Roman Catholic pope's refusal to grant that annulment helped convince Henry to leave Catholicism and form the independent Church of England, with himself as its head. (Unfortunately for his new wife, Anne Boleyn, she bore a daughter and then had a series of miscarriages without giving birth to a living son, so Henry executed her before marrying again a few days later.) Although that split with the Catholic Church did not end the power of religious institutions in the realm of marriage and divorce, by placing family regulation under the control of the state it marked a significant historical step toward separating religious from civil authority over family law in Western societies.

Still, as we saw in Chapter 8, despite the separation of church and state

**annulment of marriage**

A legal or religious determination that the marriage was never valid.

enshrined in the U.S. Constitution, the conflict persists between some religious and legal rules and customs governing marriage. Today's debate over "marriage rights" usually concerns same-sex marriage. But in the late nineteenth century, a similarly heated debate revolved around the right to marry for people who had been divorced. At the time, few Americans believed that the "guilty" party in a divorce should be permitted to remarry, but the accusing spouse—often the victim of abuse or abandonment—was seen more sympathetically. Still, conservatives feared that loosening the laws regarding remarriage would open up society to the rule of "free love," encouraging people to swap partners casually without regard for the sacredness of marriage (Cott 2000). In one case, a Catholic bishop in Nebraska declared that anyone who *attended* the wedding of a divorced man would be excommunicated (barred from the Church). Marriage rights advocates defended the principle of divorce and remarriage as a moral choice. As one radical journalist wrote, "It is dishonor to remain in a state of marriage wherein the soul cries out in agony of despair, and the bondage robs life of all its sunshine" (Harris 1906:393).

As divorce entered the twentieth century, it occurred with greater and greater frequency, even in the absence of physical abuse or abandonment. Although it remained quite rare by today's standards, the American public was riveted by the family dramas of celebrities and socialites, especially once the voices of the neglected spouses could be heard in the press (see Changing Culture, "Divorce, American Style").

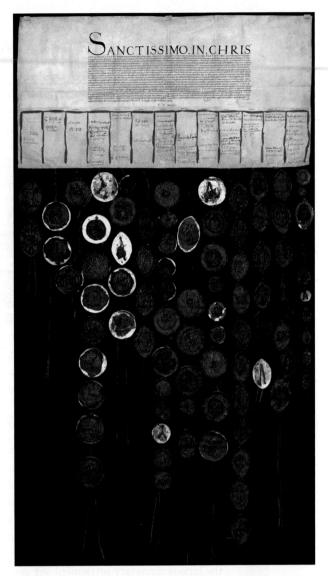

In this letter from 1530, English noblemen demanded that Pope Clement VII annul Henry VIII's marriage to Catherine of Aragon. More than 80 wax seals are attached below the lords' signatures.

# Divorce Rates and Trends

As a family sociologist with an expertise in demography, I have frequently been asked, "What is the divorce rate?" This is really two questions. First, what do we *mean* by the divorce rate? And second, what is the number itself? I will try to avoid a long, technical answer, but each of these questions deserves a little attention.

There is no single definition of "the divorce rate." To see why, consider a few numbers. In 2012, there were an estimated 1.2 million divorces in the United States. I have to say "estimated" because there is no official count of divorces:

mothers (P. Paul 2011). "I've definitely experienced judgment," said Priscilla Gilman, a writer quoted in the story. "Everyone said: 'Isn't there anything more you can do? Your kids need you to be together. They're so little.'"

These cultural skirmishes, occurring in the personal lives of many people as they make their way through a lifetime of family decisions, reflect the unresolved nature of our cultural attitudes toward families. In this case, the competitive attitude toward parenting—which encourages parents to put their children above all else and judges them harshly when they do not (as we saw in Chapter 9)—clashes with the individualist view that marriage must be self-fulfilling and rewarding (as described in Chapter 8).

six states, including the biggest (California), do not participate in the federal government's collection of divorce data. So that estimate is calculated from a large survey, the American Community Survey (which, fortunately, provides very high-quality data from all states).

But what is the meaning of 1.2 million divorces? From that number, we can produce several different divorce rates, depending on what other information we have (J. England and Kunz 1975):

- *Crude divorce rate*: 3.9 divorces for every 1,000 people in the country. This simply indicates how common divorce is in the whole country. We can report this if all we know is the number of divorces and the size of the entire population. That is why we use it for long-term trends, going back to years before there was good available data. As Figure 10.2 shows (using a different data source), the crude divorce rate rose from the earliest national estimate almost continuously for most of the twentieth century, until about 1981, from which time it has been falling almost continuously.

- *Refined divorce rate*: 19 divorces for every 1,000 married couples in the country (or 1.9 percent). This tells us how common divorce is among married couples specifically, a figure that can be further broken down into the categories of education, race/ethnicity, number of years married, and number of times married (see the Story Behind the Numbers).

- *Divorce-marriage ratio*: 1 divorce for every 1.8 marriages that year in the country. This directly compares the frequency of divorces to that of new marriages. That ratio means that there are 55 percent as many divorces as marriages—which some people have called the "divorce rate."

When most people ask about the divorce rate, they really are asking what the odds are that a couple who marry *today* will end up getting divorced. Since

**Figure 10.2  Crude divorce rate, 1860–2011**

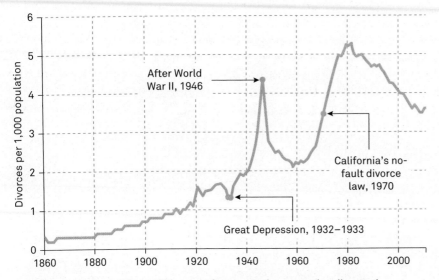

A consistent rise from 1860 to 1981, except for some major events that disrupted the trend: a dip during the Great Depression, when many people postponed divorce because they couldn't afford to move out on their own; and a spike after World War II, when many people who had rushed into marriage before the war divorced.

SOURCES: Statistical Abstracts; National Vital Statistics of the United States; Jacobson (1959). Note: For 1920–present these are official counts from the National Center for Health Statistics, and they do not exactly match those from the American Community Survey.

that question involves predicting the future, it's impossible to answer, of course, but that won't stop us from trying. There are two helpful ways of going about it. First, we can look at the marriage and divorce history of older people today. For example, of all the people who got married in the 1950s, about 40 percent were divorced after 50 years (by 2009). Among the group that married later, at the height of divorce in the late 1970s, a higher percentage—46 percent—were already divorced after only 30 years of marriage in 2009 (but many are still living, so that number will rise as more divorce). Although many people believe that 50 percent of marriages end in divorce, no cohort of couples has yet (quite) achieved that high a rate (Kreider and Ellis 2011).

Second, we can estimate how many of today's marriages will end in divorce by calculating what would happen if some recent year (in this case, 2010) happened over and over again—that is, if everyone lived through today's divorce rates for their entire marriages (S. Preston 1975). That way of estimating future events predicts that 48 percent of new marriages will eventually end in divorce (with the other 52 percent ending with the eventual death of one of the spouses).

In summary, regardless of which numbers we use, we can safely say that divorce rates are a lot higher than they were 150 years ago; and they peaked

# Differences in divorce rates help uncover the causes.

## % Divorced in 2012

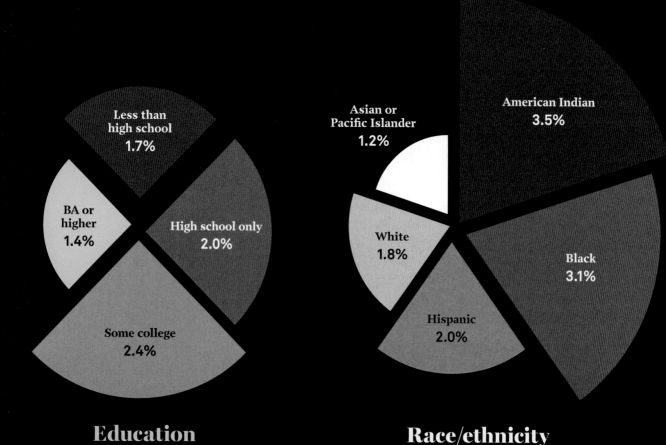

**Education**

Less than high school 1.7%

High school only 2.0%

BA or higher 1.4%

Some college 2.4%

**Race/ethnicity**

Asian or Pacific Islander 1.2%

American Indian 3.5%

White 1.8%

Black 3.1%

Hispanic 2.0%

There were 1.2 million divorces in the U.S. in 2012, which means just less than 2 percent of all married people per year get divorced. Divorce rates are higher for people who have been married multiple times, and even higher in the first 10 years of marriage. Regarding education, divorces are less common for college graduates than everyone else. Among the racial-ethnic groups, American Indians and African Americans have the highest divorce rates, while Asian and Pacific Islanders have the lowest rates, and Whites and Hispanics are in the middle.

*Source: Author's tabulation of data from the 2012 American Community Survey via Ruggles et al. 2014.*

http://wwnpag.es/sbtn10

Go to this link for an animation and additional information.

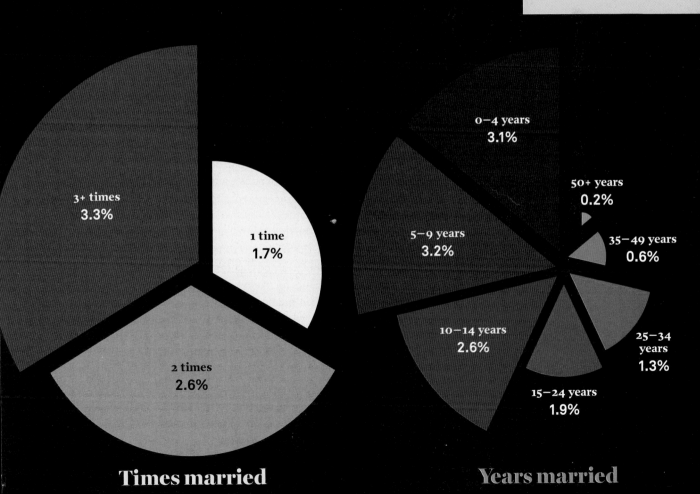

**Times married**

- 3+ times 3.3%
- 1 time 1.7%
- 2 times 2.6%

**Years married**

- 0−4 years 3.1%
- 50+ years 0.2%
- 5−9 years 3.2%
- 35−49 years 0.6%
- 10−14 years 2.6%
- 25−34 years 1.3%
- 15−24 years 1.9%

around 1980 before starting to decline. Finally, if we want to guess what percentage of new marriages will end in divorce—and it is only an educated guess—we can justifiably say it will probably be between 40 and 50 percent (Schoen and Canudas-Romo 2006).

# The Divorce Revolution

Let's return to the years 1960–1980, when there was a dramatic increase in divorce that came to be called the "divorce revolution" (Weitzman 1985). What happened? Many people associate that rise with the liberalization of family law, which started permitting easier, "no-fault" divorces. Under the new laws, which spread across most of the country in the 1970s, couples could get a legal divorce without an accusation of wrongdoing, such as infidelity, abuse, or desertion. More important, in most states, either spouse could *unilaterally* demand a divorce. In other words, the law took on the reality that marriage was a voluntary arrangement between free individuals. Although not specifically written to privilege women, the new divorce laws were part of a tide of reforms in the legal system, inspired by the feminist movement, aimed at liberating women from traditional discriminatory laws (Strebeigh 2009).

Divorce reform was probably the most radical change ever in the law governing families. But did such a dramatic break with the legal past really cause the number of divorces to skyrocket? Yes and no. As Figure 10.2 shows, divorce had been increasing for decades, and the rate was increasing rapidly even before 1970, when the first no-fault divorce law took effect in California. In fact, even prior to 1970, although the law mandated an adversarial divorce process based on finding one spouse at fault, many couples and their lawyers were able to work around the legality to arrange divorces even when no legal breach of the marriage vows had occurred (Cherlin 2010).

And yet, there is no doubt that the more liberal legal environment made divorce easier. By studying the trends in different states as they adopted the new laws, researchers have determined that no-fault divorce did in fact lead to a sharp spike in divorces, but only for a short time (Wolfers 2006). After that, the divorce rate returned to a more moderate, long-run upward trend (Schoen and Canudas-Romo 2006). Thus, whether or not changes in the law were directly responsible, the divorce rate climbed for decades and eventually reached levels high enough to have a major impact on family life.

By the time the baby boomers reached marriage age, their attitudes toward family commitments and priorities were unique in American history. People born in the late 1950s—during the baby boom—had the highest divorce rate ever recorded before or since. About one-third of them had experienced a divorce as early as age 40 (Kreider and Ellis 2011).

The fact that divorce was so common affected the decisions people made about whether to get married, whom to marry, whether and when to have children—and everything in between. By the 1970s, divorce achieved a critical level of momentum, generating ripple effects throughout society. For example, the later age at marriage and the practice of cohabitation, which we discussed in Chapter 8, are related to this reality. People fearful of divorce may postpone or forgo marriage altogether.

Finally, the divorce revolution has proved to be multigenerational (Wolfinger 2005). Whether the effects of divorce on children are positive or negative—and as we will see, either outcome is possible—one consequence is that the children of divorced parents are substantially more likely to get divorced themselves (Goodwin, Mosher, and Chandra 2010). In the view of some children of baby boomer parents—the so-called Generation X, born between 1965 and 1979—their parents' divorces were the defining experiences of their generation.

"It is a hard truism that every generation is shaped by its war," wrote Susan Thomas in her memoir *In Spite of Everything* (2011:xvi). Previous generations were marked by life during World War II or the Vietnam War, for example. But "Generation X's war," she believes, "was the ultimate war at home: divorce." Thomas, who was determined never to put her kids through the same thing she experienced, nevertheless eventually got divorced herself.

# Causes of Divorce

Our sociological perspective is useful for organizing ideas about the causes of divorce. Like other family behavior, divorce is intimate and personal, but also the product of larger social forces. This description of the causes of divorce can't cover everything, but it provides a framework for thinking about what contributes to couples breaking up (Amato 2010; Lyngstad and Jalovaara 2010).

In the Story Behind the Numbers we can see some of the larger patterns: divorces are relatively common for people with less education, for African Americans and American Indians, for those earlier in their marriages, and for those who have been married before. Some of that is not surprising given what we have learned earlier. For example, we saw in Chapter 8 that White marriages are reported to be somewhat happier than Black marriages (Broman 2005). And indeed, the higher rate of divorce among Black couples, compared with White and Latino couples, is a long-standing pattern (Bulanda and Brown 2007). But by looking more closely at the various aspects of marriage, we can learn much more about the nature and causes of divorce.

## The Matching Process

When people join into couples, through marriage or cohabitation, the nature of the relationship is affected by the way they come together and by what they each bring to the union. The clearest way to see this is by comparing those who cohabit and those who marry: cohabiting couples break up more than married couples—they're more likely to eventually split up and more likely to do so could support themselves, they would be more likely to get divorces and strike out on their own. After all, the majority of divorces are initiated by women. But surprisingly, the role of women's economic independence in accelerating the "divorce revolution" remains unclear. That is because independence actually works two ways (Sayer and Bianchi 2000).

First, it is true that when women (or men, for that matter) have the economic means to survive on their own, they are more likely to leave unhappy marriages. This has been called the *independence effect* of women's employment (Teachman 2010). Careful research—which tracks couples over time—has shown that women with jobs are more likely to seek divorces than they would otherwise, but only if they are dissatisfied with their marriage. There is no evidence that employment increases the tendency of women to leave happy marriages (Sayer et al. 2011). Still, the bottom line is that the rise of women's employment—and the independence it provides—have contributed to the upward trend in divorce.

On the other hand, ironically, independence also works to strengthen many marriages. Couples in which both spouses have higher education and earn more are actually less likely to divorce. This is called the *income effect* of employment, because higher income within the couple serves as a source of stability and reduces stress between spouses. In fact, this tendency of high-earning couples to stay together has increased in the last several decades, with a clear gap opening up in the divorce rates between those with more education—who divorce relatively rarely—and those with less education, whose marriages are more prone to break up (S. Martin 2006).

In combination, the independence and income effects of employment mean that employed people are freer to leave unhappy marriages, and people with higher incomes are happier in their marriages—maybe because richer people leave marriages that don't satisfy them. That's part of the explanation for the pattern seen in Figure 10.4, which shows happiness levels to be higher for those with more family income.

We also see how important employment is in providing stability and reducing relationship stress when we study people who *lose* their jobs (Hardie and Lucas 2010). Couples in which one member experiences a job loss often have relationship problems as a result and are more likely to divorce in the years that follow (H. Hansen 2005). This pattern is especially pronounced when it is the husband who loses a job or sees his earnings fall. That suggests that it is not just couples' financial well-being that matters, but also a continued cultural expectation that husbands will provide income for their families (Sayer et al. 2011). When that expectation breaks down, at least for some couples, the marriage bond is weakened (Lewin 2005).

There is one final consideration about the place of employment—and unemployment—in understanding divorce. With the severe economic recession that occurred at the end of the 2000s, many people were concerned that divorce rates would increase—which is what we might expect if job loss puts marriages at higher risk of divorce (Amato and Beattie 2011). However, divorce rates continued to fall for several years after the crisis (P. Cohen 2014b). Why? Future research may provide a definite answer, but I suspect that the recession both caused some divorces and prevented some divorces. Some were caused by the

e. (
f. )
g. )
h. (
i. (
j. ]
k. ]
l. /
m. (

In a gro
the first se
answers to
divorce.

Compa
class? Wha
the role of

## Adults' H

Divorced people
mean that divor
are more likely
time, the proces
symptoms of de
who get divorce
to identify a sin

For example
questions to me
recently had tro
strain, feeling l
tracked these co
with those who
years before a m
higher level of s
then fell back d
higher than the
there is at least s

On the other
people experien
Even though it ha

Figure 10.4 **Marital happiness by family income**

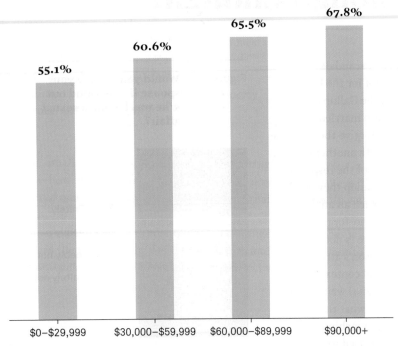

When asked how they would describe their marriage, more than half of all married people answered "very happy." But those whose family incomes are higher are even more likely to say that they are "very happy."

SOURCE: Author's calculations from the General Social Surveys, 2010–2012 (Smith et al. 2014).

stress and disruption of job loss, especially when people lost their homes as a result. But because divorce is often expensive, other divorces were prevented by the same factors. At minimum, divorce requires legal fees and the costs of one spouse moving out—and it may require selling the family home to split up the proceeds, something that was very difficult during the recession of the late 2000s. So some unhappy couples may have been stuck together by the recession as well.

# Consequences of Divorce

Divorce isn't the outcome people look forward to when they get married. So we usually think of divorce as a bad outcome. However, once people are in an unhappy marriage, divorce may be a better option than staying married, so we should consider the potential positive as well as negative aspects of the experience. There are also different parties to a divorce to consider—the adults, the children, and anyone else involved. In this section, I will introduce a few ways of looking at the question.

# Who Gets the Kids?

If parents weren't married before they had children, the children almost always live with the mother after the relationship breaks up. In those cases, the father may pay—or be ordered to pay—child support, as long as his biological paternity is established. On the other hand, when parents are married, the law no longer assumes that the children will live with the mother; that's a matter for the separation or divorce agreement or for the couple and their children to work out informally as they split up.

There are no comprehensive national statistics on legal child custody arrangements after divorce. And the legal arrangements might not be an accurate reflection of the messy reality of families' daily lives in any event. However, it is clear that the great majority of children of divorced parents live primarily with their mothers. The most recent data show, for example, that 73 percent of children whose parents got divorced in the previous year are now living in single-mother households (Elliott and Simmons 2011).

Why is this an important sociological issue? Here are two reasons. First, the care and nurturing of children is an important part of gender inequality. Because the parent who has custody of the children provides the bulk of their care, the tendency of children to live with their mothers means that the labor and expense fall mostly to women (Folbre 1994b).

Second, disputes over custody arrangements—over contact with the children (visitation rights) and payments of child support in particular—are one of the painful legacies of many divorces that have negative consequences for children and their parents and stepparents. So if the arrangements are not consensual or if they are a source of conflict, then the negative effects of divorce will be amplified.

## Changing Assumptions

Judges in divorce cases—and the state legislatures that make the rules for them to follow—face a complex task of balancing interests (Bauserman 2002). One goal is for children to maintain good relationships with both parents. Another goal is to promote a stable family life for children's development. This balance is not easily achieved, but it is one reason why many divorces today result in joint custody arrangements, in which children live alternately with both parents, with the mother and father sharing the costs and responsibilities of child rearing.

Among fathers who do not live with their children, only a small minority maintain close, supportive parenting relationships (Scott et al. 2007). When joint custody is successful, it improves fathers' involvement with their children (Seltzer 1998). If, on the other hand, it is assumed that children belong with their mothers, then the economic losses associated with divorce will be more concentrated among women and children, and men who want custody may feel bitter and left out.

Partly in realization of these facts, in the last several decades many states have changed their laws from instructing judges to evaluate custody cases based on "the best interests of the child"—which usually meant the mother—to a legal "presumption" that joint custody is the best outcome (D. Allen and Brinig 2011). Partly because more fathers now actively seek custody of their children—and they have higher incomes, which makes a favorable impression on judges—shared custody and even father-only custody have become more common (Cancian and Meyer 1998).

One recurring pattern in post-divorce disputes relates to the linking of child support with child custody or visitation rights. In an effort to reduce poverty among mothers and children and decrease the number of single-parent families receiving welfare, states and local governments have increased their enforcement of child support orders. This includes restricting visitation rights, garnishing the wages of parents who don't make payments, suspending their driver's licenses, and even arresting them for failure to pay.

Alec Baldwin and Kim Basinger's custody battle over their daughter Ireland (pictured) lasted for years after their divorce.

This situation has given rise to a new cultural genre—the custody rant. Search YouTube or another video site today for "custody rant" and you will find both men and women complaining publicly about their ex-spouses and the disputes that followed their divorces. One I found in 2011 included a man's 8-minute "rant" (his term), which included this passage:

> I don't feel I should be paying for children, who I'm not seeing—you're alienating me from their lives, I want to be in their lives—you say I'm not good enough but my money is. . . . I feel my ex-wife tries to punish me. She tries to totally alienate the children from me, yet I have done *nothing* wrong. . . . I used to love seeing the children all the time. Then all of a sudden it stops. She meets somebody. She gets married. The game now changed. I don't wanna play the game. I wanna see my kids. You want my child support and I want my visitation.

Regardless of the form the rants take, bitter divorces are likely to generate bitter custody disputes. And children's relationships with their parents—and their family stability—will suffer as a result.

different parenting strategies, as each biological parent may attempt to preserve his or her own parenting style. That causes conflict when the two parenting styles differ: which parent makes (and enforces) the rules for which child? Other common problems include money disputes having to do with the partners' previous spouses and arguments over how to manage relations with the partners' extended families (M. Coleman et al. 2005).

Finally, what about intergenerational support in and around blended families? Here, again, the informal rules and customs are being figured out as we go (Curran, McLanahan, and Knab 2003). It may seem clear that a stepfather who marries a child's mother when the child is young has the same support obligations as any other parent—including, if possible, to pay for the child's college education. And the child, in turn, might be expected to help care for him when he's old if that becomes necessary. But does it matter if the stepfather and mother aren't married but are merely cohabiting partners? What if the stepfather enters the family when the child is 17—or 27? And what about the children from his previous marriage?

The law may provide some guidance for the complicated situations and dilemmas posed by blended families, but the legal rules remain tentative and often unclear (M. Mahoney 2006). Beyond that, the questions remain up in the air—part of the cultural remaking taking place in American families—with no destination in sight. The different approaches people take to working out these issues form a vital part of the family diversity we experience today.

## KEY TERMS:

**marital dissolution**     **separation**

**divorce**     **annulment of marriage**

**stepparent**     **stepchild**

**stepsibling (stepbrother/stepsister)**

**half-sibling (half-brother/half-sister)**

**blended family**     **boundary ambiguity**